Footbinding

In this book Shirley See Yan Ma provides a Jungian perspective on the Chinese tradition of footbinding and considers how it can be used as a metaphor for the suffering of women and the repression of the feminine, as well as a symbol for hope, creativity and spiritual transformation.

Drawing on personal history, popular myths, literature and work with patients, *Footbinding* discusses how modern women feel their feet bound symbolically, as though by this ancient practice. Detailed case studies from Western and Asian women demonstrate how Jungian analysis can loosen these psychological bindings, allowing the client to reconnect with the feminine archetype, discover their own identity and take control of their own destiny.

This original book will be of great interest to Jungian analysts looking for a new perspective. It will also be of interest to anyone studying Chinese culture and psychology.

Shirley See Yan Ma is a Jungian analyst in private practice in Hong Kong and Toronto, Canada. She teaches Analytical Psychology in various cities in Asia, North America and in Zurich, Switzerland. She is an Honorary Assistant Professor of Psychology at the University of Hong Kong, and founder/director of the Jung Centre Hong Kong.

"This pioneering work is an invaluable contribution to Analytical Psychology, as well as to studies in Culture, and Consciousness. It is exceptionally informed in its archetypal depth, and reveals the power of a symbol for psychological understanding across cultures." **Marion Woodman, from the foreword.**

"I have a deep appreciation for the depth and scope of *Footbinding: A Jungian Engagement with Chinese Culture and Psychology*. It is fascinating to learn about footbinding and appalling to know of the pain that little girls endured, as they were slowly crippled to make them marriageable. Like female genital mutilation in Africa, footbinding in imperial China was done by mothers who themselves had endured this so that their daughters would be acceptable brides with "lotus feet," which measured three to four inches in length and made walking or running normally impossible. In patriarchal societies, where daughters are shaped physically and psychologically to make good marriages, the crippling that results is symbolic. This book will provide important insights for women of Chinese ancestry and their therapists especially, but it is applicable to women raised in families where the father is the most important person, and to women in the hierarchal or corporate world of masculine power. As Dr. Shirley Ma so effectively points out, when feminine qualities and women are devalued, footbinding then becomes a powerful metaphor." **Jean Shinoda Bolen, M.D., author of** *Goddesses in Everywoman* **and** *Urgent Message from Mother.*

"This remarkable book opens the door to a deeper appreciation of the struggles of Chinese women to be themselves, disclosing how the tools of their own emancipation have long lain in their own hands yet have often been misused to bind women to the expectations of others. The author shows that Chinese history and philosophy were never as firmly patriarchal as the West imagines, and she reveals that the strength of Chinese mythology, so often underestimated, lies in its images of the feminine as an agency that can survive and endure. How so destructive and limiting a practice as the binding of the feet of girls in order to realize an arbitrary aesthetic ideal for women took hold in Chinese society and survived for so long is the burden borne by the scrupulously honest author of this book, Jungian analyst Shirley Ma. Ma gives a sensitive, thorough, and fair account of footbinding's history, but where her book really comes into its own is in its moving presentation of the work of Chinese women in analysis trying to discover how to let themselves be. In the midst of their efforts to set themselves loose psychologically from the double binds of their culture, Ma's patients encounter the paradox that cultural complexes can both shield us from the difficult work of learning to be ourselves and at the same time hold the energy that is needed to move beyond the ways we have restricted our development to social goals that are too narrow. Skillful in her use of Jungian concepts, this compassionate therapist has given us a book about the therapeutic journey that is a healing experience to read." **John Beebe, past president of the C. G. Jung Institute of San Francisco, author of *Integrity in Depth*.**

"Shirley Ma has written a moving account of her personal journey toward liberation and wholeness as a Chinese woman. It is a narrative that can touch the lives of women from many cultures with the power of healing encouragement to become themselves and all-that-they-can-be if they too become liberated from damaging habits of mind and the inner forces of repression." **Murray Stein, author of *Jung's Map of the Soul*.**

"Shirley Ma's *Footbinding* is one of those rare books that take you on a journey that is both mysteriously riveting and deeply moving. Her own story is fascinating enough, but tied to it are the vivid tales of courageous but often wounded women for whom both the metaphor and the actuality of footbinding stands as historical testimony to the endurance of the human spirit. The Jungian wellspring of reverence for the seemingly inchoate longings in all of us is beautifully delineated here." **John Fraser, author of *The Chinese: Portrait of a People* and *Stolen China*.**

"A timely book, providing penetrating insights for women wrestling with the questions if they are bound for life or if they will be able to move beyond. This valuable Jungian contribution on feminine identity and creative transformation is particularly illuminating as Shirley Ma bridges East and West, culture and psychology, the personal and the collective." **Ursula Wirtz, Ph.D., Jungian Analyst, Zurich, author of *Seelenmord* (*Soulmurder*).**

"In this remarkable and groundbreaking study, Shirley Ma traces the history, from the ancient Zhou dynasty (1122–256 BC) to recent days, of the tradition of female footbinding in China. In so doing, she interweaves her personal and cultural reminiscences with Jungian oriented clinical cases from her private practice, to fashion a coherent discussion about the archetypal sources of the living embodiments of this cultural complex, as a metaphor for the suffering of women and the repression of the Feminine. Along the way she traces the myths, legends, and fairy tales arising from the physical and psychic binding of women that can be used to release feminine strength and personal transformation. A notable, mind-opening and relevant study of a culture still yet on the threshold of Western sensibilities." **Hester McFarland Solomon, Jungian Analyst, London, author of *The Self in Transformation*.**

"This remarkable book explores the psychological basis for the practice of footbinding in traditional China, and shows how contemporary women are still confined by this archetypal pattern. Dr. Ma's analysis, both historical and clinical, is original and a fascinating read. She offers detailed case histories of women who have the courage to bring their psychic binding to consciousness, thereby finding their authentic standpoint and experiencing spiritual transformation." **Lucinda Sykes, M.D., Director, Meditation for Health, Canada.**

Footbinding

A Jungian Engagement with Chinese Culture and Psychology

Shirley See Yan Ma

Routledge
Taylor & Francis Group

LONDON AND NEW YORK

First published 2010
by Routledge
27 Church Road, Hove, East Sussex BN3 2FA

Simultaneously published in the USA and Canada
by Routledge
270 Madison Avenue, New York, NY 10016

Routledge is an imprint of the Taylor & Francis Group, an Informa business

Typeset in Times by Garfield Morgan, Swansea, West Glamorgan
Printed and bound in Great Britain by TJ International Ltd, Padstow,
Cornwall
Paperback cover design by Hybert Design

This publication has been produced with paper manufactured to strict
environmental standards and with pulp derived from sustainable forests.

British Library Cataloguing in Publication Data
A catalogue record for this book is available from the British Library

Library of Congress Cataloging-in-Publication Data
Ma, Shirley See Yan, date
   Footbinding : a Jungian engagement with Chinese culture and psychology /
Shirley See Yan Ma.
      p. cm.
   ISBN 978-0-415-48505-0 (hardback) – ISBN 978-0-415-48506-7 (pbk.)
1. Sex role–China. 2. Femininity–China. 3. Jungian psychology. 4.
Footbinding–China. I. Title.
   HQ1075.5.C5M3 2009
   155.8'951–dc22
                                                            2009025534

ISBN: 978-0-415-48505-0 (hbk)
ISBN: 978-0-415-48506-7 (pbk)

To my grandmother, Yung Zhen-li (1903–1992), whose peasant wisdom inspired and encouraged me to seek and live my truth.

Contents

Illustrations

Preface

This book chronicles my exploration of the psychological meaning of footbinding in traditional China. This project was initiated as the result of a chance encounter with an old Chinese lady with tiny bound feet in the woods outside the city of Zurich. I had then just arrived in Switzerland to attend the C.G. Jung Institute for my analytic training. Meeting this old lady inevitably triggered childhood memories of footbound women in my family and in the neighborhoods in Hong Kong where I grew up. In order to further understand my emotional reactions to this experience, I delved into the cultural history of China, including cosmology, mythology, legends, fairy tales, Confucianism, Taoism, literature, as well as case histories and dreams of clients, looking for some explanations for the origin and development of this archaic practice and to find out what impact it may have on the psyches of modern men and women.

During the 1000 years that footbinding was in practice, the young girl's mother bound her feet – an excruciatingly painful practice that debilitated and crippled her, restricted her movement and grotesquely deformed her feet. Golden Lotus is the deceptively lovely name given to the tiny, mutilated and deformed bound feet of women in traditional China. This practice was carried out by the mother, but for the father – to ensure that his daughter would be a valuable, marriageable, physically beautiful bride. In other words, it was done so she would fit into and be, quite literally, confined by the strictures of an extremely patriarchal society. The practice of footbinding was abolished in the early days of the last century. Yet, occasionally, older women with bound feet can still be seen in China today, although their number is fast dwindling.

The early missionaries were appalled by the prevalence of footbinding in China and were active in their attempts to have this practice officially abolished. Chiu Chin (1875–1907) was the first female political activist to openly attack this practice and call for reforms that would end the subjugation and oppression of women in China. She found herself to be a lone voice against not only this brutal practice, but also the rigid Confucianist system that carried the weight of over 30 centuries. She was beheaded, but her martyrdom helped raise women's consciousness to continue to fight for equality and the right to freedom and happiness. Without any knowledge of Ibsen, she was the first Chinese Nora amongst the many that would soon follow to take up her cause.

This book provides special insights for women (and men) of Chinese ancestry and their therapists. It will also be of interest to women raised in families where the father is the most important person, and for women in the hierarchal or corporate world of masculine power. When feminine qualities and women are devalued, footbinding becomes a powerful metaphor. In working with men and women in Zurich, Toronto, and Hong Kong, I found that countless modern women have symbolically bound feet. Regardless of their heritage, they – like dutiful daughters of ancient China – lived their lives to please others. They struggled to meet unattainable standards of perfection; they tortured their bodies into shapes that men and society considered desirable; and they threw themselves into the dreams of their parents or husbands but never their own. Unable to stand firmly on Mother Earth, these women were cut off from their archetypal Feminine power.

In sharing these women's stories, this book reveals that while footbinding serves as a metaphor for the suffering of women and the repression of the Feminine, it is also a potent symbol for hope and creative transformation. This book offers modern women healing encouragements to redeem their instinctive feminine strength, to find their authentic identity, stand firmly on their own two feet, and walk forward into lives that will be lived truly for themselves and yet in harmony with others.

Shirley S. Y. Ma
Hong Kong

Foreword

As Shirley Ma's analyst, colleague and friend over the past 30 years, I know what the writing of this book has demanded of her. And I am delighted that she has accomplished it. This pioneering work is an invaluable contribution to Analytical Psychology, as well as to studies in Culture and Consciousness. It is exceptionally informed in its archetypal depth, and reveals the power of a symbol for psychological understanding across cultures. This book could only be written by someone like Shirley, one who knows both Chinese and Western cultures deeply.

Shirley Ma is a Chinese woman born in Hong Kong and raised there until the age of 18. Profoundly trained in that culture by her grandmother and mother, she carried this heritage with her to Canada. But on arrival she "proceeded to become as Western as she possibly could" and learned to live at ease in both cultures. She studied science, obtained a Master's degree and attained the success she longed for in the medical science field.

To hold on to an inner dream, she studied the psychology of Carl Jung. Years later, she went to Zurich, Switzerland, where she became the first Chinese analyst to graduate from the C.G. Jung Institute. While there, her dreams led her to reconnect with Chinese symbols, imagery and mythology. Recognizing the deep psychological truth of these encounters within herself, she began to ponder these symbols. One of the most powerful was the Chinese practice of footbinding. Gradually she began to see this powerful image as a symbol of the loss of self-worth in Chinese women.

Shirley's Buddhist studies, especially those concerning the koan "show me my face before I was born," brought her to an internal space where she began to recollect an anguished refugee woman on the street of Hong Kong begging for money for her child and herself. This woman could not walk. Her feet had been bound in infancy. Shirley began to bring to consciousness the women in her own life whose feet were bound in childhood.

Then she began to connect with her own feelings of loss of self-worth and saw how the image of footbinding in her own unconscious was rooted in images of lost feminine esteem through more than 1000 years. Girls' feet were often bound when they were about six years old; from then on they lived with excruciating pain.

Reading these stories can release painful images for Western women who did not literally have their feet bound, but who nevertheless learned to keep their mouths shut when they attempted to speak their truth, or stretched to be the woman they knew existed inside. Shirley's experiences as a Jungian analyst – first in Switzerland, then Canada and now Hong Kong – further opened her eyes to footbinding as a symbol of suffering for women and the repression of the feminine in patriarchal societies everywhere.

This symbol of the bound feminine that Shirley explores so compassionately, so powerfully, extends beyond the individual. We are not talking about the past alone. We are not talking only about China. We are not talking only about women. We are talking about our own dying Mother Earth, her very pulse, her trees and water poisoned by demonic patriarchal power. We are talking about the patriarchal rage that binds the feminine standpoint and poisons her soil. That power may even pass laws to shut the feminine up when she dares to speak her truth.

If our planet is to survive, the bindings have to be cut off, torn off, burned. The voices of the feminine in men and woman must take on the responsibility of learning to walk firmly, both feet on the ground, confident in the values that can save Mother Earth and allow her daughters – in women and men – to speak and love their own reality.

Marion Woodman
London, Canada
26 June 2009

Acknowledgements

I wish, above all, to acknowledge my profound gratitude to Dr. Marion Woodman, my first analyst and mentor. My work with Dr. Woodman led me to the C. G. Jung Institute in Kusnacht, Zurich, Switzerland, where I trained as an analyst and where the idea for this book was first conceived. The discovery of the rich resources of the inner life in the analytic process – thanks to C.G. Jung – also led to the rediscovery of my Chinese cultural heritage.

I wish also to acknowledge my gratitude to the many analysts, teachers, colleagues and friends who encouraged my exploration of Chinese culture through the study of footbinding, especially when I felt discouraged and needed to be reminded that this research could be helpful to others. I feel indebted to the late Drs. Marie-Louise von Franz, Richard Pope, Peter Walder, and Herren Martin Odermatt, and also to John Hill, for their loving kindness and compassion which silently supported my studies and contained my inner journey. I am grateful to Dr. Ursula Wirtz for her insights and ideas during the development of this project. I also wish to express my deep appreciation to my colleagues from the Ethics in Training Initiative in Toronto.

There are numerous unnamed contributors whose stories have been told to me under many circumstances, especially during the years of my analytic practice. It remains my privilege to be trusted by women who reveal their depths to me. In the process, they enable me to better understand their psychology and, through them, the psychology of other women and myself. My analysands are my best teachers; to each of them, my deepest gratitude.

For that first spark that ignited my belief in myself as an author, I want to express my appreciation to Dr. Jean Shinoda Bolen. Her wise words at a crucial juncture synchronistically lifted me out of lethargy and into action. My heartfelt thanks go to Dr. Ellen Shearer for her editorial guidance and direction when I first began to seriously undertake this work in book form. Her original career as a ballet dancer allowed a seasoned yet delicate treatment of footbinding and the feminine. Thanks are also extended to Christy Shum for her drawings and help in pictorial editing.

Finally, I want to express my gratitude to my family – my parents and particularly my brothers and sisters – for their emotional and spiritual support throughout my life. I also extend my deep appreciation to Dr. Ken S. Adam. A valuable source of inspiration, he provided much needed emotional and spiritual containment during my journey into uncharted territories.

I wish to thank Kate Hawes, Publisher, and Jane Harris, Assistant Editor, at Routledge, London, for taking on this project, together with their production team, and for their guidance, patience, and cooperation.

To each and every one, thank you.

Shirley S. Y. Ma
Hong Kong

Chronology of mythical and historical dynasties in China

The Three Sovereigns	*c.*3000–2700 BC
Fu Xi	
Shen Nung	
Yen Di	
The Five Emperors	*c.*2700–2000 BC
Huang Di	
Chuan Hsiun	
Khun	
Yao	
Shun	
Xia Dynasty	*c.*2000–1520 BC
Shang	*c.*1520–1030 BC
Zhou	*c.*1030–221 BC
Qin	221–207 BC
Han	202 BC–AD 220
Three Kingdoms	221–265
Jin	265–420
Song	420–479
Six Dynasties	479–581
Sui	581–618
Tang	618–906
Five Dynasties	907–960
Song	960–1279
Yuan	1260–1368
Ming	1368–1644
Qing	1644–1911
Republic of China	1912–1949
People's Republic of China	1949–present

Note on romanization of Chinese words

In this book, I have used the current Chinese pin-yin system of romanization for most Chinese words. However, I have kept the names already familiar to readers under the former Wade-Giles system of romanization. These include examples such as Tao, I Ching, names of historical figures such as Chiu Chin, Tung Chung-shu and so on.

Chapter 1

First glimpse of the Golden Lotus

When I began my training at the C.G. Jung Institute in Zurich to become a Jungian analyst, I had no idea that living in central Europe and immersing myself in the teachings of this fascinating Swiss psychiatrist (Carl G. Jung, 1975–1961) would take me on an adventure that would lead back to my Chinese heritage. I thought I'd left all that behind.

Soon after I turned 18 I left my home in Hong Kong, moved to North America and, in a concerted effort to fit in with other university students and be successful, proceeded to become as Western as I possibly could. I studied science, obtained a Master's degree, and eventually obtained the success I'd longed for with a career in the medical science field. The interest I'd had as a teenager in Chinese history, culture, and literature was long laid to rest.

However, several years later, not long after I moved to Zurich, I began experiencing dreams and having encounters that led to an increasingly deep interest in Chinese symbols, imagery, mythology, and tradition. Many of these encounters had an element of synchronicity. In Jungian terms, synchronicity is sometimes defined as "meaningful coincidence" or "meaningful chance," but a more exact explanation would be to say that a synchronous event is one that occurs in the outer world but coincides in a deeply meaningful way with some psychological aspect of our psyche. One of the most wonderful things about these events is that they often reflect some deep psychological truth that we are, at that moment in time, still completely unconscious of. This was certainly true for me, because a number of these events related in some way to the Chinese practice of footbinding, and I had no idea at the time that I would eventually embark on an extensive exploration of this phenomenon or that I would come to see it as an extraordinarily potent symbol – one that can work as a powerful metaphor to help us to heal our wounds, reclaim our power, and regain our sense of self and worth as women.

My first synchronous encounter with footbinding occurred not long after I'd moved to Zurich. One day when I was returning from my daily walk in the woods, I looked up and saw an elderly Chinese lady, probably in her late seventies, walking along the other side of the lane with a little boy. Overjoyed to see someone from my own culture, I walked up to her without any hesitation and proceeded to greet her and introduce myself. The old lady appeared surprised at my openness, but warmed to me after a few moments. She explained that she was in Zurich visiting her daughter and son-in-law and that the little boy was her grandson. As her story unfolded I discovered she was originally from Shanghai but had moved to Taiwan after the Chinese Revolution in 1949. It immediately became clear that she was inordinately proud of both her daughter and her son-in-law. They were professors at a well-known American university and were currently in Zurich as visiting scientists. She began to talk on and on about their scholarship and achievements in their respective fields, never once showing any interest in me or curiosity about what I might be doing in Switzerland.

As she continued talking, I began to feel uneasy and even intimidated. Fortunately, the little boy became impatient, and his eagerness to move on ended her monologue. The moment we began to part, I felt an inexplicable sense of relief. As I watched her moving away, I noticed she was walking with a cane in one hand and leaning on her grandson with the other. Glancing down at her feet, I was surprised to see that she had extremely small feet and wore special leather shoes. Later, when I reflected on the encounter, I was stunned to realize that the woman had actually had bound feet.

However, since I was deeply involved in analysis at the time, I was much more concerned with understanding the feelings this old lady had triggered in me than in reflecting on her bound feet. The woman's boastfulness about her family's achievements had made me feel inferior, not-good-enough, and useless. After a great deal of reflection, I realized one reason she had made such an impact on me was related to my upbringing in Hong Kong, a British colony where the sciences were considered not just more useful than any subject in the arts or the humanities, but held to be superior fields of study in every way. When I was in school there had also been considerable pressure on female students to prove themselves in what had previously been male-dominated fields. And there I was, in Zurich, having just walked away from a career in the health sciences where I'd been on a fast track to promotion, immersing myself not just in the humanities but in one of its more esoteric branches – a decision my family and many of my Chinese friends found incomprehensible and believed would be ruinous to both my career and my future security.

It was only years later that I realized the synchronicity in this event – the link between the woman's bound feet, as a powerful psychological symbol, and the feelings of doubtful self-worth I was experiencing – and made the discovery that my own feet, like those of so many of the women I would eventually work with, had been psychologically bound. I did, however, at the time at least recognize the fact that these negative feelings needed to be dealt with.

Indeed, there was no way I could have ignored them because they were so intensified by the completely uprooted state I was living in. The moment I had moved to Zurich for my Jungian analytic training, I had thrown myself intensely into what Jung called individuation, a process that is sometimes described as our journey to wholeness and likened to the way a seed, already containing within itself all it needs to become a flower, eventually blossoms. It involves casting aside the false cloak of the persona – the "I" we present to the world that generally reflects only our most idealized aspects – and coming to know your true self.

Looking back I realize my approach to this was rather extreme and not one I would really recommend. After moving to Zurich, I found a place to live in one of the many wooded areas that dot the city. It was a 300-year-old farm house – but not much more than a cottage. Although there was electricity and a limited amount of hot water, the only heat was provided by stoves that I had to chop wood for. There was no direct access to the main roads or sidewalks from the cottage so I had to hike up and down a steep hill, my backpack filled with books, groceries, or anything else I needed to carry. When I wasn't in class at the Institute, studying, or undergoing the many hours of required analysis, I recorded my dreams, practiced T'ai Chi, walked in the woods, and generally lived an isolated existence.

Driven by my need for self-realization and my thirst for spiritual enlightenment, I realize now that I had embarked on my quest with the fervor of a pioneer. And I had not for one moment stopped to realize how difficult this approach might be, especially in the beginning. Not only was I isolated, my life was turned upside down. Suddenly in a country where I didn't speak the language or understand the culture, the basics of everyday life were totally disrupted – finding my way around, making myself understood, buying food and then trying to prepare it without any of the conveniences I'd always depended upon. Disoriented, I felt isolated and completely vulnerable.

On top of my living situation, and probably to some extent because of it, I was flooded with powerful dreams, some of them returning ones about my personal past and others with deep mythological motifs that I had to struggle to understand. This placed a heavy psychic burden on what was already a difficult adaptation to my new environment. Because I hadn't considered how difficult all this might be, I was taken by surprise and totally overwhelmed. Not surprisingly, I became depressed.

In spite of all these difficulties, I knew it was the right path for me. I lived in my isolated cottage for the five years that I was training at the Jung Institute, and it gave me the time I needed, as the Buddhists say, to "contemplate my original face and eyes"; or in other words, to discover my true identity, the true self I was born with. I had been living as my persona, a false self that had been artificially identified with my job, and I had needed to abandon the job and lifestyle that went with it and live in the woods, in nature, in order to retrieve and heal myself.

There is another Buddhist expression that is similar to the idea of contemplating your original face and eyes; it is an entreaty that goes "Show me my face before I was born." It was in this context of both being consumed by a deep desire to come to know the face I'd had before I was born and being disoriented by my living situation that I met the footbound Chinese lady on the path that day. It is little wonder she had such an impact on me. And it wasn't long before the haunting image of her bound feet began to trigger childhood memories. One was the distinct recollection of walking through the busy outdoor market place in Hong Kong one day when I was about eight years old and coming across a crowd of people. The spectacle they were staring at was a young, attractive woman with an infant, sitting on a filthy red quilt laid on the ground, begging for alms. I was struck by her beautiful, classic features, which contrasted so vividly with the expression of helplessness and shame on her face. There was terror in her eyes as she gazed into empty space. Naively, I wondered to myself why on earth she didn't look for a job. Then I looked down and noticed that this woman had extremely small feet, about three to four inches in size, that were encased in a pair of filthy, red silk, embroidered shoes that once must have been exquisitely beautiful.

I then realized why she was sitting on the ground. Her feet had been bound. I was overwhelmed with pity for her immobility and her desolate future. Even at my young age I had the horrible realization that, if she weren't begging, suicide might be her only option.

In retrospect, I realized that she must have been one of the newly arrived refugees from mainland China, where the failure of the "Great Leap Forward" movement had led to widespread food shortages and a resulting mass exodus to Hong Kong. I also realized that it was her bound feet that had made her such a spectacle for the crowd.

Years later in Zurich as I pondered her fate, more memories associated with bound feet came alive to me. With shame, I remembered that my siblings and I made fun of the semi-deformed feet of our cook, whose feet had only been partially bound. Images of other old women in our neighborhood, both rich and poor, who'd had bound feet began to come unbidden into my mind. Memories also came back of a trip I took in 1982 to Hangzhou, in mainland China, and how I had seen many more old women with bound feet there than we were accustomed to seeing in Hong Kong.

As these recollections came flowing back to me, they eventually became more personal. I began to remember my parents' reminiscences and the stories they had told me. For instance, I recalled my mother sometimes complaining about how terrible her own mother's feet had smelled. And although I'd been aware that my grandmother's feet had been bound, I had never made the connection between the horrible smell my mother described and the fact that she'd had bound feet – even though it is widely known in China that bound feet often reeked from the thick bindings, the frequent sores, and the difficulty of cleaning the compressed, decayed flesh. A bit stunned, I began to fully apprehend for the first time the fact that my own maternal grandmother's feet had been bound! She must have suffered terribly because of it and I had given it little thought. In fact, I came to realize that I had taken the whole subject of bound feet, and even the role they had played in my life, completely for granted.

Realizing this, I began to think about the fact that my great grandmother, my father's grandmother, had also had bound feet. As a child my father and his mother and four siblings had been forced to move in with this grandmother when his father died suddenly. According to the stories I began to recall, my father and his siblings had frequently played tricks on her, often taking advantage of her lack of mobility. One of these misdeeds had extraordinarily far-reaching results and affected my father's entire life. It occurred one day when my father sneaked up behind her and tugged on the string that held up her pants. Being loose-fitting Chinese britches, they fell immediately to the ground. Because Chinese women in those days did not wear underwear, she was suddenly half-naked in front of her grandsons. Shamed and completely humiliated, she struggled to run after them and catch them but couldn't because of her bound feet. Later that day she took her anger out, not just on the boys, but on their mother, berating her and upbraiding her for her sons' behavior until she could no longer bear it. The next day, the boys' mother – who would eventually become my grandmother – packed up her meager belongings and her five children, left the security of her mother-in-law's home and set out on foot for Hong Kong. They walked for 11 days, the children without shoes.

Many years later I realized this story held one of the keys to the deeply synchronous link between my feelings of low self-worth and the imagery associated with footbinding. One reason for this was that this incident – so inextricably linked to the fact of my great grandmother's bound feet – changed the course of my father's life. While living with her in the ancestral home in the village, my father's family had been poor but had had adequate shelter and at least a sufficient amount of food. This was not so in Hong Kong. The already crowded city was teeming with new immigrants, and my grandmother had no skills to use to support her five children. They were forced to live in abject, grinding poverty – conditions so bad they resulted in the death of my father's two beloved younger brothers and younger sister. All this left indelible scars on my father, and was in turn one reason he would set such unattainably high standards for his own children – standards I spent years vainly trying to live up to. Naturally, living in such terrible conditions marked my grandmother for life, too. This also had a profound effect on my life for I was sent to live with her when I was an infant so that she wouldn't be alone, and she became a substitute mother for me.[1]

Of course, in those early days in Zurich I had yet to make many of these connections. Still, the powerful imagery associated with footbinding had definitely begun to do its work, making its way through my unconscious, spurring me onward, and at some deep level, exhorting me to put my own best foot forward and begin the journey that would take me into the labyrinth of myth, symbol, legend, and tradition that formed the basis of my Chinese heritage.

The practice of footbinding was a part of this heritage for more than 1000 years. During these centuries, mothers were required, sometimes forced, to bind their daughters' feet. This practice, which often began when the child was six or seven, tortured her with excruciating pain that could last for years, and restricted her mobility to an extreme degree. The girl child who galloped through the grass and leapt with her friends one year was confined to sitting in the women's quarter the next. She would never run again, and she would only ever walk with aid or, at best, with difficulty. A mother carried out this practice so that her daughter would fit into society and be desirable enough to make a good marriage, thus pleasing both her father and her husband to be. If she remained unmarried she would be considered both a shame and a liability – a great burden on the family.

My journey to understand my culture in general and the practice of footbinding in particular has had ever widening implications for me over the years. When I first began to explore the history of footbinding it was simply to discover its meaning in my own life. By the time I had become an analyst and worked for a few years in the field, I began to see it as a metaphor that could help the Chinese women in my practice with their psychological growth and healing. Eventually, however, I came to understand that it had profound implications and value for a great many Western women as well.

At first from my own experiences, and later from those of the women in my practice, I discovered just how many of us have had our feet psychologically bound. As you read throughout the book the stories of women I've worked with, you'll discover that this "binding" may take many different forms. Struggling to achieve outward success at the cost of all else; following someone else's dreams rather than our own; desperately trying to mould our bodies into the shape that society and men consider desirable – these are just a few examples.

However, as you delve into the stories of Chinese goddesses, divine Feminine beings, and heroines from both fairy tales and real life in the following pages, you will also discover that the binding cloth – no matter how tightly it has been wrapped and tied – can slowly but surely be unwound. For, while a metaphor for the suffering of women and the repression of the Feminine can be found in this peculiarly Chinese practice, the myths, legends, and sacred stories of China contain powerful images that can be used in your own journey to redeem your innate archetypal Feminine power.

Before going into detail about what the archetypal Feminine means in Jungian terms – and in terms of your own personal growth – it is necessary to look at the custom of footbinding itself. From the very beginning I wanted to understand the paradox of how such a horrifically brutal practice could have been fostered in the same highly sophisticated culture that gave birth to such spiritual classics as the *I Ching* (*Book of Changes*) and the *Tao Te Ching* (*Book of the Supreme Way and Virtue*)[2] and such profound treatises on moral and ethical behavior as the writings of Confucius.

And make no mistake, footbinding was a brutal practice. Some of my Western friends have told me that they had always supposed that foot-binding was a process that only restricted the woman's feet a little bit, making them somewhat smaller and dainty looking. In fact, it was a procedure that completely deformed and crippled the woman's feet for life. Its goal was to make the part of the foot that extended from the heel not just smaller and daintier, but – if optimum results were achieved – a narrow, curved moon shape, that was no more than three or four inches long (Figure 1.1).

In order to accomplish this, the process was usually begun when the girl was about six or seven years old. Gradually her toes, except for the big toe, were turned down and bent until they were twisted completely under, flattened out, and embedded in the sole of the foot. At the same time, the metatarsals, the bones of the foot, were squeezed as close together as possible. In addition, these bones were pulled downwards and backwards, drawing the toes as far back towards the heel as possible, so that the resulting crescent shaped appendage would eventually hang down vertically from the ankle instead of forming the normal horizontal surface of the foot. The resulting short, narrow, moon-shaped appendage which was once a foot was called a *Golden Lotus* (Figure 1.2).

Andrea Dworkin's angry exposition, *Women Hating*, contains a chapter entitled "Gynocide: Chinese Footbinding."[3] This chapter gives the following instructions in an attempt to help us imagine what it must have been like to have one's feet bound.

1 Find a piece of cloth ten feet long, two inches wide.
2 Find a pair of children's shoes.
3 Bend all toes except the big one under and into the sole of the foot. Wrap the cloth around these toes and then around the heel. Bring the heel and toes as close as possible. Wrap the length of the cloth as tightly as possible, turning the big toe upward in the shape of the new moon.

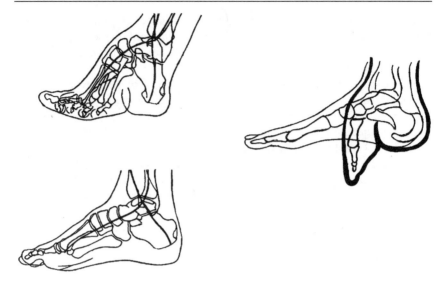

Figure 1.1 Skeletal outline of bound and natural foot (Chinese and Annamese women of the same height). The bowed effect is identical to the appearance and position of a foot in a high-heeled shoe

Source: Dr. Eugene Vincent, *La Médicine dans Chine au XX Siècles*, Paris: G. Steinheil, 1915

4   Squeeze the foot into the children's shoe.
5   Walk.
6   Imagine that you are five years old.
7   Imagine being like this for the rest of your life.

The mother's role in this was not only to bind the feet, but to also make sure the child never loosened the bindings. In his comprehensive book, *The Lotus Lovers*, Howard S. Levy quotes an older woman's recollections of how excruciatingly painful the process was:

> Born into an old-fashioned family in P'ing-hsi, I was inflicted with the pain of footbinding when I was seven years old. I was an active child who liked to jump about, but from then on my free and optimistic nature vanished. . . . (On the day it began) I wept and hid in a neighbor's home, but my mother found me, scolded me, and dragged me home. She shut the bedroom door, boiled water, and from a box withdrew the binding, shoes, knife, needles, and thread. . . . She washed and put alum on my feet and cut the toenails. She then bent my toes towards the plantar with a binding cloth. . . . She finished binding and ordered me to walk, but when I did the pain proved unbearable.

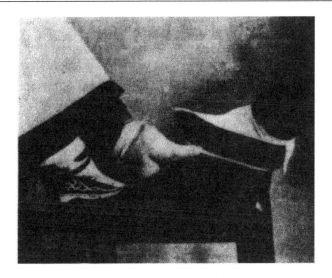

Figure 1.2 Comparison of a woman's natural foot with other women's feet, bound to 6 inches and 4.5 inches respectively

Source: Mrs. Archibald Little, *Intimate China*, London: Hutchinson and Company, 1899

That night my mother wouldn't let me remove the shoes. My feet felt on fire and I couldn't sleep; mother struck me for crying. . . .[4]

This level of excruciating pain usually gradually decreased, but not for a long time, often sometime between a year and a half and two years. For most girls the feet were generally deadened and desensitized by that time.

Mobility was, of course, never really regained. Once a woman's feet were bound it was, as you can well imagine, extremely difficult for her to walk. Just how arduous was determined to a great extent by how small her feet actually were. However, the actual final length depended on a number of factors, including how early the process was begun and how tightly the bindings were wrapped.

Generally the smaller the feet were in the end, the more assistance the woman would need to walk and perform any type of daily task. Those women who were from the higher classes and who had many servants tended to have the smallest feet. Some of these women were virtually immobile and needed to be carried from place to place. Depending on the size and condition of their feet, some women needed someone to help them walk, others needed canes, and still others were able to hobble about. But all were severely restricted in their movement, and walked – if they could walk – with an undulating gait that was likened, by the proponents of foot-binding, to the floating of a butterfly. Eventually the tiniest bound feet became the ultimate mark of beauty. Having a footbound wife became a requirement for a man who wanted to have any status at all – and the smallness of his wife's feet was an important factor in determining that status. Beyond this, as you'll read in more detail later, the small foot was considered highly erotic. The woman with bound feet was held to be a delicate, unearthly, and romantic creature whose greatest desire was to satisfy the fantasies of a man. Her lack of independent mobility kept her completely dependent on her husband and virtually confined to the women's quarters.

Although the custom of footbinding was clearly one that was created and perpetuated by a male-dominated society, it has to be recognized that women did participate in it and help assure its continuance over the centuries. In her book *Every Step a Lotus*, sinologist Dorothy Ko offers some insights into why women helped perpetuate the custom. She points out that any women who did not allow their feet to be bound would be ridiculed. A woman with normal-sized feet was called "duck foot" or "boat foot," and when seen in public she was considered fair game for mockery and would be openly laughed at and scorned. In the eyes of society small feet made a woman beautiful and desirable, and because in those days women really had no option but to marry, "desirability" was extremely important. In addition, having small feet greatly increased a girl's value for her father, whose goal was to arrange a marriage for her that would be the most financially and socially advantageous as possible for the family as a whole.

Ko adds that those women who did manage to make advantageous marriages took great pride in what they had accomplished for their fathers and their families. Also, those women with bound feet who had kind husbands were undoubtedly cherished. And although they might have been restricted from the outside world to a great extent, Ko points out that

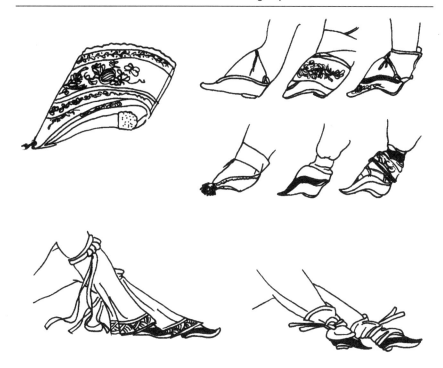

Figure 1.3 Shoes and leggings for bound feet, in various styles
Source: Drawing by Christy Shum

women ruled the roost in the women's quarters, and that many of them must have found life inside these rooms quite congenial. They enjoyed the society of other women, and they created beautiful art – often in the form of the special shoes they made for their bound feet. These tiny shoes were often beautifully embroidered and designed with exceptional creative skill (Figure 1.3).[5] Depending on the time and place these women lived, some of them also enjoyed excellent education. In some periods, in fact, they were highly literate and accomplished. Poetry and essays written by women in the inner chambers during the 17th century, for example, contain some of the finest writings in all of Chinese literature.[6]

Ko also points out that a great deal of meaningful ritual was associated with the actual act of binding the feet, the changing and gradual tightening of the bindings, and the washing of the feet. The tools used for the process were sometimes beautifully wrought and often kept in a very special box. Astrologers were consulted to find an auspicious day to begin the foot-binding so that the girl would endure as little pain as possible. The attitude of the mother was also extremely important. Not all girls were beaten or treated as roughly as the one in the vignette from Levy's book. In fact, many mothers performed the rituals and carried out the binding with great compassion for the suffering the child was enduring. According to Levy, there is evidence that this type of attitude made the ordeal easier to bear.

Of course, none of these somewhat positive aspects of footbinding offer an adequate explanation for why this practice persisted as long as it did or why mothers – many of them extremely reluctant – carried out this practice generation after generation. A better understanding of this can only come from exploring at least briefly, as you will in the next chapter, how the practice developed over the years and how profoundly women were influenced by Confucian family values – the rigid standards for the behavior of each member of the family that were set down by the men who interpreted, and many would say distorted, the teachings of Confucius.

In the meantime, it is essential to realize that the fact that footbinding is no longer practiced does not diminish its power as a symbol in any way. In Jungian terms symbols are the language of the unconscious. A symbol differs from a sign in that a sign – for example, the standard likeness of a woman that appears on a restroom door – gives specific, concrete, unambiguous information. A symbol, on the other hand, is pregnant with meaning. It transcends human consciousness, expresses the mystery of the unknown, and links the past and the future. On the personal level, a symbol acts as a transformer of psychic energy. As such, it has the power to bring about psychological healing and transformation.

For Jung, the unconscious had an aspect that was distinct from our personal unconscious, which he called the "collective unconscious." In "The Structure And Dynamics of the Psyche," found in his *Collected Works*, he defined this as a layer of the human psyche that contained "the whole spiritual heritage of mankind's evolution, born anew in the brain structure of every individual."[7] The collective unconscious can be thought of as a sort of repository of all the primordial images and mythological motifs of human kind as a whole.[8] These universal patterns and motifs manifest as what Jung called "archetypal images." These images speak to us in the language of symbol and metaphor found in spiritual traditions, mythology, fairy tales, and classic legends and sagas. They also come to us in our dreams.

Knowing this, I began my search to understand the deeper, archetypal meaning of footbinding by exploring the symbols associated with it. For Jung, the foot itself was an extremely significant symbol. The feet represent our standpoint – the stance and perspective from which we view the external world. In this way, they represent the relationship we have as individuals with reality as a whole. We stand upright on our feet to face the world, and it is our feet that carry us forward.

Although the deep unconscious meaning of a symbol can never be adequately expressed in words, we can often begin to grasp the deeper levels of significance of a symbol by thinking about the way it is used in expressions. Phrases containing the words "foot" and "feet" reveal that our feet are indeed fundamental to the way we relate to the world. "Stand on your own two feet," "put your best foot forward," "find your feet," "land on your feet," "put your foot down," "feet of clay" are all expressions that say a great deal about our actions and the way we live our lives. It is also significant that they are also all expressions that carry a great deal of emotional content.

In many cultures the foot is seen to have a phallic significance, and it has been associated with regeneration for ages. A woman's foot, in particular, has been a symbol of fecundity and fertility and has long been associated with her connection to Mother Earth.[9]

The phrase "Golden Lotus" has similar connotations. Gold has been associated with fertility, desirability, and sexuality since time immemorial. Aphrodite, the goddess of erotic love and marriage, wore a golden girdle that her image has become closely associated with. It is said that when she put on this shimmering belt her natural beauty and sexual attractiveness were so magnified that she became utterly irresistible. In the temples built in ancient Greece for her worship, the priestesses engaged in ritualistic, sacred sexual acts with male worshippers that were meant to represent union with the goddess and, hence, the divine.

Because gold's impurities are all burnt away by intense heat and fire, it has often been used to represent purity. As the most precious of all metals, it has also been used throughout the ages to symbolize immortality and the highest spiritual values. In alchemy, for instance, it represents the ultimate goal which is held to be either everlasting youth or the highest level of spiritual attainment.[10] In fact, in alchemy, gold is sometimes held to represent divine spirit itself.

It is fascinating to note that the lotus flower has been associated, exactly like gold, with fertility, immortality, purity, and spirituality. In the Tantric tradition in India the lotus flower, *padma*, is sometimes used to symbolize the female genitals; this association is based almost certainly on the vaginal shape the lotus has just before blooming, and the way it gradually opens to a full, bowl-like blossom. In Tantra this vaginal shape is known as the *yoni* and it is used to symbolize the divine Feminine in the form of the goddess known as Shakti or Kundalini.

As a plant in nature, the lotus begins in the mud of a pond, rising through the water with its long, powerful stalk to support broad leaves that float on the surface of the water. The pale, luxuriant blossom follows the sun in its path across the sky, presenting a quintessential image of ethereal beauty and spirituality. Because its pale, otherworldly blossom contrasts so starkly with the mud from which it springs, the lotus has been used to represent purity. And the way the roots stretch from the bed of mud up to the radiant blossom floating on the water has made it a perfect metaphor for the spiritual journey – one that is made even more apt by the fact that, in spite of the blossom's delicate appearance, the powerful resistance from the stalk and root system make it almost impossible to pull up out of the water.

In Tantra and Hatha yoga, the thousand-petal lotus is the image for the highest chakra, and thus the emblem for spiritual attainment. Buddha himself is often pictured sitting on a lotus. In Hinduism and some branches of Buddhism the phrase *om mani padme om* – literally "the jewel in the lotus" – is considered one of the most sacred of all chants. In this context the lotus is a symbol of the *status nascendi*, a term Jung used to refer to "future potential" in the way a seed holds the entire matrix for its future growth within itself.

The manner in which the lotus flower unfolds naturally from the centre is another characteristic that has made it a symbol for the spiritual journey. In this it corresponds to the Golden Flower in Chinese alchemy, which is a symbol of self-containment and divine bliss. In this way the lotus is a symbol of man's yearning for the spiritual aspect of the Feminine.[11]

In some ways it can be seen as cruelly ironic that the words "golden" and "lotus" symbolize all that is pure, spiritual, and divinely Feminine, and yet at the same time are identified with one of the most base, brutal, and despicable practices ever perpetrated on women. On an individual level, the bound foot known as a Golden Lotus clearly represents the suppression and distortion of a girl's feminine identity. On a more universal level, footbinding can be seen to stand for the dissociation of a woman from the Earth and from the strength of the archetypal Earth Mother. Thus, on an individual level, the Golden Lotus is a metaphor for the repressed Feminine – the devaluation of the powerful instinctive, intuitive, feeling side of our nature. On a more universal level, it is a metaphor for repression of the Earth Goddess by those who have feared her power throughout the ages.

When viewed from another perspective, however, it may be that this paradox is simply a way of making us aware of the great power that is hidden in the Golden Lotus and is only waiting to be revealed.

Notes

1 This was not an uncommon practice in Chinese families.
2 Richard Wilhelm trans. [German], Cary F. Baynes trans. [English], *I Ching* or *Book of Changes*, Princeton, NJ: Princeton University Press, 1975; D. C. Lau trans., *Tao Te Ching*, New York: Alfred A, Knopf, 1972.
3 Andrea Dworkin, *Women Hating*, New York: Dutton, 1974, pp. 93–116.
4 Howard S. Levy, *The Lotus Lovers: A Complete History of the Curious Erotic Custom of Footbinding in China*, Buffalo, NY: Prometheus Books, 1992, pp. 26–7.
5 Dorothy Ko, *Every Step a Lotus: Shoes for Bound Feet*, Berkeley, CA: University of California Press, 2001, Chapters 2–3.
6 Dorothy Ko, *Teachers of the Inner Chambers: Women and Culture in Seventeenth-Century China*, Stanford, CA: University of California Press, 1994.
7 Carl G. Jung, *The Structure and Dynamics of the Psyche, The Collected Works of C.G. Jung* (cited throughout as CW), Vol. 8, Bollingen Series XX, edited by Sir

H. Read, M. Fordham, G. Adler, and Wm McGuire, trans. R. F. C. Hull (except Vol. 2), Princeton, NJ: Princeton University Press, 1953–79, para. 342.
8 Ibid, para. 325.
9 Carl G. Jung, *Symbols of Transformation*, CW 5, paras. 356, 439, 480; William A. Rossi, *The Sex Life of the Foot and Shoe*, London: Routledge and Kegan Paul, 1977, pp. 1–13.
10   Marie-Louise von Franz, *Introduction to the Interpretation of Fairy Tales*, Houston, TX: Spring Publications, 1970, pp. 57–60, 87–8, 117; *The Psychological Meaning of Redemption Motifs in Fairy Tales*, Toronto: Inner City Books, 1980, p. 75.
11 Carl G. Jung, CW 5, op. cit., para. 405; *The Archetypes and the Collective Unconscious*, CW 9, paras. 156, 315, 389, 573, 652, 661; *Alchemical Studies*, CW 13, paras. 336, 345; Clarence B. Day, *Chinese Peasant Cults*, Shanghai: Kelly & Walsh, 1940, p. 41; Charles A. S. Williams, *Outlines of Chinese Symbolism and Art Motives*, 3rd Revised Edition, New York: Dover Publications, 1976, pp. 255–8.

Chapter 2

The Shang empress-fox and her feet

The way I had embarked on my quest to undertake my training at the Jung Institute, with the fervor of a pioneer and the rustic conditions I was living in, left me far more disoriented than I ever would have imagined. At some level I began longing for the comforts and solace of home. Interestingly enough, I wasn't longing for the comfortable modern living conditions I'd recently left behind, but for the familiarities of my Chinese childhood. It was in this state of mind that another example of synchronicity occurred. It happened when I'd been in Zurich for some time and, on a hike one day, discovered purely by chance an Oriental grocery store. Without hesitation, I ventured in and immediately felt at home. Just looking at the displays of soya sauce, dried produce like Chinese mushrooms, and so many different kinds of rice and noodles gave me a deep sense of comfort.

It was a Tuesday morning, and the store was not busy. I found an old Chinese lady sitting in a corner and I initiated a conversation with her. She told me the store was run by her son, who had come to Switzerland as a refugee from Vietnam a few years earlier. After he'd become settled in his new country, she came to join him and now helped run the store. A tiny, frail woman who was close to 80, she reminded me of my grandmother. This was especially so because we spoke the same dialect. I discovered the reason for this was that her mother had originally come from the same village in China as my grandmother and had moved to Vietnam as a mail-order bride.

Something spurred me to ask her if she knew anything about foot-binding, and she replied that when she was growing up in Vietnam women with bound feet were a common sight. She began to tell me stories about these Chinese women and to describe them to me. She told me how very hard-working they were and how, even in extreme heat, they would still be working in the fields or in the kitchen. Unable to walk, they would work seated, their legs powerful stump-hammers pounding on the flour. From the tone of her talk, I gathered she was trying to say that Chinese brides were a "good deal" because they worked so hard.

Intrigued, I asked if she had any idea how footbinding had originated. The expression on her face became very guarded and she said to me in a hushed voice, "It's the *hu-li-jing!*" *Hu li* means fox and *jing* – although one of those words that's almost impossible to translate – can be thought of as the spirit, ghost or, in a sense, the very essence of something. The way this old woman was using it, the term also alluded to the idea of an *incubus*, an evil type of being who was once believed to have sexual intercourse with women while they slept, drawing their life essence from them in the process.[1]

When she first said the words *hu-li-jing*, I laughed out loud, thinking she was referring to a more risqué, modern-day usage of the term where it means "fox ladies" and refers to the mistresses and concubines who lead women's husbands astray. My mind immediately flashed back to the stories frequently heard in my childhood of different women in the neighborhood who from time to time would be out running around the city with a group of girl friends trying to discover where their husbands' mistresses lived so that they could find them and warn them off – sometimes even getting into fisticuffs with these women, who were seen as shameless hussies.

In fact, the old woman's superstitious belief was a sign of the vitality of the mythical origins of footbinding. At the centre of the history of this practice is a mythological figure from the Shang dynasty, a period in Chinese history that probably began sometime around 1520 BC and lasted until around 1030 BC. According to legend, the last Empress of this dynasty was not a woman at all but a shape-shifting fox.

One of the elderly footbound women Howard Levy interviewed in the 1960s for *The Lotus Lovers*[2] told him a popular version of the tale. In this account the last Shang emperor was a barbaric, evil man named Chou-wang. Although Chou-wang treated everyone cruelly, he was particularly vicious to a leader of one of the feudal territories under his command, a defiant prince named T'ang Wu who wanted to bring justice back to the land. In his attempt to subdue him, Chou-wang even murdered the prince's son and forced the heartbroken prince to eat his flesh.

But Chou-wang got his comeuppance. He was madly in love with T'ang Wu's beautiful daughter, Ta-chi. When Ta-chi heard she was being summoned to the emperor's palace, she fell ill with grief. While she slept, a fox spirit – a *hu-li-jing* – entered her body in order to take over her human form. In this beautiful feminine form, the *hu-li-jing* joined Chou-wang's harem and eventually became the empress. And while the evil emperor unwittingly made love, not to the beautiful Ta-chi, but to the *hu-li-jing*, it sucked the vital life essence slowly but surely out of his body.

Now, this *hu-li-jing* was over 1000 years old and very powerful. However, it was not quite powerful enough to take on the shape of Ta-chi's entire body, and instead of feet it still had tiny fox paws. In order to hide these paws from Chou-wang, the fox bound them in white cloths. When the emperor questioned the fox about these bindings, the "empress" replied that she wore them to preserve her feet's beauty and keep them from growing. She then began to dance enticingly beside a lotus pond, where her delicate bound feet were likened to lotus blossoms. Completely entranced, Chou-wang made the order that henceforth all the women in his empire must bind their feet so that they would look like lotus blossoms. He then spent days and nights in the *hu-li-jing*'s company, ignoring the affairs of state and, unbeknownst to him, slowly having his power drained away. Before long the dissolute emperor grew so weak that T'ang Wu was able to lead a revolution against him, take over the throne, begin a new dynasty, and bring prosperity back to the land.[3]

In this strange tale, whose deep influence has clearly persisted to the present day, we find two more powerful symbols that are associated deep in the psyche with footbinding and have tremendous relevance for women today: the fox and the empress. But before I could really begin to understand these powerful symbols or start to share them with the women I worked with, I had to discover more about how footbinding had actually developed, how it fitted into the spellbinding panorama that is the history of China and, even more important in Jungian terms, how it was rooted in the collective unconscious of my enigmatic and fascinating culture.

There was, of course, the Shang dynasty. It lasted over 500 years, from 1520 BC to 1030 BC, and it is indeed said that the last Shang emperor was a cruel, debauched tyrant who was replaced by a better leader. However, it is very unlikely that footbinding began before another couple of thousand years had gone by, most likely sometime near the end of the Tang dynasty or the beginning of the Song dynasty. (A helpful chart on the Chinese dynasties can be found on page xvii)

The Tang dynasty lasted over 350 years, from 617 AD to 978 AD. The last emperor of this dynasty was a man named Li Yü. According to what may be an actual historical account, Li Yü had a consort named Yao Niang, or Lovely Maiden, who was a slender, beautiful dancer. Completely enamored of her, Li Yü had a six foot high replica of a lotus constructed out of gold for her to dance on. The inside of the lotus was encrusted with precious colored stones and decorated with ribbons to create a brilliant multicolored effect. Once the lotus was finished, Li Yü had Lovely Maiden bind her feet with gauze so that they appeared tiny and slender and were bent upward so that they had the curved shape of a sickle moon.[4] Lovely Maiden then danced in the centre of the six foot high lotus as if she were floating in the clouds, her bound, crescent-shaped feet symbolizing the new moon or, perhaps, even the moon goddess.

This account goes on to say that many women admired Lovely Maiden and the shape of her slender, curved feet so much that they strove to imitate her. And it may well be that this fashion trend was the first step, so to speak, on the road that would eventually lead to the crippling practice of binding women's feet to a length of less than three inches. This, of course, didn't happen overnight and almost certainly didn't happen any time in the Tang dynasty, a period in which women seem to have enjoyed a good deal of freedom. There are many accounts of girls and young women being encouraged to be physically active and play vigorous sports during this period. A good deal of art and literature also comes from women of this period. Perhaps most important, in terms of their freedom at least, they were allowed to divorce and remarry. In fact, there was a great deal of sexual license in the Tang dynasty, as will be seen later, due to the rise of Taoism, where the divine Feminine was honored and women, at least in certain instances and situations, were seen to embody this divine power.

Regardless of the role Li Yü had in the origins of footbinding, the popularity of the story about Lovely Maiden's exquisite dancing platform was certainly a factor in the later use of the term "Golden Lotuses" for bound feet. An even earlier origin of the term, however, came almost 500 years before, from an emperor in a northern province who is said to have created lotus shapes out of gold and scattered them on the floor for his favorite consort to parade upon. When she did, he would exclaim that a lotus arose from every step she took.[5] It seems that in creating this scenario the emperor was attempting to recreate an old legend that came to China from India – one that, not coincidentally I think, combines the elements of feminine power, fertility, and transformation that remain deeply associated with the Golden Lotus in the collective unconscious today.

In this tale from long ago, an Indian sage was washing himself in a crystal clear stream when a beautiful woodland deer came to the water to drink. Upon drinking the water the deer conceived and gave birth to a girl child who was completely human but had the feet of a deer. The sage adopted the girl and raised her as his daughter and as she grew she became beautiful beyond all imagining. One day she visited another sage in the village and as she returned every step she took left the imprint of a perfect lotus in the ground. The village seers predicted that she would give birth to a thousand sons. And in time these sons were indeed born, each one resting upon one petal of a thousand-petaled lotus[6] – an image that has been the symbol in India since ancient times for attaining enlightenment.

Regardless of its origins in myth and story, the first practitioners of footbinding were probably sensual dancers who, like Lovely Maiden, bound their feet slightly to give an appearance of a slender, delicate, and possibly moon-shaped foot. The bindings also served to make the dancers look more graceful as they moved, much the way a ballet slipper does today. Beyond this, the dancers were trying to capture and visually represent the sensuality that was associated with feet. For even though footbinding itself didn't begin in the Tang dynasty, the association of the small foot with sexuality and erotic fantasy certainly did develop in this period. One of the many poems from the era that celebrate this is quoted in *Every Step a Lotus* and is called "Ode to the Slippers":

> Glowing, glowing, six inches of succulent flesh;
> Embroidered slipper in white silk, lined in red.[7]

Towards the end of the Song dynasty, which followed the Tang and lasted about 300 years, the fashion to bind women's feet very gradually moved from the court dancers to the women who lived in the Imperial courts. From there it spread over time to an ever-increasing number of women in the higher classes. At the same time it spread geographically across China, from the North where it originated to the Southern provinces. Part of the reason for this was a shift in values that occurred during the Song as an overreaction to the more liberal attitudes of the Tang. Women began to lose much of the freedom they'd had in the Tang, for instance the right to divorce or to remarry after the death of a spouse, and they increasingly came to be seen as licentious creatures who needed to be suppressed. As the popularity of the custom of footbinding spread, it seems the tightness of the bindings also increased and, consequently, the size of the resulting feet decreased proportionally – but it is not known exactly how small the ideal foot was during this period.

One of the most telling stories about the relevant attitudes that were spreading concerning women during this era comes from Fujian province in southeastern China. Chu Hsi, a Fujian philosopher who lived from 1130 to 1200, was so adamant that a widow should remain chaste for the rest of her life that he is quoted as saying it was preferable for her to starve to death than marry again. When Chu Hsi became a governor of the southern part of Fujian province, he introduced footbinding to the area with great enthusiasm, saying it was "a means of spreading Chinese culture and teaching the separation of men and women."[8]

In his position as governor, he publically observed that women were prone to unchaste and lewd behavior and, therefore, needed to have their movement restricted. To this end he ordered that women's feet should be bound as tightly as possible. This, he believed, would curb their immorality. Following this edict, Fujian women's feet were bound to such a degree that they could not walk at all without assistance. After a number of years, the funerals and the few celebrations that Fujian women were allowed to attend became known as "A Forest of Canes"[9] for virtually all of the women needed a crutch in each hand in order to walk.

The Song dynasty ended in 1279 with the invasion by Kublai Khan and his Mongol armies. This era of foreign domination in China was known as the Yuan dynasty, and while the Mongol authorities decried the practice of footbinding it continued to spread and gain popularity among the people. This era of Mongol control ended in about 100 years and was replaced by the flourishing Ming dynasty (1368–1644). During this era footbinding received increasing degrees of popular support and official authorization and spread even further across China. The bindings also became much tighter in many areas, as they had earlier in Fujian province. By some point the Golden Lotus that measured only three inches – measuring from the toe to the beginning of the heel – became the ideal, and the woman who could no longer walk without assistance became a status symbol for her husband. One reason for this was that it indicated he was wealthy enough to provide the many servants she would need to perform household tasks and be carried around when she needed to move from place to place. In addition, the bound foot also came to be seen as the ultimate tool for keeping women from indulging in the sexual promiscuity that was common among men. As one verse succinctly puts it:

Why must the foot be bound?
To prevent barbarous running around![10]

Eventually a woman's value as both a status symbol and sexual object increased in inverse proportion to the size of her feet, and the woman with the smallest and most perfectly formed Lotuses was able to attract the wealthiest and most desirable husband. A daughter with unbound feet became a terrible liability for her family because she was virtually unmar-riageable.

Over this period the Golden Lotus also became firmly entrenched in the male psyche as a highly erotic image. Love fetishes developed around tiny, bound feet. Manuals and erotic literature were written that described in detail the ways the bound foot could be fondled as a prelude to sex and in the sexual experience itself. The belief developed that walking on bound feet developed voluptuous, enticing thighs and made a women's genitals far tighter. In spite of this idea having no basis whatsoever in fact, it eventually became so widely accepted that no amount of evidence to the contrary could dispel it.

In the inner chambers, the women who made and embroidered the beautiful, intricate shoes for their bound feet created special silken "sleeping" slippers – usually red, which was considered the most erotic of colors – for their husband's delight. In theory at least, the actual foot that lay beneath the bindings and beautiful slippers was never to be revealed, and this added to the mystery and allure of the bound foot.

When the Ming dynasty began to falter in the mid 1600s, control of China was taken over by the Manchus, a people who had once hunted, fished, and raised horses in the area of what is now northeastern China and was known as Manchuria. Although the Manchus were not Chinese, they quickly adopted the aspects of Chinese government and culture that had been successful in the past. The Manchu era lasted from 1644 to 1911. Known as the Qing dynasty, it was generally a time of peace and prosperity, and under Manchu rule Imperial China reached the height of its power and influence.

From the very beginning, the Manchus condemned the practice of foot-binding. Still the custom continued to grow and, gradually throughout this 300-year period, to spread from the very highest classes to the common folk. It has been speculated that one reason this occurred, at least in the early stages of Manchu rule, was that it was a way for the Chinese to affirm their own heritage and underscore their "difference" from the foreigners who had conquered them. And even though the Manchus opposed foot-binding and tried several times to make it illegal, the association of tiny feet with beauty and desirability gradually became so entrenched that eventually even Manchu women began to adopt the practice. Toward the end of their reign the Manchus made numerous attempts to outlaw footbinding by official decree, but their efforts repeatedly failed.

By the final years of Manchu rule – which ended officially when the Republic of China was established after the revolution in 1911 – foot-binding was being practiced by many of even the very poorest classes. This created a situation in which many of the women who worked in the fields or carried out the household tasks that the higher-class, footbound women could not perform were hampered by having their feet bound at least to some degree.

Slowly, over a period beginning with the final decades of Manchu rule and the first years after the revolution, an anti-footbinding movement and a corresponding "natural foot movement" gained strength. According to Levy, one of the reasons the Manchus failed to eliminate footbinding while the revolutionary movement eventually, if slowly, succeeded was that the anti-footbinding propaganda spread by the revolution tied the unbinding of the foot with the liberation of women in general[11] – a movement that was gradually gaining strength in China during this period just as it was in the Western world, where women were slowly gaining freedoms like the right to vote and to own property. But it wasn't until 1957 that the last attempt to bind girls' feet was put to a final stop and the custom died out completely.

Much of my exploration of this history was done during the years I spent in Zurich. And while delving into footbinding in this way helped me understand the essentials of how it spread, it still didn't explain to me how something that seemed so barbaric could have existed during the various periods in Chinese history when art, literature and culture flourished, when society was so well-ordered, and when government reached such levels of sophistication and success. One of the most significant answers to this question lay, I eventually came to understand, in Confucian family values and a concept known as "filial piety."

In spite of the rise of different philosophies and religions over the centuries, which ranged from Taoism and Buddhism to Communism, the influence of Confucian family values and filial piety has never really vanished. In fact, as you will see from the stories of the Chinese women I've worked with, these ideals are still influencing and motivating Chinese women today. Quite early on in my practice I came to see how understanding their influence on these women's lives could help them. However, it wasn't long before I discovered that delving into these two notions could be just as useful – and sometimes even more so – for my Western clients. Indeed, the very "foreignness" of looking at the world through a Confucian lens made it a powerful tool for these women and helped them see how parallel Western values were binding their feet symbolically and psychologically.

In terms of my own journey, it wasn't until I returned home after my time in Zurich that I began to delve really deeply into my Chinese roots. Although I had begun the process during my years at the Jung Institute – and had even written my final dissertation using footbinding as a metaphor – I had been immersed in Jungian, and not Chinese, thought during that time. When I came home to Toronto from my five years in the woods, I found myself in the middle of a frenetic, fast-paced North American city, and I was once again completely disoriented. But I was also conscious now in a way I had never been before, and I knew that for me the process of becoming whole required that I re-own the Chinese side of my being.

In immersing myself in North American culture as I had when I was 18 and becoming as Western as possible, I had created a Western persona. In addition to this, as I had realized during my analysis in Zurich, I had actually been taken out of my culture very early. My whole family had become Protestants, and the grandmother I had been sent to live with when I was an infant had turned into a rather fanatical Christian. Completely committed to the Christian God, she rejected the concept of worshipping the ancestors. She prayed many times a day and went to church several times during the week. She often made me go with her and taught me Christian prayers and hymns. The church she attended was an extremely conservative Presbyterian one. I remained a member there until I was 14, when I became disillusioned with it, had an open disagreement with the pastor, and left the congregation in righteous indignation! But even then I remained a Christian. Right across the street, a new church had opened up and I joined it. It was a Southern Baptist congregation. The minister and his wife were from Texas, and in spite of what I now see as their rather rigid views, they were wonderful people. English-speaking Sunday school class was held at the church every week, and I attended it until I was 18. In addition to all this, I attended a Catholic convent school all through grade school and high school.

Fortunately for me, even though my grandmother and my family had rejected worshipping the ancestors, we still celebrated the Chinese festivals. This was one of the only bits of true Chinese spiritual heritage that found its way into the strange conglomeration of Christian, and therefore Western, influences in my young life.

It was no wonder that, once my analysis and my Jungian training had helped me become more conscious, I began to long to reconnect with my Chinese heritage.

This desire was intensified when I returned home after living in the woods in Zurich and was thrust full force back into North American urban culture. Acutely aware of just how Western my persona had become, I immediately started taking seminars on Chinese culture. Very soon I realized that the way I had lived in the woods and the approach I had taken to life while there had been very Taoist in essence. The Taoists, I eventually learned, were individuals who sought a return to pristine simplicity and a golden age in which people lived in harmony with nature. In Zurich, this way of living had come to me intuitively and completely naturally. Realizing this made me long even more deeply to regain my Chinese roots. Through all this I was still trying to understand footbinding and find some way to put the whole phenomenon into some kind of context. In a sense I was starting from scratch, revisiting Chinese culture and heritage in a way I never had before.

Before long I enrolled in an institute for Chinese medicine and over the next few years studied all aspects of it from acupuncture to the use of herbs. I also began to study Chinese literature and history again. These were subjects I had been so passionate about in high school that part of me had longed to go to live in Hong Kong and study them at university there. Although I had lost all connection with this passion when I'd come to the West to study science, I began to regain it. Phrases from the Chinese classics I'd had to memorize in high school would suddenly come back to me, and I started to think about the teachings of Confucius.

Rediscovering Confucius and coming to understand his teachings on a completely different level than I had when I was a child in school was an awakening for me. Especially since I had considered Confucius despicable from the time I was in sixth grade and I first learned about his famous remark denigrating woman that appeared in his *Analects*:

> There are two things I do not understand: women and the inferior men. And I fail for the same reason to understand them: if you are stand-offish with them, they resent it, and if you are familiar, they take advantage of it.[12]

Because of comments like this and other aspects of Confucian teachings that were later used to place women in a subservient position to men, I hated Confucius with a passion. I thought he was responsible for the patriarchal and what I thought of as "anti-feminine" rules and regulations governing the Chinese family system and accountable for the suffering of all Chinese women under the sky.

Certain factors in my childhood probably intensified these feelings about Confucius. One of these was the fact that when I was growing up I was paradoxically lonely much of the time and at the same time in the midst of a large, frenetic household that I often needed to escape from in order to find solitude. This situation was brought about partly because of my grandmother's obsession with the church and there was very little real bonding with her. When I was very young I lived with her in a separate home and was often alone. When I was a bit older I moved back to my parents' home, but I hadn't bonded with my mother the way my younger siblings had. Eventually my grandmother moved in with all of us, and this did not help the situation. Not only was there a conflict between the two women as to whom I "belonged" to, I was never quite attached to either one of them as a mother figure. So while I was left feeling lonely and isolated, I was in the midst of a large family – a situation that was made fairly chaotic by the fact that our living quarters were at the back of a shop my parents owned and people were coming and going all the time. This was quite overwhelming for me. I remember crouching in the corner, trying to hide and find a place where I could do my schoolwork. Sometimes this need for solitude would drive me out of the house to the market, where I could at least be alone with my thoughts.

Wandering alone through the market I began at an unusually early age to reflect on the things I saw around me – on what I would now call the "human condition." And even then I was particularly struck by the way I saw women living and being treated. Many things I saw left a heavy imprint on my psyche. Although I wouldn't have been able to put it into these words at the time, I admired the survival instinct of the peasant women, their relentless refusal to give in to hardship, their ability to work in harsh conditions, and above all their determination to feed and protect their children. When I thought about it later, memories of these women and the things I saw would flood my mind. A memory came to me of seeing a pregnant woman who carried a bamboo pole on her shoulder with a basketful of vegetables on one end and her two babies on the other. I remembered cheering on an older woman who challenged a fit young vegetable seller to a physical fight in order to defend the honor of her daughter after he had verbally abused the girl.

On the other hand, many things I saw appalled me; they weighed heavily on me, and I developed a deep sense of burden. These images come back to me in a kaleidoscope: I would see the hawkers beat their daughters when they weren't selling enough vegetables. I was speechless to see a man beating his wife, while people watched without daring to interfere. I felt sorry for a teenage pregnant woman who looked lost with her bouquets of flowers waiting for customers. I was indignant to see a mother physically abusing her crying daughter with a burning piece of wood. When I yelled at her to stop, she shook the burning stick and threatened to do the same to me.

When I was a bit older I realized how lucky I had been that nothing happened to me as I walked through these scenes alone and unprotected. Stories of young girls being kidnapped into slavery abound – and that in itself was a testament to the reality of women's condition in Chinese society. And I laid the blame for this condition squarely on the shoulders of Confucius. How strange it seemed to me, then, that those long-forgotten lines from Confucius started rising up from my unconscious. They came to me spontaneously as I walked the busy city streets and rode the street cars, and they continued to call to me until I picked up a copy of Confucius' own writings and began to read him with new eyes. This intuitive prodding by my inner voice was once again taking me on a journey in the right direction. For, in a certain sense, when I found Confucius, I found Jung on an even deeper level. Reading Confucius' writings I began to feel increasingly grounded; I began to feel comfortable in my Chineseness, and I don't believe this would have happened if I had not begun to understand Confucius' teachings on this new, deeper level. In a way, it gave me the freedom to explore Jung, Christianity, and other Western traditions even more deeply without losing myself. Although I didn't know it then, this inner voice was also leading me to material that would eventually be essential for both my work and my writing, for no one can really understand much about the Chinese psyche – or the powerful imagery to be found in the Asian unconscious – without at least a little background on Confucius.

Notes

1 In medieval European legends and folklore an *incubus* was always a male creature, while the corresponding female was known as *succubus*.
2 Howard S. Levy, *The Lotus Lovers: A Complete History of the Curious Erotic Custom of Footbinding in China*, New York: Prometheus Books, 1992, p. 280.
3 Quoted in Levy, ibid.
4 Dorothy Ko, *Every Step a Lotus: Shoes for Bound Feet*, Berkeley, CA: University of California Press, 2001, pp. 42–3.
5 Ibid., p. 32 – note that Levy says this emperor actually built a giant lotus for her.
6 Howard S. Levy, op. cit., pp. 39–40.
7 Quoted in Dorothy Ko, op. cit.
8 Quoted in Howard S. Levy, op. cit., p. 44.
9 Ibid.
10 Quoted in Howard S. Levy, op. cit., p. 41.
11 Ibid., pp. 65–6.
12 James Legge, 'Analects' (Lunyu), in *Sacred Books of the East*, London: Oxford University Press, 1879, p. xviii, 25.

Chapter 3

The Confucian Way

Confucius' teachings have influenced virtually every aspect of Chinese culture for millennia. Two concepts, however, are of particular interest when it comes to the spread of footbinding, the effect it has had on the psyche of Chinese women, and the role it plays as a metaphor in the collective unconscious of all of us as women. The first of these notions relates to the way Confucius saw the family and the way family members should relate to one another. The other is a concept known as filial piety.

There was a great irony in the journey of exploration I took into Confucius' life and thought. This was that, while I discovered the fundamental role these two aspects of his world view had had in the spread of footbinding, I also discovered a human being who appeared to have been, in Eastern terms, living in a state of Realization or, in Jungian terms, living an individuated life. One reason he could have lived in an enlightened state and still failed to advance the cause of women was simply that he was a product of his time and place and his views reflected the attitudes about women that were prevalent then. The other is that much of his teaching was edited, misinterpreted, and misused by Confucian scholars for more than 2000 years. Confucius himself would almost certainly never have condoned the act of footbinding as it would have gone against his most basic tenets, which insisted that all human beings, and especially family members, treat each other with respect and benevolent kindness at all times.

Confucius was born in 551 BC – just a few decades after the Roman Empire had been founded in the West – and lived about 72 years. He was a descendant of the royal house of Shang, but he grew up in poverty because his father died when he was only three years old. By the time he was 19, he had married. He soon fathered three children. Even though he had managed to obtain an excellent education, he was forced to work at menial tasks until he was about 24. At that time his circumstances changed and he began to work as a teacher, moving about and teaching small groups. His renown as a man of extraordinary character and learning spread, and groups of disciples began to follow him.

His teachings, best known through the *Analects*, were concerned with ethics and morality, rather than religion in any sense. His work was in essence a protest against the time in which he lived when interstate warfare and feudalism were rampant. Having great humility, he always called himself a transmitter, not an originator, and claimed he was only propagating the tenets of the ideal state that were taught in the ancient classics and were said to have been originated by the sages who lived in the Golden Age – a period that existed in the mists of time before recorded history began in China.

As disorder spread throughout the land, he passionately advocated his idea that rulers would bring peace, prosperity, and justice to their lands if they lived the consummately ethical and moral lives he described in his teachings. When he was about 50 years old, he was given a high administrative post in his home province of Lu (now Shandong) and a chance to prove that his philosophy would work. It did, and Lu soon became so strong and prosperous that the head of a neighboring province intrigued to have Confucius removed from office. After this, he never found another ruler willing to take him on and put his ideas into practice. After this period in which Confucius spoke his truth and was rejected, his humility prompted him to consider himself a "failure" in his political career, even a "stray dog" in society in general. It was at this point in his life that he recognized what he called the Mandate of Heaven and surrendered himself to it: he withdrew from politics and devoted his life to private teaching and to writing.

During the Han dynasty, some 300 years after Confucius' death, his basic principles were adopted by China's rulers, and they became official state policy. Although the official fortunes of Confucianism rose and fell at various times over the centuries, from the Han dynasty to the Chinese Revolution that overthrew the last Qing dynasty in 1911, Confucian concepts – and various distortions of them – had a pervasive influence on Chinese thought. After 1911, Confucianism was discounted and when the Communist Party came to power in China in 1949 it was officially declared decadent and corrupt. During the late 1960s and early 1970s official government campaigns were launched to attempt to wipe out its influence.

As I followed the intuitive call I felt to learn about Confucius, I started to carry his works around with me, reading them as I rode on the subway or waited at busy street car stops. With the noises of the city – so glaringly different from the ones I'd become used to in my home in the woods in Zurich – clanking around me, I read the works of this ancient master with the insights I'd gained during my analysis and training and found much to love and admire. And as I began to see him as someone who was devoted to living toward wholeness, I found insights that would help me in my own personal growth and in my practice.

Confucius himself never wrote down the principles of his philosophy. These were written down by his disciples and gathered into the *Analects*, which are generally held to be the most accurate source on his teachings and his life. As I delved into his teaching I read the *Analects* again, but I also explored the classic works that were written before his time and contained the knowledge he believed was so essential. Known as the *Wu Ching* (*Five Classics*), these books are also part of what makes up the body of work known as Confucianism. The five books include the *I Ching* (*Book of Changes*), *Shu Ching* (*Book of History*), *Shih Ching* (*Book of Poetry*), *Li Chi* (*Book of Rites*), and *Chunqiu* (*Spring and Autumn Annals*).

Confucius' system of ethics and morality was based on the "five virtues": compassion, righteousness, propriety, wisdom, and sincerity. He also believed reverence for parents, both the living and the dead, was of the greatest importance. The most fundamental principle in Confucius' thought was the concept of *jen*. Although it is extremely difficult to translate, *jen* embodies the essence of what we associate with qualities such as benevolence, human feeling, mutual respect, love, human-heartedness, and goodness. In this sense it is the "supreme virtue" and epitomizes the best of human qualities. In relationships between individuals, *jen* manifests in terms of loyalty (*chung*) and altruism (*shu*) and is expressed in Confucius' Golden Rule, "Do not do to others what you do not want done to yourself." Additional insight into the meaning of *jen* can be gained by looking at the way it is written in Chinese, where it is composed of two characters. One is "man" (also *jen*) and the other is "two" (*erh*). Thus, *jen* embraces all those moral qualities that ought to govern one human being in his relations with another. It is on the basis of *jen* that a person can relate to others and become himself. This is reflected in Confucius' second most famous aphorism, "*Jen* is to love all men; wisdom is to know all men."

Confucius believed that *jen* was an integral part of our inborn nature. It was not, as some other philosophers have believed, a quality that was learned or taught to us by society. It was, rather, bestowed upon us by Heaven. As he says in one of his aphorisms, "What Heaven confers (*ming*) is called the inborn nature. The following of this nature is called the Way (*tao*). The cultivation of the Way is called instruction."[1]

In a more Western sense, then, *jen* can be seen in some ways as that force within us that compels us to seek a fulfilled development of our true original nature. Thus, inherent in our Heaven-endowed nature is the spiritual propensity for self-development. In another Western interpretation, *jen* can be seen as the heart's divinity. In this way, it lies very close to the Christian concept of God as the interior ground of being, and to the Renaissance conception of *imago Dei*, the image of God in human beings. Of course, Confucius would never have used images like this as his philosophy was basically a secular and not a religious or obviously spiritual one.

Still, the central focus of this philosophy was to encourage individuals to follow the Way, or the *tao*. He believed this journey was what he called *tien ming*, or the Mandate of Heaven. In his own life, once he retired to private

life, he began to understand the Mandate of Heaven. Eventually, he
realized his life-long search for the *tao* and came to actually manifest the
Mandate of Heaven in his daily life.

> At 15, my mind was set on learning.
> At 30, my character had been formed.
> At 40, I had no more perplexities.
> At 50, I knew the Mandate of Heaven (Tien-ming).
> At 60, I was at ease with whatever I heard.
> At 70, I could follow my heart's desire without
>   transgressing moral principles.[2]

Confucius called the person who pursued the Way, *chun tzu*, which can be
translated as the son of the Son of Heaven or, more loosely, as the noble or
superior man. The *chun tzu* was the true "gentleman" whose highest goal
was self-knowledge, for self-knowledge was in Confucian terms the pre-
requisite of all wise thinking and action[3] and, in an even more profound
sense, the key to knowing the secrets of the universe. "For a man to give full
realization to his heart is for him to understand his own nature, and a man
who knows his own nature will know Heaven."[4] On this journey to flowing
completely with the *tao*, the gentleman was to cultivate his moral mind,
which included his feelings as well as his thoughts. He would also strive to
develop his capacity for understanding, evaluation, and discrimination.
Confucius believed an integral step in learning to follow and flow with the
tao was taking part in certain rites, ceremonies, and ways of behaving that
had been set down by the sages of antiquity in the *Li Chi*, or *Book of Rites*,
which was one of the *Five Classics*. Even certain types of poetry and music
could help the *chun tzu* come ever more closely in touch with his inner
nature. And, as he did, he would calm his own conflicting passions and
emotions and create tranquility in the world around him. Increasingly, he
would gain in his ability to bring order to the world at large.

The *chun tzu*'s humanity was defined by his moral intention to help the
tao prevail in the world. Because of this, the desire to take on social or
political responsibility was seen as the natural corollary of following the
Way. Thus the true gentleman would involve himself actively in public life.
In turn, Confucius believed that when such men controlled government, the
natural result would be a just, well-ordered, ideal society. But this well-
ordered society didn't just appear because the ruler at the top was a *chun
tzu*. At the very basis of this ordered society was the type of sincere,
mutually beneficial relationships that were typified by *jen*.

As I read these teachings of Confucius, I found so much to identify with.
I could see many parallels between Jung's ideas and those of Confucius. I
found, for instance, a striking similarity between Confucius' description of
how following the natural, inborn nature would result in self-realization

and the way Jung's concept of individuation has so often been described as a natural unfoldment that occurs in the way a flower unfolds naturally from the blueprint on the seed within. But there were elements of his teachings that I still found extremely problematic, and were, I discovered, directly related to Confucius' view of family relationships and to the concept of filial piety – precisely the two aspects of Confucian thinking that I have found to be most intricately intertwined with the practice of footbinding and how footbinding functions as a metaphor in our lives as women today.

One of the most problematic elements in his teaching was, as stated in the last chapter, how he equated woman with the inferior man. And after I had delved into Confucius more deeply, I realized that women weren't just being equated with men from the lower levels of society, but with the man who was the opposite of the "superior" man. In other words, they were at the opposite end of the spectrum from the *chun tzu*, the man who was following the Way. Whether Confucius believed, as seems to be implied by this, that a woman was incapable of following the Way, we have no way of knowing. However, he did leave women mostly out of the picture when he described the sincere, mutually beneficial relationships mentioned above that he believed were absolutely integral to the functioning of his ideal society. These relationships are strictly defined in Confucian texts. They include: ruler and subject, father and son, husband and wife, elder and younger brother, and friends.

A moment's reflection on these relationships reveals that the only role mentioned for a woman is wife; daughter, mother, grandmother, and all the other tremendously important roles a woman was able to play even in the patriarchal society of Confucius' day are left out. Although these five cardinal relationships were to be typified by *jen*, two other virtues were also essential. These were *chung*, or loyalty to one's master, and *hsiao*, or filial piety. *Hsiao* is also often translated as duty, and filial piety can be thought of as doing one's filial duty with almost a kind of reverence.

Thus, ideally, the subject should exhibit absolute loyalty to the ruler and perform his duty with pious regard. In exact imitation of this relationship between ruler and subject, the wife was expected to exhibit absolute loyalty and duty to her husband, indeed to subjugate herself to him as her ruler. In the same way, the son was to exhibit complete loyalty and filial piety to his father. Within the hierarchy created by this framework, a younger son would need to subjugate himself to both the father and the older brother, and so on down the line.

To understand how deeply the concept of filial piety is rooted in the Chinese psyche, it is worth looking at one of the most prevalent creation stories from Chinese mythology. This legend features Nu Wa and her brother, or perhaps her husband, Fu Xi. They are said to emerge, without being born, from the dual cosmic principles of *yin* (the feminine, receptive, and dark) and *yang* (the masculine, active, and bright). Members of the

Figure 3.1 The divine couple: Nu Wa and Fu Xi

Source: Drawing by Christy Shum. Adapted from a Han dynasty stone rubbing in a Shangdong temple

trinity known as the Three August Ones, Nu Wa and Fu Xi are thought of as the bearers of civilization and culture. Reigning over the Earth, they had the power to solve problems and deal with the adversities facing human beings. It was their responsibility to make sure the Earth was habitable.

In the beginning, after Nu Wa and Fu Xi had risen up out of the primordial forces of *yin* and *yang*, they shaped Heaven and Earth and lived together on Mount K'un-lun. Both were half human and half animal. Nu Wa had the head of a human and the tail of a snake or, in some renditions, a dragon (see Figure 3.1). Because there were no humans on Earth, Nu Wa decided after a time to create them. In order to do so, she reached down into the yellow earth and began to painstakingly mould the humans who would live in China and who would come to call themselves "the black-haired people." After making countless numbers of these wonderful people, she grew tired from her exhausting efforts. Finally thinking of a way to make the people faster, she drew a rope through the wet earth and let the drops of mud that clung to it fall to the ground. These drops of mud also became black-haired people. But they, not being crafted by hand, lacked some of the qualities and abilities that the earlier people had been given. But even though all of the black-haired people were not created equal, it didn't really matter for each and every one of them was cradled securely between the yellow earth from which they had come and the bountiful Heavens above.

In this cosmology, the yellow earth, the people, and the Heavens form a trinity that has been central to the Chinese worldview for millennia. The yellow earth symbolizes something that is far more significant than just the land. The color yellow represents the power of centrality in Chinese thought. The yellow earth is special, virtually sacred. Thus, the people who come from it are blessed. The yellow earth provides them with the "hundred crops" that will nourish them. The Heavens in turn are the source of the sun and rain that will make the crops flourish. The black-haired people are cradled between the two.

In the Chinese psyche, Heaven is represented by one's father and Earth by one's mother. The ego, or individual, is the child that is cradled between them. A father and mother nourish their offspring with food just as Heaven and Earth provide for humanity. In this naturalistic view, people pay homage to the cosmos in thanksgiving for life. In the same way children revere their parents and give thanks to them for giving them life and feeding them. Thus, a kind of veneration for those who are in some way above us or "superior" to us begins at the ground level with the expression of filial piety within the family and is repeated upward through the whole of society.

Confucius placed tremendous importance on this – for he saw the family, not the individual, as the basic unit of society. He believed that with clearly defined position and authority, respect for the status of others, and the subordination of self for the benefit of the family as a whole, peace and prosperity would prevail. If the family unit functioned on these well-ordered lines, so would the neighborhood, the village, the province, the country, and the world. And the family unit could not function as it was meant to in this system without filial piety.

The fact that Confucius' vision of harmony and order was based on these clearly defined hierarchical differences made his ideas vulnerable to distortion by the emperors and politicians who would later use this aspect of his ideas to support autocratic rule. In fact, for the next two millennia, Confucian scholars would interpret his teachings in ways that supported the Imperial system. These teachings were used as ideological tools to maintain political stability and control in a centralized, authoritarian state.[5] Women especially bore the brunt of the abuse of power.

A number of scholars have recognized this and stressed the notion that Confucianism, undeniably patriarchal as it was, created a situation in which women were virtually completely suppressed or even subjugated. However, more recent research, particularly that done in the last two and a half decades, has tried to offer a more comprehensive view of the way women lived during the 2000 years of Imperial rule. This paints a picture that shows women's many accomplishments during various periods and the ways in which they managed to have influence and even power in some instances. This also shows that it is simplistic to say that Confucianism was completely anti-feminine. Works by sinologists such as Dorothy Ko, Susan Brownell, Jeff Wasserstrom, and others show that in some cases Confucian women participated actively, if often only conservatively, in the intellectual life of society.[6] As important as these sinologists' work is in terms of accurately understanding the tremendous complexities of Chinese history, it can hardly be denied that the prevailing attitude toward women during the 2000 years of Imperial rule was in general extremely suppressive. It is also well-established that without this climate of suppression created by the distortion of Confucius' ideas in the Imperial system, footbinding would have had a difficult time flourishing.

The first easily identifiable step in the use of Confucian ideas as a manipulative tool to control society occurred with the Han dynasty when "Confucianism" was elevated to an orthodox state teaching. The Han dynasty was founded in 202 BC by a peasant named Liu Bang, who led a revolt against the brutal Qin dynasty that came before it. Liu Bang was a minor official, and the emperors before him had all been noble. Recognizing that he needed some kind of authority, he adopted the Confucian idea that he was ruling by the Mandate of Heaven. Under his successor, Emperor Wu, the orthodox Confucian system that would prevail in government over the next 2000 years was developed. The credit for this is given to Tung Chung-shu, who was one of Wu's advisors.

Tung Chung-shu brought Confucian texts that had been destroyed in the Qin dynasty back into favor and essentially canonized them. Based on Confucius' idea that positions of authority in the government should be given out based on merit rather than heredity, Tung Chung-shu developed an education system in which scholars studied the Confucian Classics and were then awarded government positions according to how well they did in examinations on the material. This examination system is how the class of "Confucian scholars," often known as the *literati* (*shih*) was created. Results of these "civil service" examinations determined a man's fate and his position in society. Social prominence was not to be held as a privilege of birth, but to be achieved through proficiency in the Confucian Classics along with individual merit and virtue. To maintain their status quo, these scholar-officials learned to see and interpret the world through Confucian lenses, and often to distort it according to the needs of a particular emperor. Over time the mastery of the Confucian Classics, the examination system, and the attainment of bureaucratic office combined to form the backbone of the Chinese value system.

Under Han Confucianism the idea that the patriarchal, hierarchical structure of the family was the basic model for "government" became entrenched. Classic works such as the *Rites and Ceremonials* (*Chou Li* and *Yi Li*) from the Zhou dynasty were collected and developed, expanding Confucian rules and rites in ways that endorsed and intensified this view of the family:

> Inside the smaller doors leading to the inner apartments are to be found all the rules of government. There is fear and respect for the father and also for the elder brother. Wife and children, servants and concubines are like the common people, serfs and underlings.[7]

Han Confucianism markedly increased the negative bias of this view of women as intractable and difficult to understand. It even ascribes to woman an explicitly inferior nature.[8] In fact, the inferiority of woman to man was considered as natural as the inferiority of Earth to Heaven. The ideal woman was the *nei jen* – "she who is within." A complete segregation of the sexes was advocated. Various literary works instructed women about their inferiority and the "virtues" of obedience and loyalty.[9] One, a book called *Nu Chieh* (*Women's Precepts*), was written by Lady Pan Chao, a woman who died in 116 AD. Her strict and unrelenting instructions on women's inferiority and the need for absolute obedience to their husband were considered a shining example by Confucian scholars for centuries to come, and it inspired many similar treatises in the following centuries.[10]

The next major development in Confucianism didn't occur until late in the 13th century during the Song dynasty. By this time Buddhism and Taoism had been spreading for several centuries, and scholars who were well versed in these two traditions developed a new form of Confucianism that incorporated ideas from them. Known as Neo-Confucianism, one of its main intentions was "to restore Heaven's principle from the clouds of human desires."[11] One of these scholars was the philosopher Chu Hsi (1130–1200), who directed the revival and reconstruction of Confucianism. He organized Confucian thinking into a truly cohesive system known as School of Li (*Li Hsueh*), which became one of the foremost schools of Neo-Confucianism. This was an extremely rationalistic system that emphasized investigating the world with a mind devoid of emotions. It denied life after death, immortality, and deity, and ancient terms used in Confucius' day for spirit, soul, and demon were given technical meanings associated with physical phenomena. This was a system with a pronounced tendency to value form over matter, this-worldly over other-worldly, and the organic over the spiritual. Although not all sinologists today might agree, from a Jungian perspective, this can be seen to have imposed a distinctly negative attitude toward the Feminine and, on a concrete level, the position of women in society.[12]

It became considered unpatriotic to express doubt about the authenticity of Chu Hsi's interpretation of the Classics. Any "non-Confucianist" thoughts were treated with suspicion and everyone was expected to conform. Soon these attitudes worked their way from the government on down and began to affect the daily life of the people. The separation of the sexes and the seclusion of women began to be practiced in earnest. As mentioned in the last chapter, this was the period of history where the chastity of women began to become a veritable cult, the remarrying of widows became a moral crime, and divorce for whatever reason was considered a disgrace for life for a woman. You'll remember from the last chapter, this was also the dynasty when footbinding began to spread. And this can hardly be a coincidence, as the philosopher Chu Hsi is the same man who ordered that women in Fujian province should have their feet excessively bound in order to curb their natural tendency to immorality.[13]

For the Westerner reading this book today it may be hard to believe that these Confucian attitudes about family structure and filial piety could still be influencing the Chinese psyche today. Especially since both the Revolution of 1911 and later the Revolution of 1949 attempted to abolish and eradicate the Confucian heritage. But indeed they do, and the truth of this was brought home to me when a young woman I'll call Pearl came to me for analysis.

When Pearl phoned me for an appointment, she was brief but firm in articulating her purpose for this meeting. I was very impressed by the forthright, professional way she conducted the phone conversation. She explained that she was a clinical psychologist who had recently taken on a new position at a large hospital in the city. Feeling tremendously overwhelmed, she hoped to find some answers to her difficulties in meeting with me. To be frank, I found her manner on the phone a bit intimidating. Not so much because she was a psychologist herself, but because she seemed to exude an extraordinary amount of confidence and self-possession. I also honestly wondered a bit about her being Chinese and whether this might affect boundary issues with me.

So, with quite a bit of excitement and some trepidation, I awaited our appointment. I was quite surprised when I met her, and my earlier image of her changed completely during the session. She was dressed casually in jeans and T-shirt, looking sloppy and tired. Rather thin and petite, she looked much younger than her age of 35. She started to talk right away, telling me about her family history, her relationship with her parents, her education, and her travels. It quickly became clear that the overly confident professional I first experienced was, inside, a needy little girl who had to tell her story and was starved for such attention.

Beyond this, at the end of that first session I was struck by a very unusual thought. In spite of the fact that Pearl's appearance was so Western, and as I learned, she had been raised in the West, the words "I have China in front of me" came into my mind. I was certain the phrase that had come to me summed up something extremely basic to her nature. During the months we worked together this was proved to be the case. How this affected her and how she eventually managed to regain her strong inner Feminine standpoint by "unbinding her feet" is described in later portions of the book, but for now even an introduction to her story shows how deeply the ancient concept of filial piety was ingrained in this modern woman.

Before I came to understand this, I learned a good deal about Pearl's family background. Pearl's parents, who were born in China, were both from prominent gentry families. In the 1940s they left China to study in the West, and both earned doctoral degrees, her father in physics and her mother in literature. Although they had planned to return to China, the

Communist Revolution of 1949 occurred while they were studying, and they were stranded overseas. They took a brief sojourn in Brazil and eventually settled in London, England. Their life "in exile" was devoted to work and achievement, and they both became highly respected in their fields of scholarship. Pearl had also led a fascinating and adventurous life so far. She had not only managed to obtain a doctoral degree but had spent a great deal of time traveling. Aware that much of this travel had been motivated by a search for herself and her cultural identity, she had lived in various "New Age" communities in Europe and the United States, and in an ashram in India. She had also spent two years studying Chinese medicine in China.

When she first came to me she had finally settled down into her career. Her major concern was the anxiety she had been experiencing while trying to adapt to her new work environment. She described the hospital as a "cold, competitive, militaristic environment, devoid of feeling." Intensely afraid of her boss, Pearl felt a tremendous pressure to perform and prove herself. She also felt intimidated by her colleagues, as if she was under observation all the time. The daily tension and anxiety she was enduring had led to depression and bodily reactions that included fatigue, lethargy, nausea, and weight loss. After several sessions Pearl had a very significant dream. (These dreams are discussed in more detail in Chapter 5, pp. 58–60.) In the first part of the dream, Pearl is driving around an island in a car. She arrives at a café where a woman appears and begins to speak to her. The woman compliments Pearl on the nice scarves she always wears, but says she was expecting Pearl to be wearing her pink silk scarf from India and is surprised to see her wearing a Chinese scarf instead. Quite large and long, the scarf is covered with a map of China. After Pearl shows the scarf to the woman, the scene changes and Pearl is in the café with her father and his friend.

Pearl adds: "They are talking about making an acquaintance with a pretty young woman. Another woman comes along and says that the younger woman is only 18, but she herself is 28, and that the older men can forget about the idea of meeting the girl." As Pearl focused on the age of 18 – the age she began to struggle for autonomy – she began to reveal more about her relationship with her father. When Pearl was growing up, she adored her father who she saw as her "first love" and her "animus figure." In describing him, she used the words "quiet, powerful, intelligent." But there was also another side to this, for she also described him as omnipotent and intimidating. Then, much to my surprise, she revealed to me the fact that "she had to bow to him every day" in order to show her respect for him.

Conversation around the dream also revealed that as she was never accepted by her parents unless she achieved and achieved well, love was conditional on performance:

When my report card showed 85%, I was merely asked: Why not 90% . . . or 95% . . . It was never good enough. When something went wrong, I felt myself being questioned to my very roots, as if I had no right to exist.

When Pearl started university, she wanted to major in music and registered for classes for the fall term. When her parents heard of her decision they dismissed it as impractical. Her father insisted that she study mathematics instead so she could "help him with his research." Then without her knowing it, he personally went to the university to change her registration without her consent. Striving to be a good filial daughter, Pearl spent her first year at university as a math major, only barely enduring what she found to be a dry, boring subject. Finally after the first year, Pearl found her studies unbearable. Dropping out, she left home to begin her travels. Although this showed a spark of independence, by the time she came back and started university again Pearl's inner compulsion to honor her parents by doing what they wished reasserted itself. For, although she had no real desire to study psychology, she chose this as her major. It was, she explained to me, a compromise. Because it was technically a science, she knew it would be acceptable to her father. She also knew it was a topic that would help her avoid criticism at home because it was a field her parents knew nothing about.

When Pearl, during our sessions, began to focus on the 28-year-old woman, she saw her as a symbol of hope. The older woman was protecting the younger one from the men, and 28 was the age when she had finally finished her doctorate and was able to begin supporting herself. But it would be some time before Pearl would be able to "support" and stand on her own two feet in a more fundamental way. Even when she started her new job at the prestigious hospital, the pattern of showing filial piety to those in authority was still deeply imbedded in Pearl's psyche. This was shown when she said:

> Now when my boss tells me I have done a good job, I say to myself: I must do better next time. It never stops. I am tired of working but I don't know how to play.

And then, even more poignantly, when she added:

> I only know how to please others and I don't know how to please myself.

Notes

1 James Legge, trans., *Chinese Classics*, London: Oxford University Press, 1893–5, p. 2: 349.

2 All quotations from Confucius are from Wing-tsit Chan, trans., *A Source Book in Chinese Philosophy*, Princeton, NJ: Princeton University Press, 1963.
3 Sukie Colgrave, *The Spirit of the Valley*, Los Angeles, CA: J.P. Tarcher, 1979, pp. 77–9.
4 D. C. Lau, trans., *Mencius*, Harmondsworth: Penguin Classics, 1970, Bk VIII, part A, p. 182.
5 Michael H. Bond and Kwang-kuo Hwang, 'The Social Psychology of Chinese People', in Bond, Michael H., ed., *The Psychology of Chinese People*, Oxford: Oxford University Press, 1986, pp. 223–4.
6 Terry Tak-ling Woo, 'Emotions and Self Cultivation in Nu Lunyu (Woman's Analects)', *Journal of Chinese Philosophy*, 36 (2009), pp. 334–47.
7 James Legge, trans., *Hsiao Ching* (*Classic of Filial Piety*), in *Sacred Books of the East*, London: Oxford University Press, 1879, p. 3: 488.
8 Fung Yu-lan, *A Short History of Chinese Philosophy*, New York: Macmillan, 1950, pp. 193–5. In Tung Chung-shu's interpretation of *yin* and *yang*, for instance, there is a clear bias towards *yang*, the masculine aspect. He writes: "The constant principle of the universe is the succession (waxing and waning) of the *yin* and the *yang*. The *yang* is Heaven's beneficent force, while the *yin* is its chastising force. . . . Heaven has trust in the *yang* but not in the *yin*, it likes beneficence but not chastising." Also: "The human mind contains two elements: *hsing*, 'nature,' and *ching*, 'emotions' or 'feelings.' From *hsing* comes the virtue of human-heartedness, from *ching* the vice of covetousness. Thus *hsing* is equal to Heaven's *yang* and *ching* to its *yin*."
9 Lin Yu-tang, *My Country and My People*, New York: John Day, p. 140. See also the translation by Albert R. O'Hara, *The Position of Women in Early China*, Taiwan: Mei Ya Publications, 1955.
10 See also the translation by Florence Ayscough, *Chinese Women, Yesterday and Today*, Boston, MA: Houghton Mifflin, 1937, pp. 228–63. Examples include *Nu Hsiao Ching* (*Book of Filial Piety for Women*) in the Tang dynasty; *Nu Hsun* (*Instructions for the Inner Apartments*), 1405; *Nu Hsueh* (*Study for Women*); and a number of *Hsin Fu Pu* (*Manuals for Brides*) in the 17th century. See Robert van Gulik, *Sex Life in Early China*, Leiden: E. J. Brill, 1961, pp. 43–5, 97–8.
11 Mokusen Miyuki, 'The Secret of the Golden Flower, Studies and Translations,' Diploma Thesis, C. G. Jung Institute, Zurich, 1967, pp. 39, 65; Fung Yu-lan, op. cit., pp. 237, 287, 294, 301, 306, 319.
12 Fung Yu-lan, ibid. In Chu Hsi's new system of thought all objects were made up of two forces, *li* and *ch'i*. He called *li* the "Great Ultimate" and saw it as a universal principle that underlay everything in the universe, while *ch'i* was substance that made up matter. *Li* was immutable and constant, but *ch'i* could dissolve and change. Chu Hsi identified *li* with human nature and felt it was the same in all people. The differences in people were ascribed to differences in the quality of the *ch'i* that made up their physical bodies, some having more "turbid" *ch'i* than others. *Li* was concealed like a pearl within this turbid matter, which was also the origin of all evil. This hidden pearl could be retrieved only through knowledge gained by investigating the world with a mind free of human desires.
    Joseph Needham believes that this analytic and empirical orientation of Neo-Confucian philosophy, similar in essence to Western scientific naturalism, contributed to the development of the scientific world-outlook in China. And indeed the Song dynasty witnessed an unparalleled flowering of all kinds of activities in the pure and applied sciences. See his *Science and Civilization in China*, Vols. 1 & 2, Cambridge: Cambridge University Press, 1954, 1956, pp. 475, 490, 492–3.

13 Howard S. Levy, *The Lotus Lovers, The Complete History of the Curious Erotic Custom of Footbinding in China*, Buffalo, NY: Prometheus Books, 1992, Chapter 2: "As the national outlook on feminine morality became more stringent, footbinding became more widespread and more significant. The Yuan writer Tao Tsung I records that in his own time, ladies considered it shameful to have unbound feet. Friar Odoric of Pordenone, a contemporary of Marco Polo, who was in northern China in 1324, was the first foreigner to write about the custom. Portuguese missionaries in the 15th and 16th centuries made the following observation: 'The women were very secluded and virtuous and it was a very rare thing for us to see a woman in the cities and large towns, unless it was an old crone. They were accustomed since babyhood to bind the feet in such a way that they deform them, leaving all the toes twisted below the great toe.'"

Chapter 4

A Pearl of great price

Pearl was a client who visited me very early in my career as an analyst. The sense that she, in spite of her modern appearance, contemporary education, and New Age lifestyle, embodied all of China was a very powerful one for me. The scarf she wore in the dream that was emblazoned with a map of China later attested to this and proved to be a key symbol in her healing process. The degree of filial piety she exhibited made me think a great deal about family relationships in Chinese culture, and I was once again struck by the fact that, except for the husband and wife combination, Confucius had left women out of his conceptualization of cardinal relationships. To clarify in my own mind these "missing" relationships and the roles women played, I decided to write out descriptions of them. Later, this proved to be a valuable tool for several women, both Asian and Western, in my practice. It was as if looking at contemporary relationships through a Confucian lens allowed these women to sharpen the focus on what was happening in their daily lives. For example, a friend of mine, Jeanne, who is a fairly typical Caucasian American, had a very strong reaction to hearing me tell Pearl's story in a lecture. "She had to *bow* to her father every day!" my friend cried, "That's disgusting!"

Several days later, however, Jeanne told me she'd been thinking about Pearl and had realized, with a shock, that she too had "bowed" to her father every day:

> After dinner, which was always fairly formal at our house, I had to stand and ask to be excused. I had to look at my father, who *always* sat at the head of the table, and say, "Sir, may I be excused, please?" I don't think there's anything wrong with a child asking to be excused. But after hearing Pearl's story, it struck me that I had to ask my *father*! Never my mother. If he was out of town on business, I just got up from the table and walked away. And I always had to say "Sir"; I never had to call my mother "Mam!"

Jeanne realized that she had also had to "venerate" her father in other ways. For instance, if he was working at his desk in the den, the other family members would have to tiptoe around. "S-h-h-h-h!" her mother would say, "Don't disturb your father. He's working!" But no one, my friend realized, ever had to act like this when her mother was doing something that required concentration, and this was in spite of the fact that her mother was a hospital administrator and sometimes brought home very important work. Jeanne also realized she had been taught to tiptoe, both figuratively and literally, around the house whenever her father was upset about anything.

> When I was thinking about all this, I had this very clear image of myself as a teenager, tiptoeing around the house when my father was angry or upset. I can see myself walking on tiptoe with my shoulders sort of hunched over and bent forward, exactly as if I were just beginning to bow. When I was tiptoeing around, the thought at the back of mind was that he was the "important one," that his needs outweighed everyone else's. Part of this was, of course, fear. But I think that is part of filial piety too. There is respect and veneration, when it's deserved, but fear of the person who is "superior," higher than you in the hierarchy, is there too. My father was clearly the "alpha male" in the pack! And we were expected to show respect, whether he deserved it or not.

Several months later Jeanne told me that she had continued to think about how she had virtually always treated her father with respect, but rarely gave her mother the same accord. Because Jeanne still has a very problematic relationship with her mother, this proved to be a valuable insight for her:

> I realized this was one of the ways I contributed to the difficulties in my relationship with my mother. I always showed this "required" respect to my father but really didn't give it to her! On some level this was probably one of the reasons mother was always angry with me. And I was always reacting to this anger, usually showing even more dis-respect! And so the cycle went on and became ingrained.

Through hearing stories like this from both clients and friends, it became abundantly clear to me that we could all, as women today, gain a great deal of insight from looking at the roles that were missing from Confucius' list of cardinal relationships. It is important to point out, however, that these descriptions do not in any way depict the whole of life for Chinese women in Imperial times. As Ko and other sinologists have recently stressed, the life of Chinese women was extremely complex and varied greatly in different eras and in the various provinces. Detailed descriptions of these conditions are the subject matter for entire books.[1] My intention is simply to paint with broad brushstrokes how women generally fit into the strictly defined hierarchal structure during the 2000 years of Imperial rule in China and, in this way, provide new insights into the way hierarchical family structure and concepts like filial piety have been embedded in the unconscious for millennia.

As you will see, a curious paradox lay at the very basis of the Chinese woman's position in society. From the moment of her birth, her value as a human being depreciated because she was not a son, and yet at the same time she held within her the absolutely essential potential of becoming the producer of sons in the future. The integral importance of this was rooted in ancestor worship, a belief system that had been prevalent in China since earliest times and was later adapted to further the emphasis on filial piety and the rigid family structure that was so essential to the rulers during Imperial times.

In this system, those individuals in the family's direct genealogical lineage who had died before them were held to be intermediaries between the forces of Heaven and the daily life of the family. The ancestors were believed to have the ability to intercede in the events of the family's daily life. They could bring good fortune, prevent disease and disaster, and in general influence the course of events that affected the family's existence. Careful genealogical records tracing the family's ancestors were inscribed on tablets that were set upon an alter in each family's home. In order to insure the ancestors' active and beneficent participation in the family's affairs, rites and rituals honoring them needed to be carried out. Without successive male heirs there would be no one to continue the family lineage and sustain the needs of the ancestral spirits.

Because the woman was the means of producing sons, she was seen as the essential connecting link between the living and the dead – but this positive aspect of her position in the family structure was inextricably linked to the ability to produce a son. Failure to do so was seen as the most unfilial act of all. This paradox – the female's essential inferiority for simply not being male in contrast to her incomparable value as the indispensable link in the chain forged between the dead and the living, between Heaven and Earth – colored every aspect of her life from infancy onwards. For me, as a Jungian, coming to a deeper understanding of this paradox made it even more essential to me to try to describe the roles in a woman's life that were missing from Confucius' list of cardinal relationships. In doing so, it made sense to me to think of them in terms of the stages in a woman's development from infancy to matriarch.

The roles in a woman's life

Infant girl child and daughter

Within the confines of the family, as is already clear, the inferiority of women began at birth. Beyond the fact that she would never be a male in the ancestral lineage, she was considered a bad economic and emotional investment. Just how ancient this attitude was is reflected in a song found in one of the books Confucius considered the great classics, the *Book of Poetry*. The song describes the different customs observed for a newborn boy and girl in the palace, symbolizing their different future status in life. Regarding the boy it describes how he is "richly" cradled and how his "lusty cries" are celebrated as a sign of vigor. For a toy, he is given a jade scepter. The scepter symbolizes kingliness or royalty and jade has since ancient times been considered the most auspicious of stones. In contrast, when a daughter is born she is simply "cradled on the floor." The song says she is expected "not to cause trouble to her parents." For a toy, she is given not an auspicious royal symbol but a loom-warf![2]

A passage written centuries later shows how little this attitude had changed:

> When a newborn baby comes into the world, if it's a boy as strong as a wolf, its parents are still afraid that he might be too weak; whereas if it's a girl as sweet and as gentle as a little mouse, her parents still fear she might be too strong.[3]

Another aspect of this is revealed in an old Chinese saying: "A daughter married is like water poured out the door."[4] Although an infant girl's eventual marriage was considered her main purpose, it could only be hoped that it would bring increased social standing or create beneficial alliances for the family. For once she was married, she was gone. She no long "belonged" to her birth family. Since her marriage into another family was considered the pivotal point in a girl's development, she was in a way a "transient" in her birth family, and this sense of impermanence dominated her childhood.

Her marriage would almost certainly be arranged by her father as he was responsible for the relations of the family with the outside world and the advancement of the family position within society. It was also his right to sell her if deemed necessary. In difficult social and economic situations, a daughter might be sold to the groom's family as a child-bride when her labor was sought and expected. Among those in dire straits, and especially among the peasants, girls were also sold as concubines or servants to wealthy families, and as prostitutes. Female infanticide was practiced from feudal times. Naturally such practices created a shortage of women as prospective brides for peasant boys.

Ironically, the Confucian ideal of womanhood appears to have demanded a tougher training for daughters than sons. This was especially apparent by the time footbinding came into widespread practice. Although in a physical sense the goal of footbinding was the creation of the tiny golden lotuses that would be desired and adored by her future husband, in a psychological sense the painful ordeal was a mark of her capacity to suffer and obey. These were the most prized attributes of the ideal wife and daughter-in-law. The suffering she endured during footbinding also initiated her into womanhood; it gave her a superior knowledge and a superior maturity. It is hardly surprising that a girl appeared and behaved much more mature than a boy of her age. In comparison to boys she had an abbreviated childhood.

From the time their feet were bound, girls' lives became much more circumspect and the emphasis on their learning proper manners and behaviors intensified. In a description of the girl who has reached puberty, Lin Yu-tang wrote:

> She plays with few toys, does more work, talks more quietly, walks about more delicately and sits more properly. . . . She learns above all, demureness at the cost of sprightliness. Something of her childish fun and tomfoolery goes out of her, and she does not laugh but only smiles. . . . She learns embroidery . . . keeps herself busy with her home duties and guards her feelings sacredly. . . . She cultivates the charm of mystery and distance. . . . Thus she is prepared for the responsibilities of wifehood and motherhood.[5]

Once footbinding came into practice, it was the main task that consolidated the esteemed feminine virtues. A daughter was expected to learn her womanly skills and to work hard in the household. In her seclusion, she prepared for her proper role as a wife in her husband's home, where her real life would begin.

If you look again at Confucius' cardinal relationships you will notice that "daughter" is, in fact, not mentioned at all. In one sense this can be interpreted as meaning that none of the roles she played – mother–daughter, father–daughter, brother–sister – were officially defined by the collective.

Daughters and mothers

Within the structure of the hierarchal family a mother had very different roles to play in relation to her sons and her daughters. This was because her main duty was to serve her husband and her husband's parents by producing sons. The birth of these sons was essential to her standing in the family. In some families, even though she was married, she was not considered an official part of the family until she produced a son. In this situation the birth of a daughter – unless the hoped-for number of sons had already been produced – was, at best, disappointing to some degree and, at worst, a near disaster for the new mother, who could be seen by the family as having failed in her filial duty.

For the young mother, the need for sons wasn't just necessary to secure her position in the family. Because she had no power or position in the hierarchy in and of herself, the only way she could obtain any real security was through the love and loyalty of her sons. Because sons had some standing and power in the family structure they could intervene on her behalf, support her, and help her get what she wanted or needed. This was especially true in terms of the oldest son, whose position was second only to his father's. In this way, the sons also provided her security in old age and upon the eventuality of her husband's death. Daughters simply could not provide this for their mothers. They were lowest of all in the family structure. While this did mean that they could be of help to their mothers in performing household tasks, even this benefit was transitory. Eventually they would be made members of another family, where their loyalty would need to be transferred from their own mother to their mother-in-law.

This did not mean that mothers did not love their daughters. Traditionally, all children were adored in the Chinese family. It is inevitable, however, that these age-old values colored a mother's attitude toward her daughter from the moment of birth. Beyond this, the mother–daughter relationship was defined by the mother's need to mould her girls into ladies who had the proper behaviors, manners, attitudes, and skills that would help ensure their marriage into good homes. This included binding their feet, once this practice had become common.

Howard Levy, in his book on footbinding, gathered some important insights into the mother–daughter relationship by doing field interviews with 11 women who had been born at the turn of the 20th century and who had all had their feet bound.[6] These women all described exactly the same details of "what mother did to them." Their descriptions paint vivid pictures of the pain and fear they experienced and suggest how deep the imprinting of such a traumatic experience was upon them. They recalled their mothers' instructions:

> If one loved a daughter, one could not love her feet.

> If you don't make her feet tiny and attractive, it will be difficult later to arrange a proper marriage . . .

> When a girl first has her feet bound, one must exert pressure to make her oblivious to pain. Then success is relatively easy . . .

As mentioned earlier, Levy's interviews did show that the intensity of the suffering from footbinding was directly related to the amount of maternal care the mother devoted to the process. In other words, the girls seemed to suffer less when the process was carried out with as much compassion as possible. Still, the binding had to be done.[7] It was essential in preparing the daughter for her future marriageability, and in this way it also initiated her into the paternal order. It was the first test she had to endure in the Confucian order; it was a mark of her capacity to endure, suffer, and obey – the prized attributes of the ideal wife and daughter-in-law. This made a pair of well-shaped feet a woman's pride for life. A bride who was praised for her small feet had a feeling analogous to filial gratitude to the mother who had forced her to endure the suffering.[8] In this way, mother and daughter, the torturer and the tortured, were bound together for each other's survival in the paternal order.

Daughters and fathers

The father–daughter relationship is yet another that was not included among Confucius's five cardinal relationships – an omission that indicates this was another relationship that was not officially defined by the collective. To be understood, it needs to be compared to the father–son relationship, which was based on the authority derived from the lineage of ancestors. While the son saw in his father a potential ancestor and revered him, the father needed the son to make sacrifices to him after his death. A rite of bonding was required to formalize this relationship and place the son in the paternal order. In the old villages, for example, when a son was born his name would be written on the family's genealogy tablet in the ancestral hall. A month later, a celebration would be held in the village, a pig would be roasted and small pieces of the meat would be given out to each of the men in the village. Other rituals were carried out at other important stages of the boy's life; for instance, when he started school he would be taken to the ancestral hall to bow before the ancestors and to the god of learning. No such ceremonies or rituals were carried out for girls.

That the father's authority in this system was unquestioned is evident in the fact that he had the freedom to confer his paternity on a child he had not sired, or conversely, to simply refuse it. The father–son relationship was in this way defined by power, obedience, loyalty, and respect. Against this backdrop, a daughter was not quite as strictly compelled as her brothers to revere their father – at least not in a formal sense, since she was not part of the order of males who were potential ancestors. Her name was not entered in the genealogy tablets of her family of origin. Neither did she go through the rite of bonding with her father. Still, her need to express her filial piety to him was absolutely essential.

Since the need for "reverence" was not so formal and since it was the mother's duty, and not the father's, to strictly mould the daughter's behavior, the father–daughter relationship was one where it was possible for the father to enjoy some respite from the rigid role as head of the family that he had to maintain so rigorously with the more strategic members of the family. This more relaxed relationship was generally more likely among the gentry, where daughters were less of an economic burden than in peasant families. It was also made possible because the daughter's early marriage made any disruption of the family – caused, for instance, by a mother's jealousy – less likely. When this positive informal father–daughter relationship occurred, the bond between father and daughter could become strong, and love and affection could replace the attitude of awe and total deference. Ironically, in these situations, the father–daughter relationship often came closer to Confucius' ideal of respectful and tender love than did the father–son relationship, which was defined more by protocol and avoidance.[9]

In Chinese poetry, novels, and stories, the clever and beautiful daughter who is her father's favorite is common. In these stories, during the transient period of her life while she waits to gain her place in her future husband's family, she devotes to her father the love and allegiance that she will eventually have to transfer to her husband. One example of this that Westerners are now somewhat familiar with, thanks to the Disney movie *Mu Lan*, is the story of Hua Mu-lan. Although some scholars think Hua Mu-lan may have only been a legendary character, many others believe she was real and that she lived sometime in the 5th century. According to a poem written about her during the Tang dynasty, when Hua Mu-lan's sick and aging father is called up to join the army, she dresses as a man and joins in his place. There, according to the story that has been passed down, she is said to have fought on her father's behalf for 12 years. In both the movie and Chinese lore, Mu-lan and her father enjoy a relationship of love, affection, and mutual admiration. In the Chinese story, however, Mu-lan's dedicated filial piety towards her father is the attitude that is stressed. Another difference is that the movie, in very liberated modern-day fashion, focuses on Mu-lan's ability to do everything that men can do, while the original story lauds Mu-lan for maintaining her chastity during her time spent with so many men, and in this way maintaining her loyalty and value to her father and family. Another example of love and loyalty exhibited by a favored daughter was the brave 17th-century heroine known as the Rainbow Girl, who allowed herself to be captured by several men in succession in order to find her father's murderers.[10]

While older stories such as these emphasized the act of filial piety, in modern times the daughter's feeling for the father is described more openly. The famous writer and poet Bing Xin (1900–1999) described her relationship with her father, which included love, companionship, mentoring, and respect. She described how father and daughter would spend the evenings together in his study, at times sitting in silence, yet breathing the air of each others' presence, at other times sharing their intimate feelings and thoughts on various subjects.[11] Another description of the deep feeling of the father toward his daughter is provided by the well-known modern woman writer Ding Ling (1906–1986). In her essay "Homecoming," a retired scholar-official reminisces:

He has been longing for his eldest daughter . . . She lost her mother at an early age and her marriage has not turned out well. Among his other children, he loved her the most which often aroused jealousy among her brothers. But deep down, he also empathized and pitied her fate . . . Quietly, longingly, he recalled her childhood, her long black hair in plaits, her strong character, spirit and intelligence.

He sent her to school for an education (unusual in those days) and her brilliance did not disappoint him. She was good in her social skills and quite often represented her step-mother in important social functions. He arranged her marriage with an established wealthy family but her husband turned out to be a playboy addicted to opium and gambling. She is destroyed by her fate. Her future has become the most painful affair in his heart. Even though she does not return home to him, at least to complain about her life, he worries about her every day.[12]

The father's feeling is characterized by a sense of regret and helplessness over the fate of his daughter. For after marriage, her real life began and her allegiance was to her husband and his family. In these positive, deeply affectionate relationships, the sense of loss both the father and daughter felt must have been intense. However, it needs to be remembered that it was perhaps the transient nature of the relationship that allowed these feelings to be experienced.

This favored daughter was often referred to by the father as "the precious pearl in my palm." Although this is a lovely phrase, it also denotes possessiveness. The father has the daughter "in hand," so to speak. And this serves as a reminder that not all intense father–daughter relationships were positive. An extreme example of this relationship is described by Lao She (1899–1966) in *The Rickshaw Boy*, in which the father, a widower, refuses the marriage of his daughter, already in her thirties, and tells her that she has to decide "between him [the lover] and me." When the daughter did not occupy the favored daughter position, she often had very little relationship with her father. It was required that her attitude to her father was one of fear, awe, obedience, respect. In the segregated household of the middle and upper classes, she would spend most of her time in the inner chambers with the other females of the family and, in fact, might have very little interaction with him.

Wife, daughter-in-law

The very fact that wife and daughter-in-law need to be put in the same category is telling. In Western culture certainly they would be two distinct roles, but in the traditional culture described here, they cannot be separated. In the marriage ceremony, the bride was always clothed in red, a color which symbolizes ritual birth. It signified her entry into a new family, the beginning of a new life and her incorporation into a new family line. In contrast to a man, for whom marriage marked a smooth transition to adult status with its attendant privileges, for a woman marriage was psychologically a traumatic event. It marked the departure from her family of origin, when she ceased to be a member of her biological father's family, cut off from all affectionate bonds with her siblings and relatives. It also marked the beginning of her career as a daughter-in-law, a stranger with the lowest status in the family hierarchy, burdened with the task of integrating herself into an unfamiliar, tightly knit and disciplined family.

Although she owed complete obedience to her husband, her priority was her relationship with her parents-in-law.[13] According to the *Book of Rites* (*Li Chi*), she had to display great affection and obedience toward the parents of her husband, who was himself in a subordinate position in his father's house. Their dislike or repudiation of her could lead to divorce, which would bring great shame on her and her family – regardless of who was really at fault. She had to avoid contact with her father-in-law and brothers-in-law. The person with whom she was in closest contact was her mother-in-law, who was the person charged with the integration of the bride into the family unit. And here the real drama of her life began. The harsh treatment of the daughter-in-law by the mother-in-law was frequently a striking feature of Chinese family life. In Chinese fiction and folklore, the cruel mother-in-law played the role that the wicked stepmother plays in European fairy tales.[14] The only person who could really support the bride in her new family structure was her husband. Unfortunately for her, his role as "son" came before his role as "husband" and, out of filial piety, he was required to side with his mother, and the mother often took advantage of her position.

The relationship between the mother-in-law and daughter-in-law was extremely complex. In some ways it can be likened to a mistress and her enslaved maid. Their intimacy was anything but mutual. This relationship was also frequently emotional. At its darkest it entailed fear and hatred on one side, and contempt on the other.[15] Howard Levy cites a case, for example, in which the mother-in-law rejected her new daughter-in-law because her bound feet were not up to standard. With beating, she supervised the re-binding, which involved putting tiles inside the binding to induce inflammation and flesh deterioration.[16] One of the means of escape open to a bride in this type of situation was suicide. This was the most damning public accusation she could make towards the family that had violated her. It carried the implication that the proper, required rules of conduct had been ignored.[17] For the abused, mistreated daughter-in-law, death would bring not only an end to suffering, but power, for it was the one means she had at hand to punish her tormentors.[18] Sometimes the threat of suicide could protect the young woman to some extent, for if she killed herself, her family could sue her husband's family. The threat of a long and tiresome lawsuit and the "loss of face" were often strong enough to protect the woman to a certain extent.

From the perspective of many young women, the traditional Chinese family was a grim setting. Arthur Smith astutely observed:

> One of the weakest threads in the Chinese social fabric is the insecurity of the life and happiness of woman . . . . The law affords her no protection while she lives, and such justice as she is able with difficulty to exact is strictly a post mortem concession.[19]

In Confucius' cardinal relationships, the husband–wife relationship is the only one in which a woman, at any stage of her life, is mentioned. The guiding principle in this relationship was respect. The significance of the wife as a person was secondary, and any role she might have as a companion to the husband was low in priority. The general rule in the *Book of Rites*, which prescribed proper behavior between husband and wife was that all physical contact and intimacy should be strictly confined to the bedchamber. Overt expression of affection was considered bad taste. The *Book of Rites* even established strict protocol regulating the sequence and frequency of a man's sexual intercourse with his wife and concubines.[20] The primary orientation of the husband–wife relationship was the production of children. As stated before, in the Confucian family structure, priority was given to the continuity of the family at the expense of individual feelings and desires. Because an unmarried daughter was a financial and social burden for the family, for a woman, the only alternative to marriage was to become a nun.

Although happy, mutually respectful relationships between husbands and wives did certainly exist, the rigid hierarchical family structure and the fact that marriages were arranged presented tremendous challenges to the bride – especially until she produced a son.

Mother–matriarch

Motherhood was the most highly prized and rewarding role for a woman. Her marriage to her husband and her position as daughter-in-law were, in a certain sense, sealed by the birth of a son and his presentation to the ancestor. The son would assist her integration into the family, for she had produced the means of its continuance. Her future depended on her relationship with her sons, whose loyalty she had to cultivate. Given all this, the strong attachment of the mother to her son is easy to understand. In addition, motherhood helped alleviate her sense of isolation in a strange environment, especially with a harsh mother-in-law.[21] The mother thus played an important role in the psyche of men. Although the mother–son relationship is not included by Confucius in the five cardinal relationships, the *Sacred Books* stress that the dominant feeling of the son for his mother should be love. Chinese writers and poets write with great warmth and understanding of the mutual love between the son and his mother.[22]

When her son married and she became a mother-in-law herself, she gained a position of honor and power that was well-earned by a life of service: she was no longer an outsider. Now she was integrated into the family on the formal level. Ultimately, however, her position within the family was not truly solidified until her own mother-in-law retired as manager of the household and passed this role down to her. And only when her mother-in-law died did she fully come into her own. If she was the wife of the oldest son, she became the head of the female hierarchy. With her husband's death, she became free of male domination, especially if no other male head of the family survived. Because of the subordination of the young to the old in the family hierarchy, the elderly mother and grand-mother enjoyed respect and certain advantages. Still, her power was never as complete as that of the elderly man. He had the ability to exercise real authority and had ultimate responsibility, while the elderly woman was accorded only formal deference and provided with security.

Of course, there were – and still are – many examples of matriarchs who were *de facto* rulers of the family by dint of their iron wills or their ability to take control of weaker husbands. One well-known example of this is found in the novel *The Dream of the Red Chamber* (*Hong Lou Meng*), written in the mid 1700s, which is considered a classic of Chinese literature. One of the characters is an extremely powerful matriarch. However, on careful reading it becomes clear that her power is, in fact, derived from her son who held high office, and one of her daughters who was appointed Imperial concubine. Powerful dowagers like her did indeed exist, but their position of power was never officially sanctioned.

The concubine

During the centuries of Imperial rule, it was not uncommon for men of the middle and upper classes to take concubines. Since a concubine was recog-nized as a legal member of the family, this was a role that a woman might, depending on circumstances, end up having to play. From the point of view of the woman who was the official wife, however, the concubine's existence often created problems. This was sometimes complicated by the fact that polygamy was sometimes practiced and the first, or principal, wife had to put up not just with concubines but with additional wives as well. Because both polygamy and the role of concubines were accepted institutions, the principal wife was at least not humiliated when her husband added one more wife to the household. Still, the situation was generally far from being an idyll.

One frequent cause for concern was that, unlike the principal wife, who was chosen by the husband's parents, the concubine was chosen by the husband himself and she would have a much better chance for romantic involvement with him. It is easy to imagine that the concubine was often a source of disruption to the family, caused by jealousy, aggression, and sexual rivalry. The situation was made even more complicated when an attractive young concubine was brought into the family of an older man who had grown sons. The old *Annals* are full of stories about fights between jealous empresses, princesses, and concubines. Palace intrigues often involve tales of battles among Imperial concubines and their power struggle to get their sons appointed prince regent.[23]

Even though the concubine was recognized as a legal member of the family, she occupied an inferior position to the wife, whose standing was protected by the *Rites and Ceremonials*. Her relationship to the principal wife had certain aspects of a servant role. What's more, maternity was collective in these situations and so the concubine's children were held to belong to the principal wife. The concubine's position was also precarious. Since her main function was the sexual satisfaction of the husband, she could be sold if he lost interest in her. The same was true for secondary wives, who could easily be divorced if they no longer pleased the husband. Both these women's security in the household depended to a great extent on their relationship with the principal wife. Chinese novels and fiction abound with stories of the ill-treatment of concubines by principal wives.[24]

Among the peasants, the situation was somewhat different because a wife was indispensable economically. Because of this she had more freedom of movement and enjoyed a relationship of more equality with her husband. Still, she had to contend with the idea that her husband was likely to take a concubine if their economic situation improved. A good example of this can be seen in Pearl Buck's *The Good Earth*, which offers a fairly realistic example of Chinese rural life around 1900.

In conclusion, the psychology of a Chinese woman was shaped at every stage of life by various structural forces within the patriarchal family system. As the daughter, she was like an orphan who lived a transient life in the home where she was born. As the wife, she was a stranger in her adopted family. Her chief salvation was motherhood and the birth of a son, provided she has the future potential of her son's loyalty. Her power and authority in the family hierarchy came with age, attaining its full potential only if she outlived her parents-in-law and her husband. Even then, her power remained dependent on the loyalty and achievement of her sons.

In the paternal order, a woman's fate was defined by the patriarchy, depending on her relationship with men, and was split in three ways between the father, husband, and son. As a result of this, her relationship with the Masculine was purposive and not without calculation. Her relationship with the Feminine was even more complicated – a situation that was exacerbated by the practice of footbinding. Through it, she was abandoned by her mother emotionally and the initial bonding with her mother was severed, destroyed by rejection and lack of trust. After her marriage, the mother-in-law became the substitute mother. Like the wicked stepmother in Western fairy tales, this was usually a negative mother with whom she entered into a power struggle for the allegiance of her husband and her children. In a wealthy family, she had to share her husband with his concubines.

Within this structure, footbinding allowed women to enter the phallic order – but as its waste. It reduced the power of women, their natural connection to the Earth, and turned them into crippled slaves. In her inferior and restricted position, obedience, service, and performance were the means to survival. Thus, the patriarchy inculcated in a woman the rejection of herself and her relationship to the Feminine. Cut off from her instinctive Feminine self early in life, her identity as a woman was severely damaged by a sense of self-abasement which began with her birth.

Over the years that I have been in practice as a Jungian analyst, I have seen how many of us as women, whether from the East or West, are striving at some deep level to "do our duty" in terms of filial piety. Often this survival need is passed down from mother to daughter in subtle unconscious ways. A good example of this comes from my friend Jeanne. She eventually came to see how this attitude she'd had about her father carried over to her relationships with men and, ultimately, to her husband. In one conversation we had, she told me:

> Not long after I had the realization about how I had been "bowing" to my father by tiptoeing around the house when he was working or upset, I discovered I had, in a way, been doing the same to my husband. This was an incredible shock to me because I have always thought of myself as a feminist!

The worst part of this for her was that it was her teenage daughter who pointed it out to her. One evening Jeanne, asking her daughter to tidy up the living room, said, "Let's get this done before Dad gets home; he shouldn't have to come home to a dirty house!" Her daughter looked at her and said, "Why do you always say stuff like that? It's wrong! If we clean up the house, we should do it for everybody! Daddy doesn't deserve a clean house any more than anybody else around here!"

> I was so stunned when she said this. Right away I realized it was true. And, later when I had the realization about tiptoeing around my father, I knew I'd been doing the same thing around my husband. And modeling the behavior for my daughter, subconsciously trying to teach her that "Daddy" had more rights around the house than anybody else!

All I could think of was how thankful I was that she somehow had grown up with enough inner strength to resist this!

Jeanne's story is a good example of how, with awareness, the negative cycles can be broken. Another comes from a client I worked with for some time; it's of particular interest because it shows how these attitudes can be found not just in personal relationships but also when we deal with "collective" authority/father figures. It is also another indicator of how reconnecting to the Feminine is often the key to correcting this problem in our lives.

In Margaret's case this collective authority figure was the medical establishment. Her rather complex relationship with it began at a very early age. As a child Margaret suffered from an extremely severe and debilitating form of asthma. Her young life was fraught with long periods of illness and frequent intensive medical intervention. Doctors were a constant factor in her life. Over time, with the development of new medications and better treatment methods, the grip the illness held on her was loosened and, eventually, she was able to lead a fairly normal life. Small wonder then that medicine began to hold a very special place in her heart, and she determined at a fairly early age that she wanted to be a doctor. Since she made this decision when being a doctor was still considered mainly a "man's job," her family wasn't particularly supportive. Regardless, once she'd made up her mind, she aimed for her goal with remarkable determination, worked extremely hard, and eventually was accepted into medical school and subsequently became a medical doctor upon graduation.

She loved medicine, and for a number of years she practiced very happily; the medical model that had helped her as a child and in which she'd later been trained was an ideal to her, and it was difficult for her to believe anything could be lacking in it. But over time she slowly began to become disillusioned, not with medicine as a science, but with some of the patriarchal attitudes that the tradition was steeped in. In order to understand herself and these attitudes better, she entered analysis. Over time she came to realize that her animus, the masculine side of herself, had become out of balance and needed to be integrated and brought into more harmony with her total being. In throwing herself into first her medical studies and later her work in a field so dominated by the masculine perspective she had, she discovered, lost some of her own inner feminine perspective.

Her work on herself in analysis helped her to regain her connection to the Feminine. But she also sought out other sources. Drawn to Christianity, she joined the Catholic Church and began to sing in the choir. She also continued her spiritual search by examining other world religions such as Buddhism and Taoist Qi-gong and doing various types of body work. She also began to meditate and discovered, much to her surprise, that it had a tremendously positive effect on both her overall physical health and her asthma. For her, as a medical doctor, this was fascinating. Margaret began to explore new scientific studies that were coming out on the effects of meditation on illness and found that the improvements she had seen in her own health were no coincidence. Armed with the solid data that was supplied by these studies, she began to integrate forms of meditation into her medical practice. Soon other doctors, seeing the positive results these methods were getting, began referring their patients to her to learn the techniques she was teaching her own patients.

Interestingly enough, there is a fascinating parallel between the way Margaret brought the feminine perspective into her own healing process – meditating, developing her spiritual nature, and connecting with her physical self through bodywork – and what was happening in her medical practice. For there, too, the feminine principle was being integrated. In the patriarchal medical model of the past, the doctor was the authority figure who bestowed "healing" on the patient; the patient was merely the recipient of the treatment. But in the model Margaret was now using in her practice, the patients were recognizing that they were the "authority" on their own bodies and, even more importantly, that they were the source of their own healing. Both because of her personal experience in dealing with her own illness and the increasing number of scientific studies that support her observations, Margaret believes this more feminine perspective will be incorporated even more firmly into the medical model of the future.

In the next chapter we explore the role of the cosmic Feminine in Chinese history, mythology, and legend, and discover more about what a powerful metaphor this is in the process of becoming whole.

Notes

1 See for example: Lisa Raphals, *Sharing the Light: Representations of Women and Virtue in Early China*, Albany, NY: SUNY Press, 1998; Walter Slote and George DeVos, *Confucianism and the Family*, Albany, NY: SUNY Press, 1998; Dorothy Ko, *Teachers of the Inner Chambers: Women and Culture in Seventeenth-Century China*, Stanford, CA: Stanford University Press, 1994.
2 *Shih Ching* is a collection of poems, hymns, and folksongs that belong to oral literature from 1200 to 600 BC, compiled and edited by Confucius as one of the *Five Classics*. This song is 'Szu-kan', No. 189, quoted in Robert van Gulik, *Sex Life in Early China*, Leiden: Brill, 1961, pp. 15–16.
3 Quoted in Julia Kristeva, *About Chinese Women*, trans. Anita Barrows, London: Marion Boyars, 1977, p. 76.
4 Dympha Cusack, *Chinese Women Speak*, London: Century Hutchinson, 1958, p. 140.
5 Lin Yu-tang, *My Country and My People*, New York: John Day, 1939, pp. 153–6.
6 Howard S. Levy, *The Lotus Lovers, The Complete History of the Curious Erotic Custom of Footbinding in China*, New York: Prometheus Books, 1992, Chapter 10 and pp. 219, 229, 238.
7 Ibid., Chapter 9.

8 Lin Yu-tang, op. cit., p. 168.
9 Marion Levy Jr, *The Family Revolution in Modern China*, Boston, MA: Harvard University Press, 1949; reprint New York: Athenaeum, 1968, pp. 179–81.
10 Olga Lang, *Chinese Family and Society*, New Haven, CT: Yale University Press, 1946; New York: Archon, 1968, p. 30.
11 Cho Ju, ed., *Bing Xin*, Hong Kong: Joint Publishing, 1983 [text in Chinese], pp. 146–50.
12 Ding Ling, *Selected Essays* (*Ding Ling Hsuan Chi*), Hong Kong: Wen xue chu ban she, 1955, pp. 25–6.
13 Lin Yu-tang, op. cit., p. 148.
14 Olga Lang, op. cit., p. 48.
15 In more modern times, the fate of the young wife in the Chinese family system has played a major role in the movement toward women's emancipation and family reform. Available statistics show that the majority of suicides and attempted suicides occurred among young married women. Marion Levy, op. cit., p. 186.
16 Howard S. Levy, op. cit., p. 225.
17 Marion Levy Jr, op. cit., pp. 117–18.
18 Margery Wolf, 'Women and Suicide in China', in Wolf, Margery and Witke, Roxane, eds., *Women in Chinese Society*, Stanford, CA: Stanford University Press, 1975, pp. 111–41.
19 Arthur A. Smith, *Village Life in China*, New York, 1899, quoted in Wolf, Margery and Witke, Roxane, eds., ibid., pp. 11–14. Smith also comments: "Every year thousands upon thousands of Chinese wives commit suicide, tens of thousands of other persons are thereby involved in serious trouble, hundreds of thousands of yet others are dragged in as co-partners in the difficulty, and millions of dollars are expended in extravagant funerals and ruinous lawsuits. And all this is the outcome of the Confucian theory that a wife has no rights which a husband is bound to respect."
20 Quoted in Olga Lang, op. cit.
21 Marion Levy Jr, op. cit., p. 181.
22 It is interesting to note that Confucius never knew his own father, but his mother played an important role as his protector and his inspiration. Mencius – the great Chinese philosopher who was known for interpreting and carrying on Confucius' works – had a mother who later became known for the way she had managed to procure the means for her son to get an education. A similar case is the mother of General Yue Fei, the famous defender of China against the Mongols under the Song dynasty in the 13th century.
23 Olga Lang, op. cit., pp. 51–2.
24 Ibid. The novel *Dream of the Red Chamber* describes the reactions of one of the heroines to her husband's love affairs and her fights with his concubines: "When Phoenix hears of her husband's intrigue, she nearly swoons, feels a violent pain in her heart, almost chokes with anger, trembles with indignation. She violently attacks one of her rivals, stirs up the whole family against her, and finally drives her out. When another woman is set up as a concubine, she moves heaven and earth to destroy her, provokes an abortion, and finally drives her to suicide." In *The Golden Lotus*, the first wife cooperates with her husband's concubines in arranging house parties, mediates their conflicts, and even reprimands him when he favors one concubine to the neglect of another. However, both his wife and his concubines are indignant at his escapades in brothels, with servants, or with other women outside the family circle.

Chapter 5

Xi Wang Mu: the Queen Mother of the West

When Pearl first began her journey to self-discovery through Jungian analysis, one of the first things I did was to have her participate in an Association Experiment. This is a test that was devised by Jung to reveal complexes that we have but that we are unconscious of. It can also reveal how these complexes are affecting our lives and undermining our goals. Right away, Pearl's Association Experiment revealed that she had what is often referred to as an authority complex. This type of complex is often seen as being closely related to what is known as the "father" complex, and depending on the school of psychology the two terms may nearly be used interchangeably. The idea that many women have this type of complex – and, as a result, spend their lives looking for love or approval first from their fathers and later from other authority figures – has been bandied about so much in the last two decades that the concept has almost become trite.

But in spite of this widespread awareness – and the feeling that it's so well known it should almost be something of the past – the fact remains that a tremendous number of women are suffering from its effects. And these effects have ramifications in our daily lives that go far beyond a need that was originally grounded in a very natural longing to find the love or approval we did not receive – or did not receive enough of – as a child.

Pearl is a very good example of just how this complex can play out and unconsciously control our lives. Even if you are someone who has worked through enough psychological issues that you are no longer frantically seeking the approval of an authority figure, you may well see some of yourself in Pearl. Early on in her analysis, Pearl had the following disturbing dreams. In the first:

A woman leads me to my home, which is somewhere between two floors. I can't get there without her lead.

Two older women are lying in bed in a hospital. They cannot walk. The doctor is to take some liquid out of their backbones to examine the reasons.

In the other she saw a society where:

> . . . the people are eaten as soon as they are dead, especially the young
> people. I arrived at a place where someone has just died and he is
> butchered.

If you remember from Pearl's story earlier, she had been striving all her life
to reach the impossible goal of perfection – trying for better marks and
reaching for higher degrees. After receiving her doctorate, she obtained a
high-status job in a prestigious hospital where she felt constantly under
pressure to perform and prove herself. In our discussion of the two dreams
above, she came to realize the imagery represented, at least on one level,
how she felt about her constant drive for perfection and her job at the
hospital. The constant pressure she felt from her demanding boss and her
critical colleagues was draining her. Putting it graphically in terms of the
dream imagery, she said that the hospital had "sucked her blood."

The characteristics that had led Pearl to the job and the situation she was
in were typical of the woman with an authority complex. Pearl had been
extremely focused on achievement all her life, had been very disciplined and
was intensely results-oriented. These traits were shown in her continual
pursuit of the highest marks in school, her attaining her doctoral degree,
and her success in her career. None of these, in and of themselves, are bad
things. Indeed our society lauds them. But in Pearl's case – as in the case of
so many women today – she was never satisfied unless what she did was
perfect. And because this is an impossible goal, she was never satisfied with
what she achieved. No matter how hard she worked, nothing was ever good
enough. And she worked very, very hard. In fact, she never stopped
working. She could never allow herself to stop and take a breath. In order
to achieve all she had accomplished, Pearl had had to have a highly
developed intellectual and rational nature. Unfortunately, this had come at
the cost of denying the emotional and intuitive sides of her nature. She had
denied her own wants, desires, and emotions first in order to please her
demanding father and then later to achieve approval from the authority
figures represented by her boss, her higher-achieving colleagues, and the
hospital itself. In this process, she had lost touch with her body and
sacrificed her personal relationships.

In Jungian terms this complex is associated with the overdevelopment of
the animus – the inner masculine side of a woman. The animus – like the
anima, which is the inner feminine side of a man – is both a construct
within us personally and an archetypal image. For a little girl, the personal
father carries the projections associated with the archetypal father image.
This archetypal "father" is the principle that represents rationality, justice,
law and order, and structures such as institutions. It is the quintessential
authority figure. For a child raised in the Judeo-Christian tradition, the

ultimate archetypal father image is often the one associated with "God the Father." For a child raised in the Chinese tradition, this concept might be contained in the image of the Supreme Ancestor, or the Emperor as Son of Heaven. This is one reason a father's words carry so much weight and authority for a girl. For her, part of the process of growing into woman-hood involves becoming conscious of the human side of her father and the separation of these two "father" images. For Pearl, the older women in the dream that took place in the hospital represent the worn out feminine. They can no longer walk and cannot go forward in life. Like those women who are footbound, their backbone needs to be examined – they no longer have a standpoint as they have lost their connection to the powerful, regenerative feminine force. She needs help from a healthy feminine figure, probably her analyst, to show her the way. Pearl instinctively recognized the symbolic value of this woman in her dream, who "leads me to my home," and added "I can't get there without her help." To Pearl, the home between two floors is her "spiritual home," her soul identity between the East and the West. Her healing is in connecting with this woman, the carrier of the Self, the spiritual healing aspect inherent in her psyche.

Through the process of analysis, Pearl came to realize that in order to get out of the desperately stifling and frenetic situation she was in, she had needed to balance out her overdeveloped animus by reconnecting with the Feminine. She had to regain her own feminine standpoint. She had to swing those paralyzed legs down off the operating table and reconnect her feet with Mother Earth. And this is exactly what so many of us need to do as women today. Like the little Chinese girls who had their feet bound in order to win the approval of their fathers and husbands, we have dis-connected ourselves from the archetypal Feminine. For many of us, this has entailed letting our animus become extremely overdeveloped. We seek perfection and denigrate ourselves when we don't achieve it; we work non-stop and never take a breath; we are overly achievement- and results-oriented, and we have sacrificed our intuitive, feeling natures to the intel-lectual and rational. It is not that achievement or the intellect or some degree of striving are bad – it is that we have allowed ourselves to become terribly out of balance and the time has come for us to bring the feminine back into consciousness. Without our feminine consciousness, we are not that much better off than our Chinese sisters – our feet are bound in a psychic sense; that is, we suffer from psychological footbinding.

One reason that looking at this problem through the lens of Chinese imagery is so helpful is that it allows us to draw on the myths and legends of ancient China, which are filled with powerful archetypal images of the Feminine. The roots of this powerful imagery can be found from Neolithic times onward. At the same time as the original roots of ancestor worship were developing in those early days in China, forms of nature worship and shamanism were also being practiced. Although different in many ways, ancestor worship and the more Earth-based forms of worship were inter-connected to some degree and in many ways formed the basis of original religion in China.

Underlying both these tradition is the early Chinese world view that saw the human being as but one aspect of an animated nature. In this world view, a mysterious life force in the universe, *chi*, sustains a continuous, eternal, mutual interaction of dual cosmic forces, *yin* and *yang*. This life force follows a definite path representing the supreme order of nature, *tao*. Those who live according to the *tao* increase their *te*, mana or "virtue," and live long and happily. Those who deviate from the *tao* are exposed to misfortune and grief. *Te* is not the exclusive possession of man, but also belongs to certain birds, beasts, stones, and plants, for instance, tortoises, pine trees, jade, and certain mushrooms.

Both the masculine *yang* and the feminine *yin* have equally important roles. One cannot exist without the other. The ancestor cult, however, received reinforcement from the way the *yin* and *yang* were viewed in terms of the soul. The *yin* soul, known as *po*, comes into existence at the moment of conception and stays with the corpse until it has decomposed. *Hun*, the spirit or *yang* soul, enters the child when it leaves the womb. After death the *yang* soul rises to heaven as an ancestral spirit to be nourished by the sacrifices of its descendants on Earth. Almost certainly, the fact that *yang* is masculine contributed in some way to the idea that the men in the family were the ones whose sacred duty was to carry out the rituals of worship and to produce the male children who would continue the sacrifices in the ancestral hall. Although ancestor worship eventually became pervasive in China, in early times it was more closely associated with the landed gentry, for in those days the landless commoners had no surnames. It is likely that in early times the more nature-based and shamanistic types of worship had a greater role in the lives of the peasantry. And it is not surprising that in these naturalistic forms of worship the forces of *yin* held more sway than those of *yang*.

Although some Chinese historians have offered the idea that in earliest Chinese culture – in other words, in Neolithic times – some type of matri-archy may have predominated,[1] the view generally held by current archeologists is that no concrete evidence has been found that validates this view. As Suzanne Cahill states somewhat regretfully in her wonderful exploration of the divine Feminine in the Chinese middle ages, *Transcendence and Divine Passion: The Queen Mother of the West in Medieval China*, "no trace remains in China of a Neolithic Great Mother goddess of the kind found in Europe and Japan."[2]

We can say, of course, that early forms of Earth worship in most cultures tended to view the Earth as "feminine" – as the nourishing mother. And certainly the idea that the Earth was mother and the sky was father has long been an element in Chinese thought. Life and death were understood as part of one continuous process controlled by Mother Nature. It was she who imbued the seeds with life and she who received them into her embrace in death.

Other ways that the Feminine may have formed the link between Heaven and Earth in the earliest Chinese spiritual practices can be found in shamanism. From earliest times in Chinese history shamanism seems to have been the most pervasive type of religious practice. Shamanism holds that there are two realities, the physical and the spiritual. Of these, it is the spiritual that is the most significant and, indeed, the most real. The shaman, by entering into trance states, provides a bridge between these two worlds and communicates with the spirit realm. Although shamanism has been practiced in virtually every culture, it may actually have originated in Siberia some 10,000 years ago. From its beginning in Neolithic times, it spread to China where it was practiced for millennia. Although it gradually lost power in later centuries to the more rationalistic types of thinking that would form the basis of Confucianism, it was an immensely powerful tradition throughout the Shang dynasty – from about 1520 BC to 1030 BC – and was still in evidence to some degree right up until about 400 BC.[3]

For centuries, the shamans of China practiced divination by burning ox bones and tortoise shells and interpreting the cracks that formed. These interpretations were written on the bones, known as oracle bones. Hundreds of thousands of these bones, dating from the beginning of the Shang, have been found. They reveal how the shamans recognized the power of nature, communicated with the spirit and animal realms, and tried to determine the will of Heaven.[4] According to some authorities many of the shamans in Shang times may have been women. Known as *wu*, the shamans were not only responsible for divination, they were also in charge of contacting *Ti*, the Supreme Lord or Lord on High, and interpreting his will.

Regardless of whether all, or even some, of the earliest shamans were women, hints as to how significant this archetypal Feminine imagery was in early Chinese thought can be found in a number of places. One is that the Chinese character for "surname" consists of a combination of the characters for "woman" and "to be born." This is often quoted as proof that in ancient Chinese society children were named after their mothers. Also, the Chinese surnames that are said to have originated in the mythical times of the Yellow Emperor all had the word "woman" as their radical.[5]

Another indicator of the importance of the Feminine can be found in the history of the *I Ching*, the *Book of Changes*. Mentioned earlier as one of the works that Confucius held to be the five great classics, the *I Ching* originated in the Shang dynasty. Originally it was probably only used as a tool for divination; however, more than 1000 years before Christ it had been developed into a moral, philosophical, and cosmological work. The *I Ching* is based on 64 symbols that are in turn based on the concepts of *yin* and *yang*. According to Richard Wilhelm – whose early translations of the work have helped it become a classic in the West as well as the East – the hexagram that originally began the *I Ching* was *kun*, "the receptive."[6] This obviously *yin* symbol maintained its primary position until sometime around 1144 BC, when King Wen is said to have switched the positions of the first two hexagrams and put the masculine *yang* symbol *chien* into first place. It remains there today. The Chinese ethnologist Tu Er-wei interprets *kun*'s early primary position as an indication that Earth and nature worship formed one of the elemental phases of the original religion of China. In his view, the worship of Earth through various deities lies at the very foundation of Chinese culture.[7] It has even been suggested that the Kitchen God, a deity that has held its place in Chinese culture for millennia, was originally a goddess. Known as *Tsao Shen*, the kitchen deity combines the symbols of the household hearth and fire – the messenger of the gods. As such, *Tsao Shen* reports family affairs to Heaven, supervises family morals, and forms the most intimate link between Heaven and Earth.[8]

Although *Ti* was seen as the First Ancestor and was therefore masculine, powerful female deities also existed during the Shang. Two of these were the Western Mother, *Xi Mu*, and her counterpart, the Eastern Mother, *Dong Mu*. Although very little is known about Shang deities, these two mother deities were certainly honored with rituals; inscriptions on oracle bones indicate that they received offerings, that sacrifices were made to them, and that they were clearly seen as powerful forces to be reckoned with.[9] This Mother image, in both its esoteric and physical aspects, lingered in the Chinese psyche and later became canonized in Taoism. In fact, the *Xi Mu* of Shang times may well be the *Xi Wang Mu*, or Queen Mother of the West, who becomes the principal female deity of Taoism.

Interestingly enough, it is *Xi Mu*'s counterpart, *Dong Mu*, who vanishes from the pantheon and is later transformed into various masculine personages, some human and some divine, who play the much less important role of the goddess' consort. Although no written references to *Xi Mu* can be found for about 1000 years after those on the oracle bones, once this period has passed she appears as a goddess in several different traditions, and by the 4th century BC the Queen Mother of the West has taken her place not only as the primary feminine deity, but as the second most powerful of all the divine beings in the Taoist pantheon.

Although *Xi Wang Mu*'s roots cannot be traced with any certainty to the goddess Nu Wa, who was introduced in Chapter 3, the writers who recorded the early legends created a legendary history of the gods and goddesses that places Nu Wa first. In these writings, Nu Wa is one of the Three August Ones, the deities that rose out of the mists of time to create civilization and the human race. And, as will be seen when the Queen Mother is discussed in detail, there are many similarities between the two. One of these similarities is Nu Wa's obvious shamanistic roots.[10] These are shown, at least in part, by the fact that she is almost always depicted as having the body of either a snake or a dragon – creatures with great mythical significance that reveal her connection to both the spiritual and animal realms (see Figure 3.1).

Certainly in Jungian thinking both are expressions of the same archetypal Feminine energy. As such, in Chinese terms they are both manifestations of *yin*. As explained in Chapter 3, Nu Wa and her masculine counterpart Fu Xi are said to have then emerged, without being born, just as the forces of *yin* and *yang* came into being at the beginning of the universe. Later, in many legends, they are said to have proceeded to K'un-lun Shan, the sacred Tortoise Mountain, where they asked Heaven for permission to marry. Thus blessed, they became the first man and wife.

Nu Wa is associated with the image of the tortoise – which in Chinese culture is the quintessential *yin* creature – in many ways. One is revealed in the story of how Nu Wa saved the world and the humans that she had so lovingly created. This story begins with a war between two monstrous giants, Kung Kung and Chuan Hsu – a god of water and a fire god – who hated each other and loved fighting. Their battles raged on until one day when Kung Kung was mortally wounded. In his rage at being defeated, Kung Kung beat his head against the mountain that held up the Heavens. The mountain split. As it did, it ripped a great hole in the azure skies and tilted the Earth so that it was no longer in the correct position.

Water poured down from the hole and flooded the Earth. As it did, Nu Wa heard the cries of the people she had created. Rushing to the site of the disaster she found a giant turtle and took its four legs. Using these legs as pillars, she established the four cardinal points, thus propping up the Heavens and bringing balance to the Earth. But waters were still flooding through the great tear in the sky. Thinking quickly, she slew a gargantuan black dragon, and stuffed his body into the gaping hole. Knowing this solution would not last long, she sought out the five colored stones that represented the four cardinal points and the Earth – red, green, black, white, and yellow. Nu Wa smelted these stones in a great fire and created a mortar powerful enough to mend the rent in the Heavens. She then gathered a vast quantity of reeds from the waters and burned them in a great fire. Using the ash from the reeds, she stopped the waters that were flooding across the Earth. When she was finished with her repairs, the people were safe, the land was dry, the Earth was righted, and the Heavens were firmly supported by the pillars of the tortoise's legs[11] (see Figure 5.1).

Over time Nu Wa came to be credited with originating marriage, teaching humans how to build dams and irrigation canals, and inventing the reed pipe known as the *sheng*. Although Nu Wa's popularity seems to have faded away to some extent after Han times and to have given way to Xi Wang Mu, she is still venerated in some parts of China today. As creator and rescuer of human beings (*renzu*), she is still honored in Renzu Festivals. These ceremonies include songs devoted to her that women have learned in

Figure 5.1 Nu Wa repairing heaven

Source: Drawing by Christy Shum. Adapted from a Qing dynasty stone rubbing

dreams, fertility dances that have been passed down matrilineally, and clay figures (including vulvas and vaginas) that are used as talismans. Seen as the Supreme Matchmaker, she presides over marriages, reproduction, and fertility.[12]

Images of Nu Wa almost always show her holding a compass – the symbol of the Earth. The stones of the five colors that she used are often connected in Chinese symbolism to the five ores and elements. Combined in proper, harmonious alloys, these ores and elements have long been held to have special powers. The five colors also represent the four points of the compass and their centre which, in turn, represent the totality of the Earth and the integrated power of creation. The reeds that Nu Wa burns stand for water and the ashes that come from them, fire. The combination of water (*yin*) and fire (*yang*) is seen as an expression of the harmonious union of *yin* and *yang*. Viewed with this background of symbolic associations, Nu Wa emerges as the creator of humankind and the restorer of order and wholeness. That she is pictured holding a compass is also a reminder of how she established the four cardinal points with the legs of a tortoise and, in this way, established the cosmic structure in terms of balance and stability.

In Chinese mythology, the tortoise is associated with Earth, and the primal aspects of creation. Considered the emblem of longevity, strength, and endurance, it is one of the four spiritually endowed creatures, along with the dragon, phoenix, and unicorn. The tortoise is also used to symbolize the universe: its dome-shaped back represents the vault of the sky, its belly, the earth. It represents water, one of the five elements of creation. It is often depicted in mythology as attendant to the god of the waters and rivers, and is thus endowed with powers of diverse transformation. Since ancient times turtle shells were used like the oracle bones in divination. Nu Wa's partner, Fu Xi, is even said to have invented the eight trigrams – the ultimate symbols of *yin* and *yang* that form the basis for the *I Ching* – based on the markings on a tortoise shell (Figure 5.2).

Even today, the power of the tortoise permeates all aspects of Chinese life, including the culinary arts, nutritional medicine, and healing – and it is still firmly connected with the Feminine archetypal *yin*. Not long ago I saw an example of this in my own life when I was diagnosed by a Chinese medical practitioner as having a *yin* deficiency. I was prescribed pills that had 30% tortoise content along with a soup that had to be made with a real turtle (flown frozen from China), ginseng, and a number of other medicinal herbal ingredients. Given the age-old connection between the tortoise and the great power of *yin*, it is not surprising the Xi Wang Mu is also inextricably linked to this creature. She is even known as the Golden Mother of the Tortoise and her celestial home is on K'un-lun, Tortoise Mountain.[13]

As the principal divine Feminine being in Taoism, Xi Wang Mu, the Queen Mother of the West, is the ultimate expression of *yin*. Her consort, Tung Wang Kung, the King Father of the East, who emerged from the Tao as she did, represents *yang*. The interplay and balance of *yin* and *yang* represented by these two divine beings has been central to Taoism since its inception. As a popular cult, Taoism flourished from about the 3rd century BC onward, and was then formalized in about 150 AD by a Han-dynasty philosopher named Chang Tao-ling. However, it is generally held to have been founded by Lao-tzu, a philosopher who lived at least 500 years before this. The main classics of Taoism are the *Tao Te Ching*, which is often translated as *The Classic of the Way and Its Power* and attributed to Lao-tzu, and a book of allegories and parables called the *Chuang Tzu*.

Many of the philosophical foundations of Taoism are also found in the *I Ching*. It describes *yin* and *yang* as the dual cosmic forces that perpetuate the universe in an unending chain of permutations: "The interaction of one

Figure 5.2 Fu Xi and the Cosmos

Source: Drawing by Christy Shum. Adapted from portrait by Ma Lin, Song dynasty, National Museum of Taiwan

yin and one *yang* is called *tao*; the resulting constant generative process is called Change" and "The constant intermingling of Heaven and Earth gives shape to all things. The sexual union of man and woman gives life to all things."[14]

Taoists identify with *tao*, the Supreme Order, the "Mother of the whole universe." The Great Mother, called Tai I or Great One, rules over Heaven and Earth as the Original Oneness, creator and source of human existence:

> There is something undifferentiated and yet complete,
> Existing before Heaven and Earth came into being,
> How tranquil, how still!
> Standing by itself, unchanging,
> Revolving incessantly, reaching everywhere
> And yet never coming near!
> It might well be the mother of the whole universe.
> I do not know its name.
> *Tao* is the pseudonym we give it.
>
> . . . .
>
> Man follows the Earth
> The Earth the Heaven
> The ten thousands of things under Heaven
> Come from being
> And the being
> Comes from non-being.[15]

Tao, the Great Mother, gives birth to all things. She protects them during life and calls them to her in death. She lies at the beginning and at the end of human development. She is the vessel that contains and generates the cosmos, and guards, guides, and permeates the infant consciousness of humanity.

The Taoists sought a return to man's pristine simplicity, a return to a Golden Age when everyone would live in perfect harmony with nature, and therefore could do nothing that was not right. They believed that the artificial man-made society estranged man from Nature, and they advocated non-action (*wu-wei*) as superior to action. Some retired from worldly affairs and, practicing an austere form of meditation, tried to reach communion with the primordial forces of nature.[16] These Taoists venerated Nature and Woman because in her and in her womb, new life is created and fostered. They developed an elevated mysticism that is contained in the *Tao Te Ching* and *Chuang Tzu*. Some Taoists retreated to the woods and mountains and tried through dietary and other disciplines to attain longevity, with physical immortality as the ultimate goal. Some engaged in various alchemical and sexual experiments in the hope of discovering the Elixir of Life.

Regardless of how it expressed itself, the Taoist's fundamental veneration for Nature led to the formation of the Mother or fertility cult, personified in Xi Wang Mu, the Queen Mother of the West. The popularity of Xi Wang Mu increased from the Han dynasty onwards. It is often speculated that Taoism fulfilled a need that was not satisfied by the rather mechanistic and concrete cosmological view of Confucianism. In this sense, Taoism complemented the Confucian world view and satisfied the spiritual needs of the people. Sometimes the Confucian social and ethical system is typified as being *yang* or masculine, dominating, authoritarian, and rational, while the Taoist view emphasizes all that is *yin* or feminine, receptive, yielding, permissive, and mystical. Although contemporary sinologists tell us that viewing Confucianism as masculine and Taoism as feminine – a generalization that has often been made in the past – is a gross oversimplification, from a Jungian point of view these two worldviews can indeed be seen as influencing the collective unconscious in this way.

Certainly Xi Wang Mu provides a powerful feminine imagery. She is seen as the incarnation of the ultimate power of the Far West which is *yin*. Her ruling of the West associates her in Taoist symbolism with metal, autumn, the color white, death, and the spirit world. Her home on Tortoise Mountain is sometimes described as being in a Heavenly Walled City where there are five golden terraces and 12 jade towers that all illuminate each other. It is filled with the splendor of gems, stones, flowers, and precious plants. The most precious of these plants are divine reeds that spontaneously harmonize sounds and produce the music of the spheres, known as the eight harmonies of the universe. Other divine reeds also grow in her home. Resembling the sprouts of marsh reeds, these miraculous plants can be used to produce an elixir that can bring the dead back to life or grant immortality – a gift that Xi Wang Mu was believed to be able to bestow.

From earliest times, Xi Wang Mu's appearance has reflected her awesome power. She has human form, the teeth of a tiger, and sometimes the tail of a leopard. Her throne is formed of a tiger and dragon combined. The tiger is considered by the Chinese to be the lord of all land animals, while the dragon is chief of all aquatic creatures. These two creatures are quintessential symbols of *yin* and *yang*; their union on her throne gives Xi Wang Mu an extraordinary degree of authority and importance: she not only rules *yin*, she is associated with *yin–yang* duality. This duality is also reflected in the fact that she is usually depicted with symbols of both the sun and moon and that, even though she represents the West and death, she is the one who grants immortality. According to Cahill, this indicates that Xi Wang Mu is androgynous, independent, and complete with dominion over the entire cosmos.[17]

Xi Wang Mu's association with the tiger is pervasive. In later times, this potent animal is seen not only as forming her throne but also as her constant companion. The tiger – as the destroyer – is the quintessential *yin* creature. Tigers are believed to live to the age of 1000 years and, after 500 years, become white. Xi Wang Mu's tiger is, of course, white. She sends him as her envoy to help the legendary emperors and to perform other heroic tasks.

The dragon is the chief of the scaly reptiles such as fish, snakes, and lizards. It is believed that the dragon has the power of transformation, and can render itself visible or invisible. In the spring, the dragon is said to ascend to the skies; in autumn, it buries itself in the watery depths. The dragon symbolizes the productive forces of moisture, rain, and storms, which bring renewal in nature. It is a divine, beneficent creature, and for more than 1000 years appeared on the Imperial coat of arms. The combination of the dragon and tiger in Xi Wang Mu's retinue symbolize not only cosmic dominion, but also the continuity achieved by the fusion of the *yin* and *yang* forces. In this sense she can be said to even represent cosmic harmony.

Another symbol of Xi Wang Mu's dominance and authority is the *sheng* headdress that she is virtually always depicted as wearing. The *sheng* is a musical instrument of 17 bamboo tubes in five different lengths, inserted in a gourd with a mouthpiece on its lower end. Said to have been invented by the goddess Nu Wa, the *sheng* was intended to symbolize the phoenix, since its shape resembles the tail of this bird of good omen. In traditional China, the *sheng* was played at weddings, funerals, and Imperial religious ceremonies. In its original form the *sheng*, also invented by Nu Wa, was associated with reed whistles and thus with immortality.

According to Cahill, the *sheng* has been Xi Wang Mu's most enduring symbol and it associates her with both the stars and weaving. From early on, Xi Wang Mu was seen as a ruler of certain constellations and the stars in general. In earliest times her headdress may even have been made out of stars. More commonly, however, the shape of the *sheng* is believed to represent either a spool or a particular piece of the loom that links her with weaving. Interestingly, Xi Wang Mu's connection with both the stars and weaving can be seen in her close association with a star (Vega in the constellation of Lyra) that is known as the Weaver Girl. In the legend associated with her, Weaver Girl is said to travel across the Milky Way in the night sky to meet with the Herd Boy (Altair in the constellation of Aquila). This heavenly meeting of lovers occurs once a year on the night known in Taoism as the Double Seven. The seventh night of the seventh month, this night has also long been considered sacred to Xi Wang Mu by Taoists. Festivals on this night celebrate it as a most auspicious night for divine meetings. It is seen not only as the time when the heavenly lovers meet, but also the anniversary of Xi Wang Mu's visit to the legendary Emperor Wu in which she is said to have presented him with the peaches of immortality.[18]

On a psychological level, these rare meetings signify the *hieros gamos*, the sacred union with *tao*, which brings rebirth and enlightenment. Discussed in more detail in Chapter 6, the cosmological significance of these meetings resides in the idea that the continuity of the universe depends on the union of the masculine and feminine cosmic forces. These sacred unions occur at two annual meetings which correspond with the seasons. The one that happens on the seventh day of the seventh month is the summer union, while the winter union occurs on the seventh day of the first month. While the seventh day of the seventh month emphasizes the mystical union of the *yin* and *yang* forces, the seventh day of the first month is celebrated as the day of Man and is connected with an ancient religious ritual to invoke the blessing and power of Xi Wang Mu. These two festivals mark the progress of the agricultural year, the cycle of seasonal change. Xi Wang Mu was believed to possess the power to renew the cosmic cycle by weaving a web of continuity, the renewal of life, achieved through the union of the two cosmic forces enacted through

Figure 5.3 Images of Xi Wang Mu

Source: Drawing by Christy Shum. Based on descriptions in the Classic of the Mountains and Seas, c.200 BC. Xi Wang Mu in her *sheng* headdress riding a crane; with leopard tail and tiger teeth; from a Han dynasty stone rubbing

the two festivals. As this cosmic weaver, she is the connecting link between Heaven, Earth, and Man[19] (see Figure 5.3).

As the cosmic weaver she is also a powerful symbol for healing. An example of this comes from a Chinese woman I worked with in my practice. If I had been asked to pick a Chinese symbol for her when we first began working together, I would have chosen the white hare. The hare is a pervasive creature in Chinese legend and mythology. It is seen as pure, gentle, docile, obedient, and fertile. Xi Wang Mu is often depicted with two white hares sitting near her feet who are working diligently with mortar and pestle pounding the celestial reeds into the elixir of immortality. Traditional Chinese culture associated the hare with a young female virgin who was, ideally, supposed to be quiet, receptive, and yielding. This type of young virgin was held to be a "good catch," because she could be molded into the family structure and would be productive – performing what needed to be done without asking questions. Crystal was chosen by her husband's family for just these reasons. Although she was eventually able to look back at this and laugh, it was only after a long journey that reconnected her with the power of the Feminine archetype and transformed her from a diligent, obedient hare like the ones that sit at the feet of Xi Wang Mu into a stronger, more independent, and fulfilled woman.

The oldest of four children, Crystal was born into a very poor home in Southern China. From the time she was three, her mother was hospitalized frequently for depression. Constantly aware of her mother's fragile emotional state, she took on household tasks and the care of her younger siblings in an attempt to help. Seeing her mother as vulnerable and helpless, she tried to be protective of her and was often the one to take her mother to the hospital when her depression became severe. Crystal's father was an extremely hard-working man, but he denigrated Crystal and treated her abusively even when she helped him in his work.

Determined to better herself, she attended college where she studied computer programming. While there she met her future husband, who was studying business. Not long after they married, Crystal's father died and the young couple moved to Canada, taking his mother with them. It soon became clear to Crystal that this was a mistake, as her husband's mother kept complete control of him and demanded the final say in all the family decisions. Increasingly, the two of them treated Crystal as a servant; they were insistent that she work constantly – being the productive, docile hare – to bring money into the family. Even when she wanted to stay home for a while to care for her newborn son, they refused and forced her back to work shortly after her son's birth. As time went on her husband became alcoholic and more abusive – mistreating both her and her son. Unfortunately for Crystal, the family remained quite isolated within the Chinese community, and it was a long time before she was able to reach out for help. Only when her husband almost broke her son's arm did she find the strength to leave. Even leaving did not resolve the problems with her husband's family, and she felt incapable of completely protecting herself and her son. Eventually, she fell into a major depression.

But one day while walking through an open-air market, she came upon a vendor selling fabric scraps and leftover spools of thread – possibly remnants from some type of garment factory. Looking at their bright colors and varied textures, she remembered how her father had collected thread and fabric as a hobby. She bought the threads, returned home and began sorting and winding them. This repetitive motion was soothing, giving her peace and calm that she had never experienced in her life. In winding the threads, she began to remember her childhood and the suffering she endured growing up in such difficult circumstances. As she wound, tears continually rolled down her face. She found the solitude comforting and the silence nurturing. She began to feel, for the very first time, connected to herself.

Crystal kept winding the threads and soon a ball was wound into shape. As time went on she kept winding, the thread became her lifeline to her soul, connecting her to her deep innermost feelings that she recognized as the foundation of her being. The ball grew bigger. Day by day she felt she was coming closer to becoming her authentic self. And although she couldn't fathom what was happening to her, she didn't care because, in spite of the fact that the tears kept rolling down her face, she felt better. As the ball grew in size, more memories returned to her and her childhood came alive to her. Slowly, her depression lifted. She was regaining forgotten parts of her soul and beginning to truly heal from the wounding she had suffered.

Eventually she began to work with thread in different ways, winding it into fascinating shapes and weaving it into others. Almost without realizing it, Crystal discovered that inside the body of a computer programmer an artist had always been hiding. Today Crystal continues her analysis, going deeper and deeper into herself, and with every new creation she comes closer to healing her old wounds and weaving her new life. Her shapes and weavings have attracted the attention of galleries, and a well-known gallery has recently scheduled a show of her work.

Crystal's is a classic case of the transformative power of reconnecting with the Feminine archetype. It is almost as if she has taken the bindings from her feet, unwound the cloth, and used it to weave new patterns in her life. In doing so, she has transformed herself from one of the obedient white hares that pounds with mortar and pestle into a cosmic weaver who, like Xi Wang Mu herself, controls her own destiny.

Notes

1 Chen Tung-yuen, *Chung-kuo fu-nu sheng-huo shih* (*A History of the Lives of Chinese Women*), Shanghai: The Commercial Press, 1937; Lin Yu-tang, *My Country and My People*, New York: John Day, 1939, p. 137.

2 Suzanne E. Cahill, *Transcendence and Divine Passion: The Queen Mother of the West in Medieval China*, Stanford, CA: Stanford University Press, 1993.

3 Martin Palmer and Xiaomin Zhao, *Essential Chinese Mythology: Stories that Change the World*, London: Thorsons, 1997, pp. 16–18.

4 Ibid., p. 17.

5 Robert van Gulik, *Sex Life in Early China*, Leiden: Brill, 1961, pp. 4–8; Kuo-Chen Wu, *The Chinese Heritage*, New York: Crown, 1982, p. 21.

6 Helmut Wilhelm, *Eight Lectures on the I Ching*, Princeton, NJ: Princeton University Press, 1975, p. 26.

7 Tu Er-wei, *Religious Systems of Ancient China*, Taipei, Taiwan: Xue Sheng Publishing, 1977, pp. 4, 122–5.

8 Clarence B. Day, *Chinese Peasant Cults*, Shanghai: Kelly & Walsh, 1940, pp. 59–60, 86–90; Edward T. C. Werner, *Myths and Legends of China*, London: George Harrap, 1922, pp. 127, 166–8; Charles A. S. Williams, *Outlines of Chinese Symbolism & Art Motives*, New York: Dover Publications, third revised edition, 1976, pp. 210–1; Carl G. Jung, *Symbols of Transformation*, CW 5, para. 663.

9 Suzanne E. Cahill, op. cit., p. 12.

10 Martin Palmer and Xiaomin Zhao, op. cit., p. 9.

11 This Nu Wa story has been compiled from several of the many versions that exist and includes the main symbols associated with her. Versions of the story can be found in Martin Palmer and Xiaomin Zhao, op. cit., and Edward T. C. Werner, op. cit.

12 Jordan Paper, *The Spirits Are Drunk: Comparative Approaches to Chinese Religion*, New York: SUNY Press, 1995, p. 230.

13 Edward T. C. Werner, op. cit., p. 136

14 Robert van Gulik, op. cit., pp. 36–7.

15 Chapters 25 and 45 of *Tao Te Ching*, quoted in Mokusen Miyuki, 'Secret of the Golden Flower: Studies and Translations', Diploma Thesis, C.G. Jung Institute, Switzerland, 1967, pp. 12, 14–15.

16 Robert van Gulik, op. cit., pp. 42–3.

17 Suzanne E. Cahill, op. cit., pp. 18, 26–7.

18 Ibid., p. 167.

19 Edward T. C. Werner, op. cit., p. 72; Michael Loewe, *Ways to Paradise: The Chinese Quest for Immortality*, London: George Unwin, 1979, pp. 88–127, Chapter 4; Anthony Christie, *Chinese Mythology*, London: Hamlyn House, 1968, pp. 78–9; Clarence B. Day, op. cit., p. 94; Charles A. S. Williams, op. cit., pp. 226–8; Wolfram Eberhard, *A Dictionary of Chinese Symbols*, New York: Routledge & Kegan Paul, 1986, pp. 319–20.

Chapter 6

Yexian: the Chinese Cinderella

Just as myths and legends can help us reconnect with the archetypal Feminine, so can fairy tales. In fact, for Jungians, fairy tales are a primary source of archetypal images, and it is believed they can be a powerful tool in helping us understand our complexes and providing the clues we need to further the process of our own healing.

The Cinderella story is perhaps the most pervasive of all fairy tales – literally hundreds of versions of it can be found around the world. In virtually all of them a lovely young girl is being raised by a wicked step-mother. The stepmother, who has one or two spiteful daughters of her own, has married the girl's father after her biological mother has died. The father either dies soon after or doesn't seem to notice how cruelly his daughter is being treated. Other common elements in Cinderella tales include small feet, a lost shoe that is found, a grand ball or other special event, animals that can talk or have some type of special power, marriage to a prince or a true love and, often, a mystical personage who appears to offer help.

Although there is evidence the tale was known in Germany as early as the 1500s, the Brothers Grimm didn't actually record the German version of it until more than 300 years later. In the meantime, a version of it appeared in Italy around the 1600s. In 1697 Charles Perrault copied his famous version of the story down from oral tradition and included it in his *Tales from Olden Times* – the collection that has come to be known as *Stories from Mother Goose*[1]. It was Perrault who gave us the version with the fairy godmother, the pumpkins, and mice. This version of the story – especially as it was adapted and embellished by Disney – has become such a pervasive part of Western culture that almost anyone would readily assume it originated here. But this is not the case. The earliest known written version of the story comes from around AD 850, when a scholar named Duan Cheng-shi made a collection of ghost stories, strange tales, and plant and animal lore from the period in which he lived, the Tang dynasty. Even then, the way Duan records the tale makes it sound like it has been passed down through oral tradition for a long time. All this makes it seem quite possible that the Cinderella story originated in China, but this is not known for certain.

Regardless, this tale contains all the elements mentioned above that remained common in the folktale as it was told through the ages in and around the world, and it is important to examine this tale here for a number of reasons. First, if it is not the absolute first Cinderella story, it is one of the very earliest and thus can bring us closer to the primal archetypal energy and its healing power. Second, its imagery is so different from contemporary Disney-esque conceptions that it throws the deeper and more profoundly meaningful symbolism of the tale into sharp relief. Finally, it is a tale from the Tang dynasty. If you recall from the earlier sections on history, this is the period when the fascination with the small, delicate feet of dancers became a fashion that contributed to the eventual origin of true footbinding in the following dynasty, the Song. According to sinologist Dorothy Ko, this is no coincidence. In fact, Ko believes there was a direct link between the Cinderella myth, the cultural admiration – and later obsession – with tiny feet, and the spread of footbinding.[2] From the Jungian perspective this makes perfect sense. The woman who has tiny feet and walks with a swaying gait is one whose standpoint is weak and one who has little feminine power. This woman appears to be a "pushover." And while this connection between what Ko calls a "Cinderella complex" and the spread of foot-binding is undoubtedly correct, the Cinderella story – especially the early Chinese one – also has a great deal to tell us about regaining our standpoint and reconnecting with the archetypal Feminine power.

In the tale set down by Duan Cheng-shi, the lovely young maiden's name is Yexian. According to Duan, she lived about 1000 years before he wrote down her story. She lived in the south of China in an area that is dotted with great grottoes and caves. Her father, Wu, was a chieftain and "cave master" who was known as Wu-the-cave to his people. Wu loved Yexian, who was very wise and lovely, and he was particularly pleased with the great skill she showed at being able to pan – or "fish" as it was known – for gold in the streams.

When Yexian's mother died, Wu married a woman with two daughters, and then Wu himself died. After he was gone, the stepmother set Yexian perilous and difficult tasks, sending her up the steep hills to find firewood and down to the deep valleys to gather water. But one day a little happiness came into Yexian's life. In one of the streams she found a little goldfish with golden eyes and red whiskers, only two inches long. Yexian took him home in a basin. But he grew every day. Soon Yexian could no longer find a bowl or pot big enough to keep him in, and so she put him in a pond behind the house. The goldfish soon grew to be ten feet long. Every day Yexian visited him and brought him bits of food. When she did, the golden fish lifted his head onto the bank to be close to Yexian, but as soon as anyone else approached he dived back into the water.

One day, unbeknownst to Yexian, the wicked stepmother spied the giant fish and decided it would provide a great deal of tasty food. In order to trick the fish, she pretended to praise Yexian for all her hard work and gave her a new coat. Then, sending Yexian to get water from a faraway stream, she put on Yexian's old coat and went to the pond. When Yexian's fish friend raised its head, the stepmother stabbed it. Later she cooked it, enjoying how good it tasted, and hid the bones from Yexian in the dung heap.

When Yexian returned and realized her friend was gone she wept bitterly. Suddenly a person with wild hair came down from the sky and told her not to cry. Explaining that the stepmother had killed the fish, the person told Yexian to fetch the fish's bones from the dung heap and hide them in her room, explaining that these bones had great power and whatever she asked from them she would receive.

When the day of the great celebration known as the Cave Festival came, the stepmother made Yexian stay home and take care of the garden. But as soon as the others left, Yexian asked the bones for clothes to wear to the festival. A beautiful jade-green silk coat and golden slippers appeared. Yexian put them on and went to the festivities. While she was there, one of the stepsisters pointed out that the lovely girl in jade-green looked like her stepsister. Yexian hurried away and dropped one of her golden slippers.

When some of the cave people found the slipper, they sold it to the king of a neighboring island. The king had all the women in his court try on the slipper, but discovered that it was at least one inch too small for even the smallest foot. He also noticed that the slipper was strangely feather-light and didn't crumple in the normal way when it hit stones. Becoming suspicious of the shoe, he jailed the cave people and tortured them until he finally became convinced that they did not know who the slipper belonged to. They did, however, tell the king where they had found the shoe, and the king quickly sent his attendants to search the area.

After none of the neighboring houses yielded up the owner of the shoe, the king noticed that Chieftain Wu's cave was nearby. There the king found Yexian and had her try on the shoe. Immediately he knew he had found the one he had been searching for. Yexian, now wearing both golden slippers and glowing with radiant beauty, appeared in her jade-green coat and took delicate hesitant steps towards the king. Yexian and the king then left for his kingdom, taking the precious fish bones with them.

After they were gone, falling rocks destroyed the wicked stepmother and stepsisters, but the cave people mourned them and buried the sisters in the "Tomb of the Regretful Daughters." There the cave people came to have their prayers for daughters answered.

The king, now home on his island, made Yexian his Exalted Queen, but was also greedily begging the fish bones for riches. The fish bones granted this for one year and then stopped. The king buried the bones near the ocean's shore, covered them with 1000 bushels of pearls and created a border around the burial place with gold. But eventually there was a mutiny against the king and the pearls and gold were used to pay mutinous troops. The site was washed away by waves from the ocean. . . .[3]

Although all the classic Cinderella story elements are clearly in place in this tale, it's easy to see that it has some very important differences from the versions we are familiar with in the West.[4] Once Yexian is made Exalted Queen, she is never heard from again, and we don't know what happens to her when the troops mutiny. This means that the "happily ever after" we are used to is missing. Another difference is that the king, who is avaricious and cruel, is hardly the prince charming our Western Cinderella wins in the end. One of the most fascinating things about these differences is that they support a notion that feminist critics of our Disney-esque Cinderella tale have been making for decades. Namely, that we should not be teaching our daughters that "getting the prince" is what will make them happy and that it is not even necessarily a good thing. These critics have been pointing out that what Cinderella really needs to do is stand on her own two feet. And this is perhaps what this tale is telling us on at least one level. In Jungian terms, we could say she needs to regain her positive feminine standpoint, her connection with Mother Earth.

As Marie-Louise von Franz points out in her classic *The Interpretation of Fairy Tales*[5], folk stories can be interpreted in many different ways and on many different levels. Regardless, at their core, they are filled with archetypal content. This tale, like all classic Cinderella stories, begins with four feminine figures and masculine characters are either non-existent or weak. Only one of our feminine figures is not wicked, and she is weak and completely controlled by the wicked ones. This announces to us right from the outset that, at its most primal level, this story is about a problem with the archetypal Feminine. Since both the masculine and feminine within need to be present and in balance for us to achieve inner wholeness, this tale is going to tell us what happens when the feminine is either overdeveloped or distorted or both. It will also provide hints as to how we can solve these problems and restore harmony in our psyches.

Looking at this from another perspective, we see that the Cinderella tale is about loss and abandonment. In the course of both the most well-known Western versions and the Chinese tale, Cinderella loses her good mother and father; she loses her precious slipper and, after only a brief moment of glory, she loses her magical animal helpers and all the beautiful finery she has worn to the ball. But, of course, this is also a tale about redemption – in this case, finding and reclaiming what she has lost.

Looking at Yexian's story from this perspective, we see that one of the most significant facts is that right from the outset we are told that Yexian is wise and, not only that, she is also able to pan – or fish – for gold. Panning for gold is a process that retrieves gold dust and nuggets from the sediment in rivers and streams. Since water almost always symbolized the unconscious and/or the feeling, intuitive nature, this tells us that Yexian has the ability to go deep within and find the nuggets of gold that are hidden there. It is significant to note that her father, the good masculine, loves and admires her for these traits. These intuitive, instinctive, feeling-toned abilities are, of course, associated with the positive feminine. As long as Yexian is under the influence of the negative feminine, these instincts are suppressed and the wicked stepmother is able to control her and make her suffer, sending her out on dangerous, arduous tasks. But Yexian is not completely beaten – she looks in the deep water and finds the beautiful red and gold fish. The fish has long been associated symbolically with fecundity and regeneration and with all the aspects of the Mother Goddess as a generative force.[6] Thus, Yexian is beginning to go deep and reconnect with the natural elements of Mother Earth. She has opened up to the possibility of renewing herself, of reclaiming her lost connection with the archetypal Feminine. We know she is on the right track when she allows the golden fish to grow – from two inches to ten feet! But, of course, when it becomes this big, the negative mother recognizes the danger. If Yexian's connection with the archetypal Feminine becomes much stronger, the negative mother knows she is doomed. Acting quickly, she kills the fish. When Yexian discovers her loss, she is devastated. But all is not lost, a wild-haired person – someone symbolic once again of the connection with the wild and naturalistic elements and, thus, the Feminine – appears and tells her that if she will look under the dung heap, she will find the fish's bones and be reconnected with the eternal Feminine again. The dung heap (in some versions translated as a cesspit) stands for the negative elements of our selves we must explore and face on our journey to wholeness. Yexian does as she is told and discovers the source of untold treasure. But she keeps the treasure hidden from the wicked stepmother. All these riches – all this potential and possibility – remain hidden until the day of the ball when Yexian can endure being so totally repressed no longer. She puts on her jade-green silk and her golden slippers and ventures forth, *but* she only goes forth in disguise. She has come close, but she has not totally reclaimed her archetypal Feminine, and so she drops her golden slipper and loses it again. And until she finds that slipper again, she is right back where she was: disconnected from the archetypal Feminine and under the control of the negative, distorted feminine.

But the power of the archetypal Feminine cannot be suppressed forever. It rises up when Yexian finds her lost golden slipper and comes forth as her true self, radiant and clothed in eternal jade and gold. She is made Exalted Queen and she becomes reconnected to and comes into balance with the masculine. While our Western Cinderella's story ends here, Yexian's story goes on – and provides us with an incredibly important insight: the king that Yexian has found is not so exalted. Not only did he throw the cave people in jail and torture them, once he gets his hands on Yexian's fish bones – her shamanistic, natural, feminine power – he becomes greedy and abuses it. Consequently the power deserts him. Fortunately, however, he redeems himself. Once he sees what he has lost, he honors the fish bones. He buries them by the ocean, their natural home. He covers them with 1000 bushels of pearls and rings them with gold. Thus in our Chinese tale, both the archetypal Feminine and Masculine are redeemed.

It is extremely important to note that Yexian is not able to show her true self until she has found her lost slipper and has slippers on both her feet. While this is true in both the Western and the Chinese tales, the Chinese version tells us far more about them and, thus, more about their true meaning. Yexian's slippers are made of gold. As was mentioned in the analysis of the "Golden Lotus," gold symbolizes all that is pure, strong, and of great value. Right away the king notices there is something special and magical about them. Yexian's slippers are not thick or cumbersome like normal shoes. They are feather-light and ethereal – and yet they are mysteriously strong. They don't crumple, the story tells us, when they come into contact with a stone. Clearly, these are marvelous shoes: they are exactly what Yexian needs. She may have small feet, but they are her standpoint. They are her connection to Mother Earth and she has to protect what she has. What's more, since ancient times shoes have symbolized freedom and liberty. From ancient times onward, when people were taken into slavery and deprived of their freedom, their shoes were immediately taken away. Those who had shoes had liberty. They could walk on Mother Earth on any terrain and in all kinds of weather. Thus, when Yexian regains her golden slippers, her "standpoint" is now protected. She is able to step out as her true self and walk forward on her journey to find the wholeness that comes when the inner feminine and masculine are in harmony and balance.

During my years as a Jungian analyst I have worked with many "Cinderellas" who have had to come to terms with their "wicked step-mothers." These women all suffered from a sense of being abandoned by the positive mother and experienced, instead, a negative mother. Because the archetypal imagery associated with this negative mother appears so often in fairy tales as either a wicked stepmother or a wicked witch, Jungians often refer to her simply as the Witch Mother. In terms of the footbinding metaphor that we have been using throughout the book, this would be the mother who binds the daughter's feet without kindness or compassion – the one who willingly restricts her daughter's feminine standpoint and cuts her off from Mother Earth. Sadly, of course, this negative mother is often only treating her daughter the way she was treated. This is how she was mothered and so this is how she mothers. This negative cycle continues until one of the daughters – the Cinderella – manages to struggle up from the cold, dark, ash-strewn hearth of unconsciousness, reconnect with the power of the positive feminine, and become conscious.

How this happens – and how the feminine can be redeemed – was very clear in the story of Amy, one of the clients I worked with when I was still living in Switzerland. Amy was an American who had met a man from Germany while traveling in Europe, fallen in love, and married him. When she first came to see me she was the mother of a one-year-old daughter and was living with her husband in a German city near the Swiss border. Neither living in Europe nor her marriage was living up to the fairy-tale fantasies she had envisioned. Her husband was a white-collar worker whom she now found incredibly boring, and they couldn't afford to do the traveling and studying she wanted to do. Although she was working on her BA by correspondence through an American university, Amy was having trouble finishing. Her home was disorganized and she had so much trouble handling her infant daughter that she had put her in day care full time. Her situation was complicated by the constant interference in her life by her mother-in-law, who was extremely domineering and critical and who could not accept the fact that her son had married a foreigner. By the time I met Amy she was suffering from depression and crying spells; she felt lonely, isolated, helpless, inadequate, and trapped in her marriage.

When Amy first came to me she reminded me of the Cinderella who, at least at the beginning of the classic German tale, was sitting by the cold hearth, smeared with ashes, and weeping over her terrible plight. This is not to say Amy did not have real difficulties and challenges to overcome. It became clear that her life had been extremely difficult when she was a child, and it wasn't surprising that she had sought out a handsome prince who she thought was going to create a happily-ever-after life for her. And although Amy did spend some of her first months in analysis weeping and complaining about her plight, she had had the courage to begin the process in the first place, and it wasn't long before she began, like Cinderella, to find a way out of the dungeon she had found herself in.

One of the most significant turning points in her progress came, certainly not coincidently, when she had the following dream:

> In a party, we were playing some sort of child's game and each of us was allowed to pick a prize from a container. I picked and got two small books, one of them was Cinderella. I felt embarrassed and surprised that my life story was to be summed up in the story of Cinderella.

When she came to understand that this was, at its very heart, a story about abandonment, she began to understand many aspects of her life. Up until she was five years old, Amy had been raised by an aunt, one of her mother's sisters. When her mother did finally take her back, she was often both emotionally and physically abusive. There was a great deal of drinking in the home and the aggression that so often goes with it. Amy could remember times when she would hide in the closet, crying and telling herself over and over that "This is not real, this is a dream." Interestingly, she could remember comforting herself in the closet by playing the music from the Disney Cinderella on her cassette player. Although the physical abuse stopped as Amy got older, the emotional abuse continued. When Amy was 15, her mother decided to go back to university. By this time Amy's mother was sometimes punishing her by grounding her for as long as three months at a time. When confined to the house during these periods, Amy would do chores and work for her mother, for instance, typing her mother's term papers for her. During this period her aunt, the one positive mother figure in her life, died of cancer.

Again like Cinderella and Yexian, Amy's father was not there to give her any support. An alcoholic, he was given to violent outbursts when he'd been drinking. He was also emotionally distant and spent much of his time at work. Amy experienced him as being extremely selfish and self-involved. Even though he was a bank manager and made a good living, he refused to help his children with university, telling them they had to make it on their own. Soon after Amy had the Cinderella dream, she began to get some inkling of the true nature of the journey she had undertaken. She began to see that, rather than being some magical Disney-esque frolic, she was on an archetypal journey. Like Yexian, she was going to have to travel arduous trails into the deep valleys and even deeper waters. She also realized that if she was ever going to live happily ever after with her prince, she had to improve her relationships with the masculine side of her being – her animus. As a first step on this journey she began exploring her relationships with the men in her life, her father and her husband. In particular, she realized she had to come to terms with the fact that the "father" had been absent at the beginning of her tale.

The instinctive, intuitive awareness that she needed to explore this area of her life was a sign that Amy had begun to dive deep enough into the waters of her unconscious to find her golden fish. This integration of her instinctual nature allowed her to consider her father's life in new ways. As she did, the reasons for his absence became clear to her, and she realized the significance of the fact that he, too, had been abandoned at an early age. He had, in fact, been orphaned at five years of age. After this he had lived in several different homes until he was seven, and was then dropped off at the door of his older brother. As her understanding, compassion, and forgiveness for him increased, she began to integrate her own inner masculine. Not surprisingly, as this happened, her attitude towards her husband began to change.

One of the interesting effects of this was that the recurring dreams she had had throughout analysis in which she was chased, threatened, and/or attacked by a violent man with a gun began to subside. She also began to have dreams in which her husband played a more positive role. In one, while she clung desperately to a ledge on a tall barn, her husband stood valiantly below with a basket ready to catch her when she called out that she had to jump because she could hang on no longer. As Amy's attitude toward her husband changed, she was able to see him objectively rather than as a stepping stone to a fantasy paradise. She began to appreciate the fact that he was a sincere, honest, dependable person who was dedicated to providing for his family.

Once Amy felt more contained and supported both by the therapeutic process and by her husband, she was able to begin the even more difficult job of looking at the negative mother and reconnecting with the archetypal Feminine on an even deeper level. Here she is like Yexian, who allows her tiny goldfish to grow from a mere two inches to ten feet long. Amy was able to begin to explore her mother's life and, eventually, to see it more from her mother's point of view and understand why her mother had had so much difficulty mothering: her mother had had a very difficult life. Married at the age of 16, by the time she was 17 she had a baby. Within the year, her husband had died. By the age of 18 she had remarried. Soon after this Amy was born. During the next five years, three more children followed, and her mother suffered a nervous breakdown. As Amy began to understand what her mother had been through, dreams she'd been having of violent abusive arguments and fights with her mother began to diminish. At the same time, her ability to deal with the ugly confrontations she was having with her mother-in-law increased.

Naturally, like anyone in the process of deep analysis, Amy had some setbacks in the process. This was the wicked stepmother – the Witch Mother complex – within her rising up from time to time and trying to destroy the golden fish. When this connection to the archetypal Feminine was broken, Amy had to work hard to get it back. In order to reconnect with the essential, elemental nature of the fish – its bones – Amy had, like Yexian, to dig deep into the dung heap to find them. Soon Amy had a dream that told her this in no uncertain terms. In the dream Amy is with a woman who is holding an unusually small baby. When Amy stands behind the woman, she re-experiences the miraculous feeling of being one with the cosmos that she'd had when she was pregnant. Suddenly she realizes the woman must be pregnant again. The woman then asks for a drink of water, but complains that it tastes bitter. A nurse tells her it must be the time in pregnancy when water has a bitter taste.

This is a sign that it was time for Amy to face some of the bitter truths about her own role in her misfortunes. This was the dung heap she had to plow through to find the magic bones. For Amy this involved looking at the immature, whining behavior she'd been exhibiting and facing how she had been blaming her husband for her problems and been unconsciously bitter about having a child. In particular, she needed to consider how she had sent her infant to day care, not out of necessity, but because she couldn't handle being a parent. Over time Amy came to realize that she had been resenting her daughter and blaming her for her "unlived" life, just as her own mother had done. Also, as she came to see that her inability in child rearing was a reflection of her own childhood experience, she was able to see that this was a problem that could be solved. She became determined to learn to parent better and bring her daughter home from day care.

Amy now had the magic bones in her hand, and she was able to go even deeper, reconnecting with the Feminine on an elemental level. Up until this time Amy had been having recurrent dreams in which she would lose or leave her daughter in the woods, restaurants, motels, and various other places. These dreams subsided.

Over the final months of her analysis Amy had more powerful transformative dreams about her connection to the Feminine. In one of them, Amy is in an elegant room where some type of convention is going on. In the beginning, she looks more like a man than a woman. She is carrying a gun and is ready to shoot people. Forcing her way into a private reception room, she sees that other men, her colleagues, are there. They are ready with their guns, and she knows that if she shoots, they will too. Then, her husband comes into the room and comes to her:

> Suddenly, my gun power begins to disintegrate. I become more of a woman and my gun becomes a feminine energy. Then it is amazing that all the other men's guns also experience this metamorphosis. There is a strong feeling of femininity among us as we encircle the group of convention people. There is a sense of knowing, a sense of warmth, a strong sense of femininity.

The dreams Amy had had throughout her therapy of a man with a gun had symbolized on one level her negative experience of father and the phallic mother – the mother who has taken on aggression and other negative "masculine" characteristics. This phallic mother is the wicked stepmother found in all the Cinderella tales. Here the disintegration of the gun's negative energy shows that Amy had integrated the positive masculine; the wicked stepmother no longer had power over her, and she was able to connect on a deep level with the archetypal Feminine.

An even more beautiful dream shows this. In the dream Amy is in a beautiful cathedral in Italy. She feels as if other people are looking at her because she isn't following the conventions properly, but this does not distract her from what she knows she wants to do:

> I wish to light a candle. I take one and light it, then begin to search for the Madonna and Child under which I will place my candle. I find the Madonna and Child and decide to place my candle beneath a blue hurricane lantern on the altar.

This fragment of the dream shows a deep level of experience of the spirit of the Feminine and of motherhood. As soon as the energy from the negative mother is released, her inner feminine is free to develop. Soon after this Amy discovered she was pregnant again. At the same time, Amy felt stronger and more rooted in life. As her therapy progressed, she became more organized in housekeeping and time management. She managed to care for her daughter, complete her degree, and give birth to a son.

As a result of her transformation, her husband felt contained and supported, was able to grow and develop, and became very successful in his career. Eventually Amy started a home business and received much acclaim for her contribution to the community – she was even covered by the media for her success in integrating a balanced home life and career! Her fantasy marriage to her prince turned into a true Cinderella story in which Amy became able both to connect with the positive masculine and to reach down into the depths of her being to find the archetypal Feminine.

Amy and the other Cinderellas I met in my work spurred me to look for other Chinese fairy tales on this theme. One I found appears to be a much more modern version. Although it was collected and recorded in 1936, it is not known exactly when it first originated.[7] Like the other Cinderella stories found around the globe, it contains all the classic elements. However, it also has a number of unique features that make it well worth examining. In this tale our Cinderella's character is known as Beauty. Her father is never mentioned, and she lives with her wicked stepmother and the stepmother's daughter. This daughter is spoiled and evil. And, as in many fairy tales, her bad inner character is reflected in her outer appearance: she is so ugly that she is known as Pock Face.

Apparently, unbeknownst to Beauty, when her mother died she was transformed into a yellow cow. The cow now lived behind the house, and Beauty loved it very much. The stepmother, however, hated the cow and treated it miserably. One evening the stepmother decided to take her daughter to the theater and refused to let Beauty come along. But she told Beauty she would take her the following evening if Beauty straightened out a huge stack of hemp. This was an impossible task, and after Beauty broke down sobbing, she went to the cow for help. The cow magically sorted the hemp for her. Still, the next evening the stepmother took her own daughter to the theater instead, and told Beauty that if she sorted a huge pile of beans and sesame seeds, she would take her the next day. She tried sorting the seeds one by one, but it was too hard and she went again to the cow. The cow chastised her for not realizing for herself she could sort the seeds by using a fan. Beauty used the fan to blow the sesame seeds into a separate pile, and when the stepmother came home she found the nicely sorted beans. Realizing that she now had to take Beauty to the theater, the stepmother said no lowly servant girl like her could possibly have done this and demanded to know who helped her. When Beauty told her it was the cow who helped, the stepmother was enraged. She killed the cow and ate it. Completely distraught, Beauty took the bones of the cow and hid them in an earthenware pot in her bedroom.

Time went on and the stepmother continued to refuse to take Beauty to the theater. Finally, one day Beauty became so angry she started to smash things in the house; she even broke the pot where the cow's bones were hidden. Suddenly, there was a loud noise and, out of the pot, came a white horse, a new dress, and a beautiful pair of embroidered shoes. Once over the shock of this, Beauty put on the dress and shoes, jumped on the horse, and rode down the road. As she did, one of the shoes fell off. Unable to get down, she didn't know what to do. One by one, three different merchants came by and offered to retrieve the slipper, but only if she would marry them. She turned each one down – and then a handsome scholar came along. When he offered to fetch the shoe in exchange for marriage, Beauty agreed.

After they had been married three days, they went to Beauty's home to pay the customary respects to her family. The stepmother and sister pretended to treat Beauty very kindly and begged her to stay with them for a few days. Fooled, Beauty agreed. As soon as her husband left, Beauty's stepsister tricked her into leaning over the well in the back yard and pushed her in. Beauty drowned, and when her husband came looking for her he was told she had become ill. After several days the stepsister convinced the husband that she was really his beloved Beauty by saying she looked different because she had been scarred by her illness. The scholar took the wicked stepsister home. In the meantime, Beauty came back as a sparrow and peeped outside the scholar's window. Suspecting the bird might be the real Beauty, he brought it into the house and kept it for a pet. The stepsister, of course, killed it. But Beauty came back again, this time as a bamboo tree in the back yard. The stepsister chopped it down and made a bed from it. Although the scholar slept comfortably on the bed, the stepsister felt pricked by needles and threw the bed away.

An old woman next door took the bed in and slept well on it. For the next several days she found her breakfast had been prepared for her. Enjoying this, but suspicious, she hid in the kitchen the next morning. When she spied a dark shadow preparing the meal, she captured it. Beauty's spirit then told the old woman her whole story. With the old woman's help, Beauty was able to regain her former body and convince her husband she was alive. The scholar was overjoyed and the two were reunited.[8]

One of the most valuable points about this Cinderella tale is it stresses, as most others fail to do, that the process of becoming whole almost always requires the death of the "old" self before the new one can be born. This can be seen in another client of mine named Eleanor. When other people looked at Eleanor's life, it appeared to be a Cinderella story come true. Her father died when she was very young, and she was raised with very little money. After she grew up, she worked her way through university and met a man who was about as close as you can get to a "prince" in North American society: he was handsome, very wealthy, and quite politically powerful. Eleanor married him, raised a successful family, and became known in society for her good works.

But in her mid sixties Eleanor entered analysis. In spite of the fact that she apparently had everything – wealth, power, influence, prestige, and lovely grandchildren – she was filled with tremendous sadness and a deep sense of futility. The night after our first session, she had this dream.

> My two bare feet are floating alone in space beside a square white envelope. It is not addressed to anyone. I open it, it is set up as a formal invitation, but I can't read any of the words. . . .

In analyzing the dream of the disconnected feet, Eleanor said it was telling her that she had "lost her footing." The invitation was one to begin a spiritual search that would reconnect her with what she called the "ground of being." It brought with it, she explained,

> the pain of the realization that I have cut off my two good feet. I have been bought into the patriarchy . . . Only now do I recognize how I longed for a father who had died and how my father complex has affected my life's choices, how I lived it out in the family I married into, and how it is responsible for my spiritual crisis. . .

For all of her married life Eleanor had lived not only exactly the way her husband had wanted her to, but also according to the rigid standards set by her mother-in-law. The matriarch of the wealthy and politically powerful family, Eleanor's mother-in-law was a tyrant, and Eleanor had spent virtually all of her adult life fulfilling her wishes and acquiescing to her demands. In one session, when Eleanor was sharing with me her experience of her tyrannical mother-in-law, I spontaneously blurted out: "Your feet have been bound! You should have been in China a hundred years ago!" Then I shared some information about the practice of footbinding with her and told her about this awful mother-in-law who forced her new daughter-in-law to rebind her feet because they were not small enough. Eleanor could see right away how she had been psychologically footbound and how this related to her need to get back to her "ground of being," in other words to reconnect with Mother Earth and the archetypal Feminine. In fact, it turned out that Eleanor had been unconsciously aware of this for a long time. In the following session, she brought in a poem that she had written three years earlier.

I'm walking in borrowed moccasins
       so that
            I will not awaken
                the warrior in his tent.

I'm walking in borrowed moccasins
       because
            I am afraid.

Afraid to leave my footprints
       on the forest floor.

MY footprints!
Unlike any other!
Undeniably ME!

I want to bare my feet
      to dance,
          pounding my soles in the hard ground
         to the rhythm
            of an ancient dream.

But I am afraid.

I'm walking in borrowed moccasins
      so that no one will hear me,
      so that no one will know
      I was here.

This poem cries out with the anguish Eleanor had felt for years at not being able to express her true self and her fear of the powerful negative masculine had forced her to disguise her own unique footprints, keeping her from dancing on Mother Earth. In terms of the Cinderella story, Eleanor needed to get rid of the borrowed moccasins and put on her own golden slippers. In all the Cinderella stories the slippers fit *no one* but Cinderella – and Eleanor needed to put on the slippers that were uniquely her own. She needed to show her true identity. But before she could do this, Eleanor had to find a way to put that false self to death. Unfortunately, the persona Eleanor had put on for her husband and her mother-in-law – the life of the proper, constrained society matron – was so diametrically opposed to the free-spirited woman dancing on the hard ground that it would take repeated efforts to abolish it completely. This is what Beauty's story is telling us when she is killed not just once but three times in the tale: often we must undergo psychological death in order to be transformed and reborn, and sometimes we must undergo it more than once.

Again, Eleanor was already aware of this. At some deep instinctive level she was, like Beauty, in contact with the age-old feminine wisdom that is represented by the old woman in the tale. This instinctive knowledge made its way up from the depths of Eleanor's unconscious and expressed itself in a poem that she wrote that began as an ode to a friend who had recently died, but quickly turned into a realization that there was something in Eleanor that needed to die too. In the poem Eleanor cries out for her own "lost self":

When I cry
                for my friend
I cry
                for my own lost self
                    for the One Who Was
                        for the One Who Never Was

I breathe deeply to swallow the sadness
                And it sits in cells throughout my body

Destructive process! My cells rebel!

Bury The One Who Was! Release The One Who Has Not Been!

But bury the One That Was
                gently
                    into a shallow grave
Gather
                both flowers and weeds
                  that grow from it

For they will nourish the understanding
Of The One Yet To Be

She will be whole
                yet becoming

She will not look back with regret
Nor forward with expectation

Rather

Looking backwards with wonder at the mystery of growth
And forward with quiet knowledge that growth will continue
She will be

Significantly, Eleanor called this poem "An Invitation to Life." When using active imagination to work on it, Eleanor recalled an image of herself as a barefoot three-year-old in a simple brown dress. The child appeared to be named "Deirdre." Although Eleanor had no conscious knowledge of it at the time, Deirdre was a Celtic goddess whose story dates back to the 1st century in Ireland. The name Deirdre means one who causes trouble. Deirdre is the personification of the romantic and the mystical as well as the type of passionate desire and reckless love that flouts convention and the social order. Deirdre deviates; she is considered dangerous and must be suppressed. Thus, Deirdre is the personification of that aspect of the feminine that is feared and rejected by the patriarchy. It was quickly obvious to Eleanor that Deirdre represented the powerful feminine self that she had suppressed in order to fit into her husband and mother-in-law's world.

Every time Eleanor used active imagination to work on the image of Deirdre, a beautiful, wild white horse came into the vision. The white horse is connected to the Mother archetype; it symbolizes instinct and psychic energy. Interestingly enough – and again unbeknownst to Eleanor – according to Jung, the Celtic goddess of creativity is often personified as a white mare. Not long after this, Eleanor expressed the power of this imagery in a poem about a wild, untamed white horse that gallops across the fields and exists totally in the moment. In the poem Eleanor referred to the horse, "My truth, my white wild horse truth!"

It is no coincidence that this wild white horse features in both Beauty and Eleanor's stories. It is only when Beauty shows her true feelings and finally expresses her anger that the new dress and slippers – the new persona – and the wild white horse break free of the earthenware jar. In the same way, in the process of finding her truth, Eleanor had to express the passionate Deirdre side of her nature – she had to let herself feel and express the anger and frustration she had felt for so many years.

During the ensuing time she spent in analysis, Eleanor became increasingly in touch with her true emotions and her true self. The inner journey expressed itself in Eleanor's outer life in many ways. This new attitude allowed her to develop closer relationships – and a better one than she had ever had before – with her adult children and grandchildren. She became able to appreciate the good points of her marriage, especially her husband's loyalty and the ways in which he had supported her over the years. It is in these ways that the spirit of the white horse remains alive in Eleanor and continues to express itself in her dreams, in her poetry, and in the conscious relationships she is able to form. The deep feminine wisdom she has gained in this process of transformation has brought peace to her life and more harmony to those around her.

Notes

1 Philip Neil and Nicoletta Simborowski, *The Complete Fairy Tales of Charles Perrault*, Houghton Mifflin Harcourt, 1993, p. 126.
2 Dorothy Ko, *Every Step a Lotus: Shoes for Bound Feet*, Berkeley, CA: University of California Press, 2001, p. 25.
3 Ibid., pp. 26–7.
4 Marie-Louise von Franz, *The Interpretation of Fairy Tales*, Houston, TX: Spring Publications, 1970, p. 29. This Tang dynasty version has a very short additional ending that just seems to be tagged on: the text states baldly that there is a mutiny against the king, the pearls and gold are used to pay the mutinous troops, and waves wash the site away. In her book von Franz explains that the type of unexpected and seemingly out-of-context endings are common especially in very primitive fairy tales and have the effect of bringing the listener, in essence, out of the "dream" world and back to reality.
5 ibid., Chapter 1, pp. 1–23.
6 Jean C. Cooper, *An Illustrated Encyclopedia of Traditional Symbols*, London: Thames and Hudson, 1982, p. 68.
7 Arthur Waley, 'The Chinese Cinderella Story', *Folklore* (1947), pp. 226–38.
8 Wolfram Eberhard, *Folktales of China*, London: Routledge & Kegan Paul, 1965, pp. 156–60. Original text in Lin Lan, *San-ko yüan-wang*, Shanghai, 1933, pp. 70–80.

Chapter 7

Chiu Chin: the beheaded martyr

I learned about Chiu Chin when I was in grade three, at about eight years old. I remember the silence in the classroom when Miss Mui told us the story of Chiu Chin.[1] Born in 1875, she lived during the tumultuous times when the last of the Chinese dynasties was falling, wars with foreign powers were weakening China, and young revolutionaries were struggling to bring the first Chinese republic into existence. Towards the end of her short life, Chiu Chin became one of the most passionate and influential of these revolutionaries, and was beheaded by the still-ruling Manchus when she was only 31 years old. Before her death she fought valiantly for the rights of women, the poor, and the oppressed. Miss Mui explained to us that she was a martyr and had died as a *nu ying xiong*, a female hero. Although we were too young to grasp the whole story – let alone the social and psychological meaning of her death – we were speechless; some even wept, and her story was deeply imprinted on our young minds.

Shortly after I entered analysis, the memory of that day in primary school and the story of Chiu Chin was triggered by a dream that I had:

> I encounter a Chinese woman who looks like me. I ask her where she's going. She tells me she's on her way to the gym, and shows me a cloth bag she's holding, made out of a pale-blue Laura Ashley printed cotton. She says she's going to have her head cut off and keep it in the bag.

I was baffled by this dream and spent a long time pondering why, on a subjective level, I apparently needed to have my head cut off. I began research on the motif of beheading which I discovered had been a standard punishment for criminals and murderers in the Chinese penal system since antiquity. The extreme severity of this punishment is that it ensures the criminal dies without his body intact – the soul loses its abode, and is forever banished to the underworld. This means the spirit-soul (*hun*) will not be able to ascend to heaven to become an ancestor. His descendants will not be able to honor him in sacrificial rites. He will not be available to bless and protect his descendants. In a culture that worships ancestors, where the living and the dead are closely bound to each other, this punishment is extraordinarily severe.

According to Zurich analyst Marie-Louise von Franz, "cutting off a human being's head is a very widespread motif in alchemy where it has to do with the separation of the intellect from the instinctual aspect."[2] Psychologically speaking, this separation enables a certain mental detachment or objectivity in looking at oneself, so that one's intellect becomes a purely mirroring, detached factor. Beheading also suggests a sacrifice of the intellect in order to allow other forms of psychic realization to take place. Beheading of a human being thus symbolizes the possibility of symbolic thinking, which is invaluable for understanding the raw material of the psyche and the unconscious. This sacrifice allows for an overall development of the personality that counteracts the neurotic tendency to one-sided domination of the intellect – one aspect of the over-developed masculine that has been referred to throughout the book. In other words, this symbolic beheading is a step that is necessary for many of us to take before our feminine side can reconnect with its power.

When I first had the dream about the need to "cut off my head," of course, I did not yet understand all the symbolic implications it had for my own healing process. However, it did immediately trigger my memory of that day in the classroom with Miss Mui and revived my childhood fascination with Chiu Chin. I came to realize I had unconsciously identified with Chiu Chin and her passion to save China – the child in me had decided that I also wanted to be a *nu ying xiong*. As I became increasingly aware of the value of symbolic thinking, I eventually became aware that the need to "cut my head off" was linked to how my innate, intuitive nature had been so thoroughly overshadowed by my Western, academic training. This discovery was essential in giving me access to the exploration of the mystery of the unconscious that I had begun. Thus I came to understand that Chiu Chin's story had profound meaning on both a concrete and a symbolic level. In terms of the tangible aspects of her life and her heroism, she stands as a model for us all of a woman who was able to connect with inner feminine power, stand tall on her own two feet, and fight the system that had oppressed her and other women like her. On a symbolic level the lessons and the inspiration we can gain from Chiu Chin's life are equally, if not more, important. The symbolic meaning of beheading reminds us how essential it is that the over-developed intellect be brought into balance with the instinctive, emotional, intuitive sides of our being. The meaning of her life on this symbolic level is made even more significant by the fact that one of her revolutionary acts was to speak out radically against footbinding and to actually go through the excruciatingly painful process of physically unbinding her own feet.

Chiu Chin was born in 1875 to a respectable gentry family from Shao-hsin in Zhejiang province. Her family name is Chiu, meaning autumn. Chin means the hard, brilliant gem. Her ancestors had been scholars, holding various levels of government posts. She grew up in Amoy, where her grandfather was the Prefect of the city. Chiu Chin was close to her siblings and to her mother, who was well educated and became her mentor. There is also evidence that Chiu Chin was her father's favorite child. Unlike most of her contemporaries, she was educated with her elder brother and her younger sister and brother (from a different mother) in the family clan school. There she studied the Classics and learned to write poetry. In general, hers was an extremely advantaged upbringing – she even learned to handle a sword. From her early poems, one gets the impression that she enjoyed time with her girl-friends, reading and composing poetry instead of learning women's work such as embroidery, which she disliked. Chiu Chin took her education seriously rather than treating it as an "extra" for her dowry, and spent much of her time reading history and literature. She also traveled widely with her father through his posts in the provinces of Zhejiang, Fujian, and Taiwan, where he served in the governor's yeoman, and subsequently, Hunan.

While in Hunan her father made an arrangement for Chiu Chin to be married to the son of a local wealthy merchant. Chiu Chin was 21 at the time, and this was considered a rather late age to marry. After this, there was a radical change in Chiu Chin's life which had once been so contented. Her unhappiness is documented in her letters, particularly those that reveal how little she had in common with her husband who, she soon discovered, lived the life of a playboy and spent his time engaged in lavish entertainment, antique collecting, gambling, and liaising with prostitutes. In these letters, Chiu Chin described her husband as "untrustworthy, a liar, selfish, obnoxious, pompous, a good-for-nothing." It is also clear that it was very difficult for Chiu Chin to get along with her mother-in-law, who was described as "ill-tempered, unreasonable, and abusive."

Even the births of a son and a daughter were not enough to make Chiu Chin's situation more bearable. She wrote frankly that her marriage was "a big waste of her life" and stated, in more poetic terms, that it was a "life-long bitter regret lodged in her throat" and that she was "entrapped behind the baton doors"[3] – the baton doors being in this case a symbol for the way women's lives were lived mostly behind the door that closed them off in the women's quarters of the home. Just how great the contrast was between her childhood and her married life was also reflected in her poetry. While her early poems reflect the self-image of a dignified scholar who shunned the decadence of the profane world, her later work is filled with the recurrent themes of loneliness, bitterness, sorrow, and melancholy.[4]

The next major change came in 1902, when Chiu Chin was 26 and her husband purchased a post as Circuit Commissioner in the capital city, Beijing. Once they'd established themselves in their new home, Chiu Chin became exposed to Western ideas and influences. At one point, she even studied English and was impressed by such a widely divergent range of

Western figures as Napoleon, George Washington, and Joan of Arc. During this time, Chiu Chin was also exposed to the corruption in the government and the decadent lifestyle of the rich. She became increasingly aware of the political crises that had been besetting her country. If you will recall from the earlier section on history, the turn of the 20th century was the time when the Manchus were ruling China. Their rule, which was known as the Qing dynasty, would be the last of the Imperial dynasties in China, which would end officially with the birth of the Republic of China in 1912.

The events that dismayed Chiu Chin included the one-year Sino-Japanese War that ended in 1895 with Japan victorious and China in a greatly weakened state. A few years after came the disastrous Boxer Uprising in 1900. Originally a revolt by a group of Chinese nationalists who wanted all foreigners and Christian missionaries expelled from the country, it culminated in Western powers moving in to protect their people and then remaining in the country, where they occupied Beijing and eventually took a great deal of control over Chinese commerce and trade. These incursions by foreign powers convinced Chiu Chin that China was in a struggle for survival against the more vigorous imperialist West. Afraid that her country was in fact on the verge of extinction, she began to develop a strong nationalist concern about China's future. The seeds of her later revolutionary activities were also sown during her days in Beijing by her exposure to the "modern" ideas held by a group of women friends who gathered frequently to exchange their poetry and discuss current events.

Before long Chiu Chin began to speak out on behalf of women's rights and soon she was even involved in founding a natural-foot society. As her political and social concerns gained strength, Chiu Chin's interests departed further from those of her conservative husband. At the age of 29, she made the decision to leave her husband and children so that she could study in Japan. Her letters to her brother reveal that she blamed her fate on the institution of arranged marriage, and she reiterated that she felt her eight married years were a waste of her life. She felt she had to leave her marriage "to restore her dignity."[5] Chiu Chin's decision to break with her husband and tradition was an extremely radical one in her time and place. She was not only rejecting the high degree of security and the potential influence the traditional family offered, she was also risking homelessness and an unknown fate. Not surprisingly her husband tried to block her trip, and she was forced to rely on financial support from her mother and elder brother. Her husband's family took her son, and she left her baby daughter in the care of a friend.

Before she began on this stupendous journey, she unbound her feet. For Chiu Chin this act was clearly a very physical way for her to express her rebellion against a society she believed was oppressive. However, as she was a woman who was steeped in the symbolism of poetic imagery, it is easy to imagine that she also saw the act of unbinding her feet as a profoundly symbolic one that represented freeing herself from the unbearable strictures that had bound her soul for so long. Indeed, once she was in Japan, Chiu Chin attained an amount of freedom that was unheard of for a Chinese woman of her day. Her personality blossomed and she truly came into her own. Before long, she had thrown herself into three areas of activity that were tightly interwoven in her own mind: emancipation of women, Chinese nationalism, and revolution. Apart from studying Japanese, she devoted most of her time to radical politics and wrote articles on women's emancipation. One of her many important activities in Japan was, along with a small group of women students, to reactivate the Humanitarian Society (*Kung-ai Hui*), an organization dedicated to the promotion of women's rights and education. She also encouraged women to take part in military activities. Chiu Chin believed that the emancipation of Chinese women was tied to the abolition of the Confucian system and that such a sweeping change could only be attained through revolution.

Her dedication to the emancipation of women remained a dominant theme in both her activities and her writing throughout her life. In fact, the main theme of Chiu Chin's writings was an intense, unequivocal total rejection of the traditional woman's role which she associated with the evil of "oppression, blackness, numbing confinement, and degrading ignorance." In the early chapters of her unfinished semi-autobiographical novel, *Stones of the Ching-wei Bird* (*Ching-wei shih*), she describes five independent girls who come from gentry families. Incarnations of heroines who are sent to Earth by Xi Wang Mu (Queen Mother of the West), these young women bravely rebel against forced marriage, footbinding, and seclusion.[6] In one piece she wrote:

> In the black prison created by darkness and ignorance, women did not even realize the danger inherent in being divorced from the reality of the world, and even those who did wish to save themselves and others were robbed of the will and capacity to act.[7]

The darkness pervading the world of women appeared to Chiu Chin as a particularly painful manifestation of that greater blackness that enveloped the whole nation. As she became increasingly certain that the liberation of women was directly linked to the liberation of the country, she became more and more dedicated to a revolution that she believed would eradicate the stifling prisons of traditional Confucian society.

Chiu Chin also believed that equal rights and education for women would contribute to the Nationalist dream, which she shared, of creating a strong, independent China. Like the emancipation of women, she believed nationalism also demanded revolution. This was the only thing, she believed, that would sweep away the rottenness at China's core and awaken the people.[8] In her desire to help bring about the overthrow of the Manchu government, she began to meet with like-minded people from all walks of life. These included known revolutionary figures, reform advocates, and even members of the Triad Society. Some of them would later be individuals she would work closely with when she eventually returned to China to continue her revolutionary activities. At the invitation of its leader, she became the first woman to join the Revolutionary Alliance Society (*Tung-meng Hui*). When she returned to China, she would become the chairman of the branch Society and a party recruiter in her home province.

During her stay in Japan, Chiu Chin became liberated and emerged as a compelling, somewhat flamboyant figure. People who knew her described her as "courageous, excitable, light hearted, decisive, impulsive, and energetic." In addition to working on the publication of a magazine to promote revolutionary ideas, Chiu Chin established a society for public speaking. It became increasingly clear that Chiu Chin had a tremendous sense of mission. As one commentator wrote, "her enthusiastic radicalism propelled her to discuss politics tirelessly, and prompted angry despair over what she considered the apathy of many students."[9] Her devotion to the cause was absolute, and she was intense and direct in expressing her ideas and opinions. She soon became the leader among the students, but while many admired and idealized her, others found her intimidating. Increasingly, she saw herself as one of the leaders shepherding the Chinese into the future.

While in Japan, Chiu Chin also sought to develop what she referred to in her writings as her "sword power." To do this she enrolled in Jissen Jo Gakko Training College for Women, attended a martial arts society, practiced swordsmanship and shooting, boxing and fencing, and even learned the skills of explosives and bomb making. While these activities were significant in terms of her revolutionary goals, they also held a great deal of psychological meaning for the imagery associated with the "sword," which was a recurrent motif in Chiu Chin's poetry. In these poems she revealed that she prided herself on being "given" a Precious Sword by the Lord. This sword was identified with the Light. With it, her only companion, she felt endowed with the energy to carry on the dragon fight to "recover her lost country, to take the heads of the enemies and drink their blood." Here the Sword symbolizes the penetrating power for the divine task. And, at least at times, Chiu Chin clearly felt she held a great deal of power in her hands.

However, her poetry from these years reveals that she was also sometimes assailed by grave doubts. These poems reveal moods that range from intense exhilaration to great despair and many contain a persistent strain of melancholy. Some passages reveal her enthusiasm, her confidence, and her belief that she would achieve both success and fame, while others are saturated with sadness, loneliness, and uncertainty about her chosen path. The motif of herself as a "lonely wandering soul" is recurrent.[10] In a poem full of quiet despair, she "begged Nu Gua to show her the way to develop the Stone." This Stone, possibly a reference to the mythical stone that Nu Gua melded from the five colors during creation, may well have symbolized for Chiu Chin the eternal truth and self-knowledge she longed to find.

The following two poems reflect her psychological state and the inner conflicts she endured during this period. The first poem shows the depth of her feelings of loneliness and vulnerability:

> Be slow to say this woman is not brave, heroic.
> Mounting the wind, she goes alone, ten thousand miles east.
> Her poem describes a single sail on a vast and empty sea,
> Bright moon a carved gem. Her soul dreams of three islands.
> She gazes sadly towards home:
>   here bronze camels, symbols of empire, crumble to ruin.
> Sweating chargers go forth in vain; their courage has no reward.
> Grieving for home, grieving for country, her heart is deeply pierced.
> How can anyone protect a lonely traveler ferried by spring wind?

The second poem reveals her sense of both isolation and frustration:

> Once more the road from home stretches three thousand miles.
> Turn your head, gaze at clouds,
>   suffer the anguish of the frontier pass.
> In a high hall you have a mother with white hair on her temples.
> No clear-eyed comrade helps harmonize my work of reform.
> Heart and brain vexed, harassed, I find unstrained
> Wine brings no relief.
> My emotions are tangled threads. I dread
> Hearing the oriole sing.
> Spreading branches, peaceful moon:
> I am thin, exhausted
> In the capital city.
> My lonely pillow is cold and desolate, my dreams
> Unfinished.[11]

As Chiu Chin's revolutionary ideas became progressively more militant during her stay in Japan, she joined the Restoration Society (*Kuang-fu Hui*) and became an ardent adherent of the party, enjoying close comradeship with several students. At this point, the suicide of a close friend in protest against the corrupt Manchu government affected her greatly. Chiu Chin began to see death as the inevitable end of her mission and began to nurture the idea that she would be the first woman to die for her country. Now 29 years of age, she decided to return to China to dedicate herself to revolutionary action.

On her return she settled in Shanghai, which at the time was the main centre for the women's movement in China. Within a year she had single-handedly founded the *Chinese Women's Journal* (*Chung-kuo nu-pao*). This was a high point of her feminist activities and expressed her views on women's emancipation very clearly. In the introduction to the *Journal*, she attacked such obvious targets as footbinding, arranged marriages, enforced chastity, seclusion, ignorance, and the male disposition to view women as "horses and cattle," or to adorn them as playthings.[12] She gave generously to aspiring young revolutionaries, especially women, in support of their education and travel. She provided moral and political support to several women to help them leave the bondage of enforced marriage and concubinage.

Just as Chiu Chin herself acted on her ideas, she challenged other women to do the same. On a practical level, she stressed that girls should seek an education and women learn occupational skills to achieve economic and social independence as well as self-reliance.[13] Speaking from her own experience, she encouraged women to unbind their feet. She saw the footbinding cloth as a symbol of slow torture that had turned women – who were half of those living under Heaven – into crippled slaves. On a grander scale, she believed that women could wash away the shame of their former subservience by performing heroic deeds that would demonstrate their great abilities.

Soon after she returned to China, Chiu Chin's mother died and she became depressed and threw herself into preparations for an uprising in Zhejiang province, which was to coincide with a chain of uprisings in several selected cities being organized by Revolutionary Alliance members and secret societies. Now fully committed to overthrowing the government, she actively engaged in contacting army officers and military students, connecting with secret society leaders, meeting a broad spectrum of people, and raising funds for her cause. During this period she was also made principal of Ta Tung School, which had over 1000 students. Chiu Chin used this opportunity to organize, with the help of Restoration Army radicals, military training on the premises.

When the astonishing degree of independence that Chiu Chin attained is considered against the backdrop of the society she lived in, it's easy to imagine that one of the most difficult issues she faced was the struggle for a new identity: once she had quite literally unbound her feet and cast off the rigidly defined role for a woman in Confucian society. Who was she then to become? In this struggle to find a new identity, Chiu Chin looked to the heroes of Chinese history for guidance in her identity search. She found inspiration in the self-sacrificing model of Jing Ke, who died in 227 BC trying to assassinate the First Qin Emperor on behalf of a small state threatened with annihilation.[14] She also admired the poet Qu Yuan, who committed suicide as a protest against the corrupt government, and

General Yue Fei, who died in his struggle against the invading Tartars in the 12th century. However, it is easy to imagine that it was the heroic women and female generals and fighters – small though their number may have been – who gave her the greatest inspiration. And it is known that she identified with Hua Mu-lan who, as described in Chapter 4, disguised herself as a man and served for years in the army in her ailing father's stead.[15]

The anxiety caused by Chiu Chin's belief that she might have to sacrifice herself and the frustration she must have felt in living in such a male-dominated society undoubtedly caused her a great deal of inner conflict. The tension brought on by this conflict was expressed in both her poetry and her flamboyant behavior. And it is not surprising, especially considering her fascination with Hua Mu-lan, that one of the behaviors she adopted was to dress in men's clothing. Throughout the centuries of female seclusion in China, women were known to disguise themselves in men's clothes when traveling to protect themselves. For Chiu Chin, it was also a way of protesting against the restrictions imposed on women. She first tried it during her early days in Beijing when, neglected by her husband and bored with enforced idleness, she dressed as a man and went to the theater accompanied by a manservant just as a man would normally do. Unfortunately, she encountered her husband, who recognized her and was so enraged that he slapped and beat her then and there.

Beyond this desire to protest the restrictions on women, however, Chiu Chin's dressing in male clothes was almost certainly a facet of her struggle to find a new identity. Once she had rejected the role of the traditional woman, there were few if any appropriate female models for her to look to, and she had perforce to choose the male model. Interestingly, the alternative model she chose was closely linked to power and physical prowess – the direct antithesis of the ideal Confucian woman. Once Chiu Chin was living in Japan she began to express this more openly. Some photographs taken of her there show her dressed in men's Western-style suits. Others show her dressed in a kimono but expressing her masculine side by grasping a naked dagger in her hand. By the time she returned to China from Japan, Chiu Chin began to frequently wear a man's gown and tunic, comb her hair back into a queue, and carry a leather briefcase. On her feet she wore men's black leather shoes or sometimes even boots – which may have had the additional purpose of providing the desperately needed support for her once-bound feet. At times, she also rode on horseback in a black uniform and guided the students to practice military drill. But even after she adopted this strong masculine persona, Chiu Chin seemed to be conscious that it was just that – a persona – and that she was still struggling to find her true identity. The conflict and confusion she continued to experience around this issue are reflected in a poem she wrote called "Reflection on a Photograph of Myself in Man's Clothing":

Wondering who this person is,
A hero reincarnate, regrettably
In this body.
Passing through this life – an illusion,
Facing the future – perhaps the truth:
Sensing a misfit, re-asserting
A sense of right.
One day, I see this friend from the past,
Then I hear
She has left the floating dust.[16]

In spite of the growing support and admiration Chiu Chin was receiving from many, her extraordinary dress and unusual behavior made her the object of curiosity, suspicion, and resentment among the local conservative gentry and merchants. This, in turn, made it even more difficult for her to form deep friendships or find the true kindred spirit – the "clear-eyed comrade" she cries out for in her poem – whom she believed would help ease her loneliness and sense of isolation. It is worth mentioning, however, that after her return to China, Chiu Chin did meet two women, the Hsu sisters, with whom she developed a deep friendship and this must have eased her loneliness to some degree. Still, she never really found the "soul mate with whom she could share her thoughts and feelings" and this remained a recurrent theme in her poems. Alone and without social and emotional support, she experienced more acute loneliness and despair, which increasingly led her to see death as the ultimate means of redemption. As time went on, her dedication to the cause began to approach a religious zeal. As one scholar writes, she came to a point where for her the "only serious reason to continue her life was to work for the revolution."[17]

Sacrifice through death for her country was a recurrent motif in her last letters and poetry. The following poem reflects not only her despair over not being able to find a true comrade, but also the depth of her anguish. The word for filial piety, *hsiao*, mimics the dismal sound of rain dripping off the eaves and poignantly expresses her misery over what the Confucian patriarchy and the system based on filial piety had done to women.

Alone in the back room, where Heaven's influence descends
a woman chants sad songs.
Hsiao, hsiao, water drops from the eaves,
Flooded by rain. A comrade whose arrow
Of knowledge finds
The target of my soul
Is difficult to meet.
In the turn of an eye the light of time flows past.
Hair on temples tossed

By wind, disheveled. I lack any way to express
The depth of my passionate grief.
I count the times the sun has set on my impoverished road.
I exist in bitterness, alone.
This land is to be pitied
Sad that it should bring forth a miserable pitiful woman.[18]

Chiu Chin increasingly saw herself as a frustrated heroine "who was coming to the end of the road, alone." A few days before her actual death, she wrote to her friend expressing her readiness to die for her cause.[19] At this time, she had a dream which also foreshadowed her tragic end:

I came to a beautiful, rich countryside and saw a palace standing in the distance. I walked toward the palace and entered. Seated in the centre of the hall was a huge, strange-looking man, holding a decree of some sort with four big characters and rows of smaller characters written on it. Standing on either side of him were two rows of strange-looking men, all holding big steel knives. Kneeling on the floor in front of them were several headless human beings. I was shocked, wondering what had happened to them.

Suddenly, a thunderous roar, then darkness, and the palace disappeared. A big flood came upon the land and drowned the whole area. Only a small piece of land remained floating in the ocean of water. On this land, several human heads were rolling back and forth at great speed.[20]

Chiu Chin was greatly disturbed by this dream and interpreted it as a bad omen. Shortly after she had it, she received news of the death of her comrade and close friend, Hsu Hsi-lin. By this point in time Chiu Chin was actively involved in planning and coordinating specific revolutionary uprisings. One of these was a chain of carefully timed and synchronized local revolts that was to commence with an uprising led by Chiu Chin herself. Tragically, circumstances forced the revolt led by Hsu to begin action prematurely. It failed and Hsu was brutally executed, his heart taken out while he was still alive.

One result of this was that the government immediately launched an investigation into the group's activities. Although Chiu Chin was forewarned of the impending danger, she refused to flee, believing that if she allowed herself to be a target, the lives of many other students and other revolutionary activists – whose numbers amounted to almost 10,000 by that time – might be spared. She also believed that her death "would hasten the revolution by at least five years and would thus save thousands of lives."[21]

Figure 7.1 The beheading of Chiu Chin, 15 July 1907

Source: Drawing by Christy Shum

Chiu Chin waited calmly for the Imperial troops to arrive and was arrested without much struggle. She refused to testify and was tortured and hastily beheaded the following day on 15 July 1907 (Figure 7.1).

Chiu Chin's brief but valiant life ended at the age of 31, but her spirit and her aspirations for reform lived on after her death for at least that period in Chinese history. Her death was followed by the Revolution of 1911 and then, in turn, by the May Fourth Movement in 1916. Individualism, with its concomitant ideas of equality, human rights, and personal development was a dominant theme of this movement. Scholars, writers, and social scientists began to openly attack the impact of Confucian ideology on the Chinese family for promoting nepotism and for its oppressive influence on family life and the individual. The "Woman Question" was considered the most urgent in terms of its implications for national survival and development. Footbinding was considered the prime evil that weakened the health and morale of the nation. A program for women's emancipation was proposed, stressing women's right to enjoy economic independence and freedom to choose their mates, and the right of widows to remarry.[22] In 1919, the Beijing National University admitted its first female students. By 1922, an estimated 665 women were registered in the universities and technical colleges.[23] It is fairly safe to say that a heroic soul like Chiu Chin would have believed her sacrifices were worth these gains.

On that day in my childhood when I first heard the story of Chiu Chin, it was this heroism and bravery that inspired me. Over the years since then I've discovered that there are several other aspects of her life that can provide us with valuable insights – particularly when her life is looked at from a more symbolic Jungian point of view. One of these can be found in the dream she had about beheading; another is in her struggle for identity.

Dreams, of course, have meaning on many different levels. On one level the scene of the beheadings in the dream was a foreshadowing of what could – and actually did – come about in her life. On another level it might be seen, at least in part, as a message from her unconscious to her conscious mind that might have eventually had great meaning to her if she had chosen to continue her life. On this level, the message from the dream might be seen to be very similar to the one from the dream I shared at the very beginning of this chapter, which warned me that the intellectual, rational side of my being had become far too out of balance and that in order to truly unbind my feet I also needed to free myself from the tyranny of being dominated by my "masculine" side. Both sides of my nature, as I said before, needed to be in balance for my soul to survive. It is even possible – although this is certainly complete speculation – that, had Chiu Chin been able to do this psychologically, she may have been able to find an alternative to martyrdom and may have lived to fight another day and continue her battle for freedom and equality.

It is worth digressing for a moment here to point out that by making this comparison between an element in one of my dreams and in Chiu Chin's, I am not in any way comparing myself to her – she was, in my opinion, an extraordinary soul and a great heroine and I am an ordinary person! That said, it is exactly this meaning that Chiu Chin has for us as ordinary people that is so significant. This is true both for her dream about beheading and for the epic struggle she underwent to find a new identity. Given the time and place she lived in, it makes perfect sense that Chiu Chin, having cast off the role of dutiful wife and mother she was meant to play in the Confucian order, could see no other option but to begin to act like a man.[24] It was simply not in the consciousness of her time to realize that a woman acting like a woman could have real power. Her soul in exile could only find homecoming through death. But even though we live in very different times, her struggle underscores the fact that even today when we, as obedient filial daughters, cast off the ties that have been binding us and making us circumscribe our own lives in order to please others, we often have to struggle to find our true identity as a woman. However, women today are better equipped to take on this task, especially with the help of the analytical psychology founded by Dr. Jung. Their stories will be told in the following chapters in this book. But first, I will tell the story of Julia Ching, a friend who regrettably did not live long enough to enjoy her hard won feminine wisdom.

Notes

1 This psychological interpretation of Chiu Chin's life is based on the following: Mary B. Rankin, 'The Emergence of Women at the End of the Ch'ing: The Case of Chiu Chin', in Wolf, Margery and Witke, Roxane, eds., *Women in Chinese Society*, Stanford, CA: Stanford University Press, 1975, pp. 39–66; Florence Ayscough, *Chinese Women, Yesterday and Today*, Boston, MA: Houghton Mifflin, 1937, pp. 135–77.

  [Texts in Chinese]: Chiu Chin, *Chiu Chin Chi* (*The Collected Works of Chiu Chin*), Shanghai: Chung Wah Publishing, 1960, subsequently cited as CCC; Chiu Tsan-chih, *Chiu Chin Ko Ming Chuan* (*A Revolutionary Biography of Chiu Chin*), Taiwan: San Ming, 1963; and Guo Yanli, *Qiu Jin shi wen xuan* (*Selected Works of Chiu Chin*), Beijing: People's Literary Publishing, 1982; Guo Yanli, Yanli *Qiu Jin wen xue lun gao* (*Literary Discussions on Chiu Chin*), Xian: People's Publishing, 1987.

2 Marie-Louise von Franz, *The Psychological Meaning of Redemption Motifs in Fairy Tales*, Toronto: Inner City Books, 1982, pp. 117–19.

3 'Letters to Elder Brother', in CCC, op. cit., pp. 33–4.

4 See her poems in CCC, ibid., e.g. 'Chu' (Chrysanthemums), p. 80; 'Chiu Yen' (Autumn Geese), p. 65; 'Wu Yeh' (Leaves of the Wu Tree), p. 63; Yanli Guo, op. cit., 1987, Chapter 5, pp. 66–77.

5 'Nine Letters to Elder Brother', in CCC, op. cit., pp. 33–44.

6 Ibid., pp. 117–60.

7 'A Warning to my Sisters', ibid., p. 15; Mary B. Rankin, op. cit., p. 57.

8 Yanli Guo, 1987, op. cit., Chapter 10, pp. 147–74.

9 Mary B. Rankin, op. cit., p. 52.

10 See various sword songs in CCC, op. cit., pp. 73–5, 77–8, 80, 81, 89; untitled poem, pp. 82–3; 'Letters to Elder Brother, June–December 1905', pp. 33–4; 'Letter to Hsu Chi-chen', p. 89.

11 Florence Ayscough, op. cit., pp. 147, 154.

12 Mary B. Rankin, op. cit., p. 57.

13 CCC, op. cit., pp. 5, 12; Guo Yanli, 1987, op. cit., Chapter 10, pp. 147–74.

14 CCC, ibid., p. 80.

15 Mary B. Rankin, op. cit., p. 53.

16 Guo Yanli, 1982, op. cit., pp. 94–5.

17 'Letter to Wang Shih-tse', in CCC, op. cit., p. 44; poem 'Che Ku Tien', p. 107–8; 'Tu Chiu', p. 84.

18 Ibid., 'Thus Our Rivers and Mountains', p. 107; 'Sword Songs', pp. 80–1; 'To Chiang Lu-shan', pp. 77–8; Ayscough, op. cit., pp. 159–60.

19 Poem 'To Hsu Hsiao-shu in Contemplation of Death', ibid., pp. 26–8.

20 Chiu Tsan-chih, op. cit., pp. 151–3.

21 Guo Yanli, 1987, op. cit., pp. 21–3.

22 This movement was led by Hu Shih and Chen Tu-hsiu *et al.* See Olga Lang, *Chinese Family and Society*, New Haven, CT: Yale University Press, 1946; reprint, New York: Archon, 1968, pp. 109–15; Lin Yu-tang, *My Country and My People*, New York: John Day, p. 180.

23 Chen Tung-yuen, *Chung-kuo fu-nu sheng-huo shih* (*A History of the Life of Chinese Women*), Shanghai: The Commercial Press, 1937, Chapter 9.

24 It is also of course possible that Chiu Chin's choice of men's clothing was a reflection of gender issues that it is beyond the scope of this book to examine in detail.

Chapter 8

Julia Ching: a journey from East to West and back again

I met Dr. Julia Ching at a conference where she was presenting a paper on the great Neo-Confucian philosopher Chu Hsi. I had trepidations about meeting her. As a professor at the University of Toronto, she had acquired a formidable reputation for her intellect, and also for a tendency to speak her mind freely. Some people described her as being extremely short-tempered and acerbic.

When I ended up sitting next to her at lunch, I felt a little apprehensive. However, we soon entered into conversation over lunch and discovered that we shared the same alma mater, a well-known convent school in Hong Kong run by sisters of the Canossian Order of Rome. She was interested in my Jungian training and told me that she had taught at the University of Tübingen with the theologian Hans Küng and had even published a book in conjunction with the world-renowned philosopher. When I learned she had been a nun for 20 years, our conversation developed further. I began to share some of my experiences in the convent school and some of the strange stories I heard from my convent friends with her, and before we knew it we were laughing uproariously. Our animated discussion attracted the attention of other professors at the table, and they joined in our conversation. Before long we were communicating with a depth of understanding and level of camaraderie that was exceptionally unusual on such a short acquaintance. In spite of the fact that we were from different generations – Julia was only four years younger than my mother – we fast became friends. Later that afternoon, however, Julia became unwell after her presentation and had to lie down to rest. I noticed that she became quiet, distant and withdrawn, and although I wondered a bit about it, I didn't think much of it at the time.

It was quite a while before I saw Julia again at another conference. Soon after, Julia sent me a draft copy of her memoir, *The Butterfly Healing: A Life between East and West*, with a request for an endorsement that could be put on the cover of the book. I devoured the manuscript at once. It was then that I realized why she was sometimes perceived to be so short-tempered – she was, in fact, in pain almost all the time. But I also realized more clearly than I ever had before why I felt such a strong connection to Julia: she was a perfect example of a person who had truly made the journey deep within her own soul that Jung said was the route to not only finding solutions to your problems in life but, ultimately, to true wholeness and inner healing. As you will see from Julia's story, she first sought these answers outside herself and then went within to find them. During her long journey of spiritual and psychological healing, she first abandoned her Chinese heritage. However, she eventually came back to her Asian roots, where she discovered she needed to know herself not just as a Chinese person but as a Chinese woman who needed to reconnect with her own body and learn to honor the Feminine.

When I first met her, she was in the midst of a prolonged recuperation from a major gastrointestinal operation called an esophagectomy. This operation is considered as serious and invasive as having three triple heart bypasses, and the rate of survival for more than five years after surgery was only 8%. In fact, most patients die within two years. This operation, also called "gastric pull-up," entailed removal of the esophagus and wrestling the stomach up from below the diaphragm to place it between the lungs. After undergoing this procedure, Julia had not only had to adapt to a completely new diet, she also had to learn new ways of chewing and swallowing. This operation took an immense toll on her immune system. Making the process of recovery even more difficult was the fact that this was the third major illness Julia had endured in her life, as she had suffered two bouts of cancer when she was younger. During these illnesses she had had operations and radiation treatments that had weakened her body and left her with chronic physical disability that she endured for the rest of her life.

Julia managed to survive several years after the esophagectomy, and never allowed her illness to interfere with her work. She continued to teach in her position as professor, supervise doctoral students, organize conferences, and present papers around the world. Honored with the special title Professor of the University, she also continued to write, publishing several scholarly books in addition to her earlier books, a total of 14, not to mention articles in major journals and other publications.[1] Over the years she received many honorary titles, including the Order of Canada, which is the equivalent of being "knighted" in Great Britain.

Knowing Julia was a humbling experience for me. She considered her life a gift from God: she had a profound sense that it was her duty to "manifest" God's miracle and to be of service to her family, the university, and the community. Her perseverance was fuelled by her passionate sense of her personal mission. She could be thought of as heir to and an interpreter of the spiritual traditions of the East. Although Julia only lived until 2001, there is no doubt her legacy will live on.

Julia's life history reflects the historical development of modern China. Born to a prominent family in war-torn Shanghai in 1934, Julia lived her formative years in a world in a state of flight and flux. During the war with Japan (1937–1945), the Japanese Occupation of Hong Kong (1941–1945), and the civil war between the Nationalists and the Communists (1945–1949), Julia's family fled back and forth from Shanghai to Hong Kong. All of Julia's early memories were of air raids, house searches, fear, hiding, and of having nightmares about Japanese soldiers and their bayonets. These nightmares and others, along with insomnia, ongoing anxiety, and a feeling of exile, dominated her early memories.

During their many flights back and forth, Julia's family ultimately took refuge in Suzhou, a small city outside Shanghai. But after the Communist Revolution in 1949, they finally settled once and for all in British Hong Kong. Eventually Julia was sent to a boarding school for her high-school education. At age 17, she left for America to attend the College of New Rochelle in New York for her higher education, an opportunity made possible by a scholarship.

Julia's memories of her father are of a remote and unavailable man. Because he was so inaccessible, she and her siblings felt deprived of a real father. At one time, he had been a very prominent lawyer with a thriving practice in Shanghai. He had been president of the bar association and was elected to the National Assembly. He even took part in the drafting of the Constitution of the Republic of China. However, the ongoing wars and political upheaval eventually disrupted and destroyed his career. As a refugee in the British colony of Hong Kong, he did not adjust well, and Julia can only remember him working a few years during her life. He was much older than Julia's mother, who was his second wife, and Julia experienced him more as a grandfather than a father.

Her mother was only 17 when Julia was born. She barely knew how to tend to babies, and Julia was put in the care of a wet nurse. Three siblings followed in close succession, two brothers and a younger sister. After the family moved to Hong Kong, her mother learned English quickly and took up the task of supporting the whole family. Partially as a result of their substantial difference in age, her mother eventually divorced her father, and he later died at the age of 70, a disappointed and broken man.

While she was growing up, Julia felt neglected by her inaccessible father, and by her mother, who was too busy to pay attention to her. The most care she received was from their housemaid, whom Julia found more accessible than her parents. Julia was unable to confide in anyone in the family and in her memoir states "[I] grew up very much by myself, even though I was in a big family."[2] For comfort during these years, Julia took refuge in Chinese novels and prayed for protection to the goddess Nu Wa.

Years later, when Julia looked back on the trauma of the war-torn early years, she would become aware that "the constant wandering, uprooting and re-rooting, became a theme in my life. Later I would shuffle between countries and continents, always aware of my smallness and aloneness in the sea of humanity, whose waves threaten to engulf me . . . I have always felt insecure, like a leaf flipping, blown about by the wind . . . My life has been a series of disruptions, of being torn from my roots, of not being able to grow new roots"[2] (p. 19).

Amidst the chaos of her childhood years, it was in the Catholic college that Julia found peace and solace in God. During her youth, she was comforted by reading St. Augustine's *Confessions*. Searching for certitude and commitment, she came to believe that faith was the answer. At age 16, she was baptized in the Catholic Church. After arriving in America a year later, she felt the need to "prolong the religious consolations I was receiving as a student, and a good student, at the Catholic college. I loved its nurturing environment. I felt I had finally found people who understood me, who could help me make life meaningful" (p. 25).

This sense of calling continued and, when she was barely 20, Julia entered the novitiate in a New York state Ursuline Order – a tradition she would later describe as a "culture of monastic piety that was transplanted to America from nineteenth-century Europe" (p. 25). After finishing her novitiate less than two years later, she took her vows and became a nun. This decision to commit herself to a religious order and through it the institutional church gave rise to conflicts that would never be completely resolved. One of these conflicts grew out of the Chinese family tradition that, as the eldest child, she was expected to support her mother and help raise her siblings. When Julia left the family for the convent she felt like a traitor for abandoning her family and forsaking the duty and responsibility of a filial daughter. This resulted in her feeling, on a deep psychic level, torn between her loyalty to the Church and to her ancestral tradition, her cultural roots and values.

Inside the religious order Julia received a rigorous, highly disciplined ascetic training, but this was also fraught with conflict and resulted in an ongoing struggle. She experienced what Augustine had experienced, that "my inner self is a house divided against itself" (p. 30). Julia fought these battles within herself with a sense of religious vocation that enabled her to endure and to overcome her doubts in what she saw as an internal battleground defined by complete silence and solitude. She fell under the spell of the *Spiritual Exercises of St. Ignatius of Loyola*. A series of prayerful, contemplative exercises, they were developed in the early 1500s by Ignatius, the founder of the Jesuit Order. Focusing on the three cardinal virtues – faith, hope, and charity – the exercises were designed to help one see God in all things and discern the movement of the Holy Spirit within. These teachings had a profound effect on Julia's thinking.

From the days of her early training onward, Julia was taught that, in order to become a true bride of Christ, she had to believe in the superiority – and the ultimate victory of – the mind and soul over matter. It was made clear to Julia and the other novices that the form of "matter" they needed to be most concerned with was the body. In college she had already discovered how, in the writings of Augustine for example, the body was seen as at best merely an instrument and, at worst, as "a prison, a tomb," and now she was finding out how the religious order was a place where the novices walked along the edges of the corridors, looking down as if they could not be seen. In essence they were being trained to act as if they existed only as souls – beings with no physical body whatsoever. "The body," she learned, "was seen to be a burden, and had to be subjugated, tamed and humiliated as a possible source of evil words, thoughts, and deeds" (p. 30). In order to carry out this humiliation of the body, the nuns were given small chain whips with which they were, in private, to beat themselves across the thighs. This practice was known as "taking the discipline." To help give themselves the fortitude needed to carry it out, the young nuns read about how the illustrious saints of the past had whipped themselves.

This training created a split in Julia between her mind and her body, and gave rise to nightmares, insomnia, and psychosomatic symptoms that were suppressed and ignored. For her, it was indeed the "dark night of the soul," in the words of St. Theresa of Avila. Yet Julia realized that for her it was also the dark night of the body. The internal struggle took its toll on her body and soul when, 12 years after she entered the Order, Julia discovered a lump on her breast. By this time, Julia had been transferred from the convent in New York state to one in Taiwan. When Julia reported to the Mother Superior, the woman ignored Julia's symptoms and delayed sending her for medical treatment. This delay led to a radical mastectomy and heavy radiation treatments. Eventually Julia came to believe that if the cancer had been treated earlier and the massive radiation avoided, her later health might not have been affected so adversely – and much of this could have been prevented if her early symptoms had been taken seriously.

Five years later, the cancer erupted in her body again. By the time this occurred, Julia had been transferred from Taiwan to a convent in Australia, but was living temporarily in Europe, where she was studying. By this point Julia had become more tuned-in to her body symptoms and their messages, and discovered the lump when it was still fairly small. Because the United States was much closer than Australia, she was allowed to return to the east coast, where her sister lived, for her treatment. Her sister's husband was a physician, and was able to help expedite her treatment. She was able to have a lumpectomy rather than a radical mastectomy and to avoid the radiation treatments.

Even though these issues and other philosophical questions had led Julia to begin questioning her place in the Order, the strength of her commitment kept her there for 20 years. During these two decades, Julia was dedicated to service in the community. Fortunately, however, Julia's intellectual gift was recognized by the Order, and she was also encouraged to further it through formal university studies and eventually managed to obtain her doctoral degree.

A major turning point came in Julia's inner life, when she was sent by the Order to work in the mission in Taiwan. There she began to rediscover her Chinese roots. "I had started out moving far away from things Chinese toward the compelling attractions of Western civilization. I only came back to the study of China as an adopted child looking for its natural parents" (p. 60). There, in the Catholic Mission in Taiwan, she returned home to Chinese culture and became fascinated with Chinese thought and the way it contrasted with what she had been taught in the convent: "I was deeply interested in the spiritual and religious dimension of Chinese thought. At a time when the Cultural Revolution made some disturbing headlines, and when the survival of Chinese civilization was at stake, I felt a personal mission to keep the flame alive." During her time in Taiwan, she rediscovered many great thinkers, including Confucius and his follower, Mencius. She found that the essence of Chinese philosophy reflected her own spiritual experience in the unity of heaven and earth and all things, especially the unity between body and soul – the human body as the microcosm and the universe, the macrocosm. One of the things that impressed her the most was that the Chinese philosophers' worldviews were not separate from their lives, and body and soul were not split into two irreconcilable halves, the way they were by so many Christian theologians.

With discoveries such as these, her mind broadened. At the same time her intellectual interests were being developed by her doctoral studies, which she chose to do in Chinese Studies. Her travels around the world for the Church were also giving her a much wider outlook on life. Over time, her identification with the religious community gradually lessened. As her doubts and uncertainty grew in her unconscious, she found herself drifting away. She came to question her motivation and faith, the militaristic environment with its rigid rules and regulations and the lack of respect and care for the individual's needs. Finally she decided to leave the Order.

From a Jungian point of view, the years Julia spent in the convent can be seen as an incubation – a period of time that gave Julia a safe container in which to develop herself. Fortunately, when Julia finally left the convent she did not experience her departure from the Order as an emotional trauma. She greeted it rather with a sense of relief. She writes that it was "as though a big burden had been lifted from me" (p. 68). Although at the time she was left feeling somewhat puzzled and confused and wondering what it had all meant, there was not much time to dwell on her experience. Nor was there time to explore her feelings. For, at age 41, she was confronted with the challenges of adjusting to the secular world and the need to make a living by establishing herself professionally as an academic. Fortunately for Julia in this regard, the counterculture of the 1960s had led to a flourishing of interest in Eastern religion, and she was soon in demand for her expertise. She taught at Columbia and Yale, and eventually joined the Faculties of Religious Studies and East Asian Studies at the University of Toronto.

On the home front, Julia had reconnected with her mother, who had remarried, and with her brothers and sister. She also for the first time created a family of her own by adopting the teenage son of her cousin in China and bringing him to Toronto, where she became in essence a single mother in her middle age. A few years after this, at the age of 47, Julia married her widowed colleague, Dr. Willard Oxtoby. A well-known scholar of Comparative Religions, Oxtoby became a loving companion for Julia. She came to describe him as not only her lover but best friend.

Until Julia was 56, she settled into her happily married life and extremely successful career. Then cancer struck again, for the third time. One of the most frightening aspects of this illness for Julia was how quickly it seemed to appear. One moment she was completely healthy and busy lecturing at the university and speaking at conferences around the world, and the next she was desperately ill. In a few weeks time she went from noticing that she was having a little difficulty swallowing to being diagnosed with a malignant lump in her esophagus. She soon found herself once again in a hospital facing surgery – one that would this time be more invasive and difficult to recover from than anything she had experienced before. Faced with this trauma and the long period of post-operative recuperation that was required, Julia bravely took the opportunity to reflect and reconnect with her past emotions, which now appeared to be making a claim on her body and soul.

When Julia emerged from her surgery, disoriented by the trauma, she felt small, as though "I had been placed in a cradle." Still under the influence of morphine, she remembered the following dream:

> I was at a banquet. I was sitting there, in the company of a group of happy-looking people, my own family among them. But I kept looking at the beautiful table full of delicious Chinese food and was frustrated because I couldn't eat anything.
>
> (p. 78)

This dream suggests ancestral benevolence, as she is surrounded by her family and the abundance of Chinese food. In Chinese culture, since antiquity, a communal meal has been an important ritual in which food is shared with family and clan members, and sacrificed to the ancestral gods and spirits, and to other traditional gods. The banquet is the most concrete ritual expression of religious and social bonding, in the celebration of major rites of passage such as birth, marriage, and death. This dream reassures Julia of her safe passage from rebirth. Psychologically, she is supported by her family and community, and assured that nourishment is available in abundance in her new life.

But the fact she could not eat reflected her intense suffering and all that she had not been able to participate in.

Yet, in the hospital Julia felt like a prisoner, passive and powerless in a hospital bed that reminded her of the monastic cell. She felt dehumanized, "like a laboratory animal," and her body was being "treated somewhat like a used car ready to be discarded." In her vulnerable, dismembered state, her ego could no longer defend against the onslaught of her unconscious. Memories of the past, accompanied by repressed emotions, returned to haunt her. She dreamed:

> A male giant with powerful muscles flexed them, then stared at me and laughed. He represented all the forces gathered against me, I felt. He bore a vague resemblance to the Hulk on television.
>
> (p. 78)

The giant symbolized primitive raw emotion mocking the dreamer, challenging her for a confrontation. For a long time, Julia suffered from insomnia, menaced by nightmares in her sleepless nights: "grotesque images such as canine teeth that threaten to bite, sharp blades that threaten to stab." She was "tormented by the [dark] night of both soul and body . . . as [her] mind wandered, revisiting the past, seeking to find unity and meaning in fragmented memories" (pp. 27–8).

Julia came to believe that the rejection of the body and the repression of her feelings were mainly responsible for the cancer that would eventually take her life. Her ascetic training helped her later to enter the secular world and succeed in her academic career. But she believed it was also responsible for undermining her health. One reason for this was that the climate of "denying the body" that was so much a part of convent life was no doubt related to why her Mother Superior discounted Julia's fears when she reported finding the first lumps in her breast. This lengthy delay almost certainly had a profound negative effect on her body and her later prognosis. On a psychological level, the attitudes she absorbed during those years also adversely affected her sense of self-worth and her self-image as a woman. Paradoxically, her will to live and the spiritual resources from her former training also helped save her in the fight for survival that was brought on by her recurrent illnesses. For nearly 20 years, Julia seldom talked about her previous life in the Order, for she didn't want to re-open the wounds. But, as she states after learning that she had cancer for a third time, "life in the order had already etched its character on my body and on my soul. I would not be able to erase it" (p. 68). During her period of deep introspection after her third surgery she wrote:

> My past religious life is coming back to haunt me. It's made its mark over and over again on my body and my health. It's nearly de-sexed me. It's given my body the look of a Somali famine victim.
>
> (p. 108)

Even though she became disillusioned during this long period of recuperation, Julia was not defeated. She continued to look for meaning in life, to
work on regaining her health and finding wholeness. Her ego strength
supported her efforts in creating a life for herself in the second half of her
life. But she could not defeat the demon in her psyche. She feared and
avoided the unconscious which presented her with truths that she tried hard
to rationalize. When she thought back to her time in the Order, for instance,
she realized that even though she had been unhappy in the Order and had
had such great doubts and anxiety, she had felt such a deep need to honor
the promise she had made that she stayed. Even after her third operation,
her anger and frustration were still erupting in her sleep, revealing the naked
truth in her psyche. She dreamed:

> I am in St. Peter's Basilica in Rome, down in the crypt. It is like a
> marketplace. I see priests in their black cassocks and nuns in their old
> habits. They are sitting around with their legs crossed, bantering. Or
> they are actually buying and selling little trinkets and bric-a-brac,
> maybe also relics of this or that saint. And all over the place, rats and
> cockroaches are running around.
>
> (p. 134)

The crypt of St. Peter's Basilica symbolizes the unconscious of the Catholic
Church. It is often a dark, deep pit (i.e. the foundation), where the bones of
the martyrs are buried. The behavior of the priests and nuns, coupled with
the infestation of rats and cockroaches, suggest the corrupt and degenerate
nature of the Church, which needs to be cleansed and reformed. It is
reminiscent of the incident in the Bible when Jesus chased away the buyers
and sellers in the temple in a rage.

On reflection, Julia could see clearly that this dream signified her deep
unhappiness with the Catholic Church:

> But in my conscious moments I have never criticized the church that
> much. And I have never spoken out against my former life in a
> religious order. This dream made the church out to be really corrupt
> down underneath . . . I know it's only a dream, a nightmare of sorts.
> It's not reality. In reality I think there's a lot that's wrong with the
> church, but I wouldn't use any stronger language.
>
> (p. 134)

Julia's recuperation was like a battle with the unconscious. She suffered
from insomnia and whenever she did manage to sleep, she had intense and
disturbing dreams. Accordingly, in addition to naturopathic medicine, *qi
gong*, and energy work, Julia entered psychotherapy and explored biofeed-
back and dream work. Most of her nightmares were religious in nature,

further exacerbating her conflict and frustration with religion, which was not a problem in her conscious state. Her inability to feel, to connect was reflected in another dream:

> I was praying to a bejeweled statue of the Madonna and Child, praying for healing. But I was frustrated, for the statue was encased in glass. I got the feeling that there is no communication. Just as if the modem hasn't been plugged into your laptop, or portable, or desktop computer. You can't reach the modem in your dream. And you can't know that your prayers have been heard.
>
> (p. 145)

In this dream, the dream ego asked for healing from the Madonna, who symbolizes the highest essence of the Feminine in Western culture. She is the counterpart to Guan Yin, the Goddess of Compassion in the East. That the statue was encased in glass suggests a problem with disconnection to the source of healing. Glass, not a heat conductor, transparent but brittle and cold, reflects the deep inner suffering of the dreamer. Disconnection is a common symptom in trauma survivors and a major feature of chronic post-traumatic stress disorder, which Julia may well have suffered from in her early years in a country torn by wars, rebellion, and revolution.

On one level cancer forced Julia to establish a relationship with her body, which she had once rejected. She was forced into the path of healing and wholeness in an all-encompassing way, not just in her mind. It was a crisis that brought about the opportunity for self-knowledge and rebirth. Her will to live and to fight for her survival gave her insights into herself and the human condition. It also helped her to integrate her knowledge and experience of the spiritual traditions of the East and West. Towards the end of her life she wrote:

> I have spent so much of my life fighting the body and have missed such an important lesson as loving myself, taking care of my body. In fact, I've been doing harm to the body. And now, when my body's not well, I can't even help those I love.
>
> (p. 170)

Speaking symbolically, my tiny personal universe was damaged by a patriarchal church, just as Nu Gua had to cope with cosmic damages coming from male giants. But speaking more realistically, I realize that many problems have come from my neglect of my own health over the course of many years. Religion also played a role in my earlier life, giving me a low opinion of the body and its needs.

But in seeking for healing on all levels, I'm also doing a religious duty. I'm protecting God's great gift of life. Healing means becoming whole again. Healing is the essential meaning even of salvation, a word with a Latin root, salus, which means health. To be whole in body and soul is itself one way of achieving one's salvation – and that of others. In fact, this is the basic goal in every life.

(p. 217)

My religion? I would have to say that I still consider myself a Christian, even a Catholic, but that I am spiritually also a Taoist and a Buddhist and even a Confucian. The spiritual traditions of the Orient permit much more pluralism. I'm from the Orient, and sickness and the expectation of healing have spurred me to return home, culturally.

(pp. 211–12)

Meaning is also called wisdom, even compassion – loving others as we do ourselves, or at least trying to do so. Call it Buddhism, Taoism, or Christianity. The labels don't matter. Meaning is found in living and loving, in giving and receiving, and hopefully, also in dying when the time comes.

(p. 218)

The wisdom Julia gained through her life experiences is reflected in the symbol of the butterfly, for her a symbol of new life and hope. Before she succumbed to cancer, at the end of her accomplished life, her sense of completion is shown in an active imagination detailed in her memoir as follows:

In St. Peter's Basilica. And I noticed that the statue of St. Peter was no longer there. In its place stood a statue of St. Catherine of Sienna, the advisor and admonitrix to former popes. St. Peter had been moved, maybe on advice of his podiatrist, to the crypt, to be nearer his own holy remains. And nearer to the rock upon which the church is founded.

The crypt was now spanking clean. Except for one butterfly. And it was talking to me. It said: "While one's dreaming one doesn't know it's a dream. And in the dream one may even try to interpret a dream. Only after one wakes does one know it was a dream. Someday there'll be a great awakening. And we shall know that this is all a great dream."

"It's a dream if we make it a dream," I told the butterfly. "And it's real if we make it real. There is something of the real in the dream, and something of the dream in the real."

The butterfly added: "Just as the soul is in the body, and the body is in the soul. One isn't more real than the other. One isn't more illusory than the other. If we understand this, there'll be no conflict between the two."

Then the butterfly disappeared. And I told myself:

We can live our smile, day by day. This is the smile of Mona Lisa. People aren't sure if she's a real person or a myth. But her smile's legendary and precious to humankind.

This is the smile of the Buddhas. Some Buddhas are myths. One Buddha was real. But the smiles of all the Buddhas have real meaning.

If we live a smile, then we shall find meaning, whether life's long or not so long.

And we shall witness the dawn of a new age, and enjoy the view of the sunrise over a rejuvenated horizon.

(p. 220)

Julia's journey in search of meaning began in the East, took her across the oceans to the US, Australia, Europe, and Canada, and finally into herself, her body, and her psyche. Her search was a journey from the East to the West and back to the East again. It was a journey from the outer to the inner, connecting mind and body, the Masculine as well as the Feminine. Throughout her difficult life in which she survived the trauma and ravages of war, dislocation, and uprootedness, endured betrayal and abandonment, and lived with the anxiety about the unknown, Julia persevered and learned to go deep within to find the answers she needed. Her discoveries in her quest reflect the living truth of all religions – the love and respect for oneself and for others. Although she never had her feet bound, Julia certainly provides us with a vision of a woman who, like Chiu Chin before her, was able to unwind the bindings metaphorically and stand on her own two feet.

Notes

1 Julia Ching's principal publications include: *To Acquire Wisdom: The Way of Wang Wang Ming*, New York: Columbia University Press, 1976; *Christianity and Chinese Religions*, with Hans Küng, New York: Doubleday, 1989; *Probing China's Soul*, San Francisco: Harper & Row, 1990; *Moral Enlightenment: Leibnitz and Wolff on China*, with Willard G. Oxtoby, Sankt Augustin: Institut Monumenta Serica; Nettetal: Steyler, 1992; *Discovering China: European Interpretations in the Enlightenment*, edited by Julia Ching and Willard G.

Oxtoby, Rochester, NY: University of Rochester Press, 1992; *Mysticism and Kingship in China*, New York: Cambridge University Press, 1997; *The Religious Thought of Chu Hsi*, New York: Oxford University Press, 2000.
2 Julia Ching, *The Butterfly Healing: A Life between East and West*, Maryknoll, NY: Orbis Books, 1998, p. 18. All quotations that follow are taken from this book, and subsequent page numbers will be given inside parentheses within the text.

Chapter 9

Ruby and her new vision

When Ruby first came to my office, I was surprised to find that she was Chinese by ethnic origin, since her Canadian-born parents had Anglicized the family name. She was formal and polite in the way she carried herself, appearing more White Anglo-Saxon Protestant than Oriental. She was short and small, very soft-spoken and gentle. She was controlled in her feelings while she told me about herself, but I sensed much turmoil hidden within her tiny frame and the expressionless face behind her glasses.

Trained as a professional musician, she excelled in this field for many years. Yet throughout her working life, she had suffered from severe migraine headaches and serious somatic problems that disappeared whenever she withdrew for brief periods from work. Eventually she decided to leave her profession – one that her family had greatly approved of and her father had pushed her into. Close to the same time she also decided to leave an unhappy marriage. After this, both of her parents' families saw her as a "failure" in both her careers. Believing she had brought disgrace to the family, many relatives pretended not to see her when they passed her on the street, and the family in general ostracized her in many other ways.

After leaving her profession, Ruby tried other work and met with a good deal of success but was not really satisfied with what she tried. When she entered analysis, she said, "I want to find out what is wrong with me." Eventually, of course, Ruby came to realize that nothing at all was "wrong" with her. She just had not completely finished unraveling all her bindings and she had not yet found an identity she was comfortable with. In her case this search for identity and her reconnection with the Feminine go hand in hand.

Ruby's plight is not uncommon among the Baby Boomer generation, as witnessed among my Canadian clients. However, her suffering reflects a socio-cultural dimension from her ethnic background. In telling her story, it was important that Ruby located herself in a historical context and derived a sense of meaning of herself as an individual who carried the psychic burden of her immediate ancestors. In so doing, her psychic and physical exile could come together for integration and healing.

Ruby was born in Canada to parents who came from Chinese immigrant families. At the turn of the 20th century, both of her grandfathers had risked their lives and defied government decrees to leave the turmoil of China, only to risk their lives again in a foreign country where they faced hostility, persecution, and an uncertain future. Her paternal grandfather left China for Canada in 1905 while still a teenager. His bride from an arranged marriage arrived a few years later. They started a small grocery store serving the Chinese community. Unfortunately he died in middle age, leaving a young widow and a large family. The children worked in the store and subsisted on donations from neighbors and clan members in the close-knit community. All the sons managed to attend university for their professional training. Ruby's father became an engineer and eventually owned his own consulting firm. While Ruby was growing up, he worked long hours and weekends and was seldom home. She felt she never really got to know him. This was a source of great regret to her later, for when Ruby was only 20 he died in a tragic accident.

Ruby's maternal grandfather left Southern China for Canada in 1910 at the age of 20 in order to work on the Trans Canada Railway. His mother chose a wife for him who knew him only from his picture. Several years later the "postal-bride" arrived at the dock wearing his picture around her neck so that he could identify her. When work on the railway petered out, he took various jobs, including running a laundry, and later waiting on tables in a restaurant. Eventually he bought his own laundry, which would pay for his children's university education. He went on to own many businesses and became a successful entrepreneur. Ruby says her mother never talked about her childhood and refused to speak Chinese, even though she was fluent in it.

In general, both of Ruby's parents were almost obsessively committed to integrating completely into the dominant WASP society of Canada and disavowed their Chinese heritage in the process. Although this made Ruby's search for an identity more difficult, she was able to understand their feelings as they had grown up in difficult socio-economic conditions when racism against the Chinese was prevalent. When the Trans Canada Railway had been completed, the contract labourers – the "sojourners" (who had intended to return home after amassing some riches overseas) – found themselves stranded in a foreign country as their contractors failed to fulfill their promise to pay their way home. They had to enter the local labor market, and were met with resistance and dissent from among the local white workers. This discontent eventually led to organized pressure for discriminatory legislation. A heavy head tax, eventually raised to $500 per person in 1904, was levied on the limited few who entered the country. This was a prohibitive sum when the seasonal wage was 25 cents an hour. In 1923, the Chinese Exclusion Act was passed, closing the door to Chinese immigration specifically. Under this Act, wives and sons were not allowed to join their husbands and fathers in Canada. The Chinese population was cut by more than half, while the sex ratio was ten to one in favor of men. External pressures prevented the migration of the Chinese from the "Chinatowns" and contact with the rest of society. Chinese communities were seen as close-knit ethnic enclaves, consisting mostly of men who were without their families and the opportunity to intermarry.

Both of Ruby's parents grew up in this hostile environment in the 1920s and were faced with a double dilemma. There was social and political pressure to stay in the "ghetto" where they belonged by virtue of their ethnic visibility, especially after witnessing the Japanese internment during the Second World War. However, with their Canadian education, there was considerable internal psychological pressure to conform to collective values, to dis-identify with the "ghetto" and join the mainstream. Naturally, the intensity of this conflict was displaced onto striving for success, for materialistic achievement at any cost, with an accompanying rejection of their social and cultural roots. According to Ruby, members of this generation made no bones about what it was like to be Chinese during these years:

To be Chinese meant to be poor, uneducated and unsuccessful. The sole ambition for each of us was to become assimilated into Canadian life and establish ourselves as first-rate professionals with good positions, evidence of material success and investments for security.

In 1947, the Chinese Exclusion Act was repealed and Canadian-born Chinese were enfranchised and no longer "resident aliens." This change brought in a limited number of Chinese women, who nevertheless contributed to the growth of the emergent second and third generation of Canadian-born Chinese. In the early 1960s, changing political and socio-economic circumstances resulted in a new Immigration Act, allowing people from all nationalities to apply for entry to Canada on the basis of their education and professional skills. This policy drastically changed the structure of the Chinese community in Canada from a small, homogeneous peasant folk colony (about 35,000 in 1947) to the current sizeable community of about a million with members that are multi-lingual, professional, entrepreneurial, and well connected to the global economy.[1]

Ruby's parents moved out of "Chinatown" in the 1960s to join the mainstream and cut off most of their contact with the Chinese community. Ruby grew up in the shadow of her parents who, cut off from their cultural roots, feelings, and spirituality, lived an encapsulated life devoted to work and achievement. Throughout her life, Ruby has felt tremendous pressure "to make something of myself, so as not to disgrace the family." Thus when she left her profession and her marriage with the combined sacrifices of prestige and financial security, she was indeed challenging her parents' entire value system, the foundation upon which the family identity had been built and the basis of their survival in a hostile social environment.

Ruby began her analysis with the following dream:

> I looked into the mirror and found that my right front tooth was loose and could be falling out. I worried about how to eat and how to get in touch with my dentist over the weekend.

Looking into the mirror, the reflection of her soul, she saw the truth. The mirror symbolically points to a process of reflection, of contemplation with the purpose of self-realization. The reflection in the mirror represents the deepest truth in the soul, the knowledge of oneself.[2] This knowledge of her true self was what Ruby needed to find for her identity. Teeth are often associated with attack and defense, in other words, aggression and self-protection. As an instrument for biting and chewing, teeth prepare food for assimilation. In Jungian terms, the teeth are "transformers" and are associated with the ability of the ego to relate to reality. In alchemy – which is often used as symbolic reference point in Jungian analysis – the right side is connected with the realm of the conscious, as compared to the left side, which generally pertains to the unconscious. The front teeth are also related to aesthetics, the presentation of oneself, the persona. Psychologically, the loose right front tooth suggested problems in the ego's rootedness in the world, and Ruby's relationship to external reality. The dream ego was worried about "how to eat" and "getting in touch with her dentist"; that is, the direction of psychic energy was focused on issues of survival in both a physical and psychic sense, and on the possibility of healing.

One of the main problems Ruby experienced after leaving her marriage and profession was an inability to "get her teeth into anything," to engage with life. She felt that she was living a provisional life, particularly in the area of work and career. At one point she told me she didn't know how to "market" herself in order to get a new job because, she said, "I don't even know what I'm marketing." This underscored Ruby's need to discover who she really was – to find her true identity. This dream occupied Ruby throughout the course of her analysis, in which she questioned her whole being in her journey into herself.

One aspect of Ruby's story that makes it particularly interesting is that one might think that Ruby's being a musician would mean that she was well connected to the instinctual, feminine, intuitive side of her being. But this was not the case. Although Ruby was extremely proficient technically, she did not really play from her heart. The reasons for this became clear as Ruby's story unfolded.

Ruby grew up in a rigid, authoritarian household in which scholarship and academic excellence were demanded, to the exclusion of play and passion. She described her father, an idealized authority figure whom she feared, as "a nice, kind man" but also "a critical authority figure." A sensitive feeling child, Ruby was a disappointment to her parents, who wanted "a tough scientist with brains." To help develop this "useless" daughter, her parents signed Ruby up for all kinds of lessons without consulting her wishes. Her father gave her extra math lessons and assignments for her spare time and during her summer holidays. He became an added source of pressure to excel. A grade of 96% was unsatisfactory and merited such comments as: "How could you be so stupid! How could you have missed four marks?" Her mother was equally, if not even more, critical of her as she was growing up. Recalling this, Ruby said, "basically I was treated as if I had no validity or worth as an individual, unless I achieved and was a perfect child who did not cry or make any mistakes."

As a child, Ruby was given violin lessons and expected to practice rigorously and be "very good at it." Eventually, when she showed an aptitude for music, it was made clear to her later that, since she was a "good-for-nothing" – in other words an individual who lacked a culturally acceptable rational mind – learning to play a musical instrument and having a professional career in the music field was the least she could do. If she achieved these goals, she might at least in some small way bring honor to the family. When it came time to go to university, Ruby's parents, in particular her father, decided that she would enroll with a major in music. This decision was made without consultation with Ruby and without any realistic appraisal of her aspiration and her talent. And it was done in spite of the fact that she had actually won scholarships in other academic areas.

Ruby's relationship to music was complex. Because her father was so enthusiastic about music, it represented a connection to him. Continuing in this field provided a way for her to feel close to him and win his approval. By succeeding and becoming a reasonably successful musician, Ruby was being a good filial daughter. Her music provided solace during his frequent absences and gave her meaning in the cold and hostile home environment created by her mother. So, even though music was not Ruby's passion, it did provide some comfort for her and ease her suffering and loneliness. For a long time it provided a cocoon that shielded her from facing the challenge of reality and finding her true self. However, in the end, because the decision to become a musician was not her own and not anything she really wanted, it ultimately represented the binding of her feet and her disconnection from her Feminine standpoint. All this was made more intense for Ruby by the role she played for her father. Her father probably lived his repressed feeling through Ruby's music. In Jungian terms, his musician daughter carried his soul projection or anima. For him, this became the means of filling to some extent the emotional vacuum in his life in general and, in particular, in a marriage that was a very unhappy one.

In short, even though one might normally associate music with the inner Feminine nature, in Ruby's case leaving music was a necessary form of "chopping off her head" and, in this way, beginning to finally disconnect from both her yearning for approval from her father and the dominant Masculine that had developed within her because of it. Without this radical "detachment" Ruby would never be able to begin to reconnect to the Feminine and regain her own standpoint.

Soon after Ruby entered analysis, she was in a bad accident in which she broke her left leg. Her injuries left her relatively immobilized for several months, and she lost the job she had taken after leaving music. The physical injuries to her left side symbolically suggested that her wounded Feminine standpoint needed to be examined and healed before further progression in life could take place. With the loss of her job, Ruby was experiencing, for the first time in her life, freedom from duty and work, from active doing. In myths and fairy tales, the motif of being confined in a tower or a cave (i.e. imprisonment) implies the psychological need for individuation, which is made more urgent as one cannot escape any more. This motif usually occurs at the beginning of the analytical process. Thus, although all this represented a tremendous challenge for Ruby, she was able to rise above it and use the time to enter the process of looking deeper and deeper into her soul to find her true self.

Shortly after the accident, she had a series of dreams. In two of them she was a teenager involved in an activity with her parents. Here is one of them:

> I am with my father and mother somewhere in the street. I want to eat something. My father said: "If you want to eat, let's do it right here." We walked into the closest restaurant at once and ate.

The dream ego appears to be in her early teens and her parents in their mid-forties. The dream brings the dreamer back to that stage in her life when certain psychic issues need to be addressed and dealt with. According to Ruby, her father was practical and decisive and these are the qualities Ruby needed in relating to the world. Ruby's personal association of this dream related to her father's newly awakened interest in psychology shortly before his death. He was reading Jung's autobiography, *Memories, Dreams, Reflections*. Ruby believed he might have considered going into analysis had his life not been cut short. This realization helped her to see the meaning of her own analysis – that she was also redeeming her father's unfulfilled task. With this realization, she felt a sense of connection with her father spiritually. With this dream, Ruby felt validated in her decision to embark on her analytic process to satisfy her longing for spiritual sustenance and felt less guilty about not working and not being productive.

In another dream, Ruby recalled:

> I am thinking of asking father how long it'd take to learn Chinese and how difficult it will be . . . I am with father and mother, all in the front

seat of the car. Father is driving. I saw a white lump of tissue paper coming toward us, drawing a white line dividing the opposite lane. Father stopped the car and we looked at it. . . .

Because Ruby was never exposed to Chinese language and culture on a conscious level, her dream suggests on one level her psychic orientation towards her ancestral heritage, the collective unconscious. On another level, this search for her heritage represents her search for her identity. The fact that Ruby was a child points to the notion that at that point in her journey she needed to reconnect with her youth in order to differentiate her relationship with her parents and the parental *imago* – the internalized image of the mother and father. This dream told Ruby that she must, at the moment at least, pay particular attention to this in terms of her father, for it was he who had occupied the driver's seat up to this point in Ruby's life. The tissue paper may suggest that the process of recollecting and reconnecting may not take too long. Because of its transitory existence and quick, easy disposability, it suggested the urgency of her task at this stage in her life.

After a series of dreams and revelations that helped her clarify her issues with her father, Ruby began to work on her relationship with her mother. This was also an essential part of her reconnection with the Feminine for, as Ruby eventually came to realize, it was her mother who in classic fashion was the one who actually bound her feet.

> My father was definitely an authority figure – I was always afraid that I wouldn't measure up to his expectations and he would be angry and use the word "stupid" . . . But my mother was an authority figure too . . . I was not free to be myself . . . I have a lot of difficulty saying how I feel or what I want because I was programmed by my mother to think that if you said "I want this," you were selfish. We were not allowed to express our feelings. I was always told by her that I was selfish for wanting things. Even as an adult, I don't know what I want and don't feel comfortable saying how I feel. I see now that it's not selfish to say "I want" or "I like," and I have to get in touch with my feelings so I can know what I want.

As Ruby explored the ways in which her mother had bound her feet and sabotaged the development of her feeling standpoint, she began to recount her memories of how badly her mother had treated her. On a deeper level, she realized how she has internalized the negative mother principle symbolized by the witch in fairy tales, and how this has distorted her own instinctive make-up. She was shown this by a series of dreams that featured animals (which often represent the natural world and the instinctive nature) that had turned against her or were attacking her. For example:

> On a sun deck, a large cat came out of the house, leapt at me, aimed at my right index finger and bit it so hard that it split on the side. I struggled with the cat, screaming and trying to shake it off. The whole finger was cut open, all red, but no blood came out.

The cat represents the primitive, instinctive Feminine nature of woman. It can be a symbol of *joie de vivre* and gaiety. The right index finger represents one's direction in the world. Associated with the planet Jupiter, it corresponds to the solar plexus, which is the seat of emotion. The cat wounding the right index finger suggests problems with existential fear, which is common among children who have not received enough maternal love. The repression of the cat energy inhibits Ruby's direction in life. This dream suggested the need to redeem the cat in herself, that is, the need to look after herself with the recklessness of nature – to know her needs and wants and to satisfy them without feeling guilty. When one considers that Ruby was a professional musician, the injury to her finger appeared as a "direct hit" on a more immediate level. Although cats are playful and spontaneous, here the dream ego screams at it, and can't shake it off before she is hurt. The lack of bleeding perhaps suggests that this is an old wound and that time helped Ruby to gain a perspective in looking at her wounding more objectively. This dream reflected her deep anxiety, which was exacerbated by her difficult situation, being jobless and immobile.

Another dream followed:

> I opened a box and saw two live lobsters in it. I freaked out and screamed. One jumped out and got me. I jumped into the air up to the ceiling, the lobster dangling from my left leg . . .

The lobster, like the crab, an unfeeling, grasping monster, is often associated with a negative mother complex. For Ruby, cut off from her Feminine standpoint, it signified a life without contact to this essential part of her being – and that part of the inner self was moving increasingly into consciousness. Existential fear suggests problems with repressed aggression. In women, the negative mother complex often engenders a lack of basic vital security, taking away one's ability to meet life. In trying to be good and obedient, Ruby developed an artificial persona that did not allow her to protect herself adequately against aggression and to relate to the world in her own authority. This is the deeper issue of the loose right front tooth in her initial dream. The recurrent dream motif of being shot by bullets, detailed below, reflects the directedness and explosive nature of her repressed anger. Increasingly, her aggression expressed itself in fights with her shadow figures in the dreams. To keep in touch with instinct, represented by the cat and other animals, will help bring fear and aggression into the right balance. Ruby needed to find her own true nature and learn to be herself naturally. Thus, her ability to scream as she felt her fear and pain in both dreams was healing in the right direction!

In another dream, she related:

> I am being shot to death slowly. My body was gradually being punctured with bullets and I was left to die. I don't know what I have done to deserve this. I felt dizzy, and weak, trying to crawl to the carpet for comfort. I positioned myself on the left to expose the right side to be shot. Mother came in and said she will give me money to rent a presidential suite in a hotel so that I can die in comfort.

This dream was especially significant because it brings together her struggle to find her new identity and the need to reconnect with the Feminine in order to do it. Her dying here represents the need for the symbolic death in order for her to be reborn as her true self. At the same time, it's clear to Ruby that the bullets to her right side symbolize sabotage from her mother throughout her growing up. From the very beginning of Ruby's life, her mother had taken a dislike to her and had blatantly favored her brothers with both her approval and her affection. Ruby came to understand that she had to confront this issue before the internalized negative mother could be transformed into the positive one. It is this positive internal Feminine that appears in the dream and offers her "money" – a symbol that very often represents energy – to assist her in this transformation.

However, when Ruby first tried to confront her feelings towards her mother, she was overwhelmed with a mass of blackness that paralyzed her. Fear and guilt incapacitated her. Then one day Ruby discovered the diary she kept when she was young. Her account detailed her feelings and thoughts about the negative treatment she was receiving from her mother and also outlined some of Ruby's fears, anxieties, and nightmares. Reading this diary marked a turning point in her analysis. She now felt validated in her feelings toward her mother, since it was now clear that they did not grow out of her imagination, as she had been led to believe. She became increasingly sure of herself and more open in expressing her negative experience of her mother during childhood. Rejected for the way she was, she took responsibility for her "badness." At a very young age she told her mother: "Mommy, if I were dead, you wouldn't have any more trouble with me."

In Ruby's recollection, there was never any physical expression of affection in the family. The expression of negative feelings was never allowed. In fact, expressing any emotion was not allowed in her childhood and adolescence. At one point Ruby told me, "I never cried after I left babyhood." Once Ruby began to "chop off her head" and disconnect from the overbearing Masculine, she became able to cry. Eventually she reached a point in her journey where she was able to cry frequently and express her emotions through tears. As she reconnected with the eternal Feminine in this way, one day she found herself laughing with her partner. Shocked, she realized she had gone for years without laughing. Although this realization saddened her, it was also concrete proof that her inner transformation was moving forward and that she was getting in touch with the positive mother within and, in turn, with her true self.

Another sign that she was both finding herself and developing the ability to stand on her own two unbound feet came with her increasing ability to "stand up" for herself. Throughout her life Ruby was socialized to say "only the nice things." During Ruby's analysis she gained a great deal of insight into how this had affected her, both through her dreams and in doing an Association Experiment. The AE, as it's known, is a word association exercise that was developed by Jung as a means of discovering what he called "complexes," which are groups of emotionally charged ideas or images. Because we are often unconscious of these complexes and how they are affecting us, the AE can be a very valuable tool in helping bring these issues to light. When Ruby took the AE, the way she responded was like a student in an examination; she was careful, serious, and controlled. She did not show any signs of enjoying herself or of having fun in experiencing something new. The way she responded also suggested a "still water runs deep" type of personality, someone who may have deep feelings and emotions that are hidden and controlled. Not surprisingly, the responses themselves suggested three major areas that she was struggling with: the father, the negative mother, and the positive relationship to the Feminine. After taking the AE, Ruby realized that she must work through her negative relationship with her mother if she ever wanted to resolve the negative attitude she had toward herself.

The AE showed that one of the most destructive ways the negative mother had influenced Ruby was in "programming" her to always be nice, polite, and obedient; to be, in other words, the perfect filial daughter. Ruby's responses in the AE indicated she had problems with freedom, restrictions, limitations, and mobility that were directly related to the negative mother and, further, that these were virtually the main factors inhibiting her progression in life. The rules governing her life, she declared, have always been "somebody else's rules." After she had this realization, Ruby made a number of inroads into expressing her true self. She made a conscious decision to use her new level of understanding to gain freedom from old patterns. She decided not to be "nice" any longer if this attitude was a pretense and began to examine her friendships and reassess them:

> I have been trying . . . to decide who I really care about and want to keep in contact with. I've realized that I need to ask myself: Am I happy when I'm with this person? Would he/she be loyal to me when I'm going through tough times?

One of the most positive outcomes of this introspection was that she realized that she was not solely responsible for the failure of her marriage, and she also became more confident and committed to her current relationship, realizing, she said, that he is "much more than the man who is my lover – he is a true friend, my best friend."

Another positive sign came with the following dream:

> I got a call from my music teacher, who asked me to go to her house to drive her around because she has been injured. I told her the same thing has happened to me and that I can't believe she could ask such a favor of me.

She remarked: "In questioning everything right now, I feel like I'm starting a new life." And this was indeed exactly what she was doing: she was starting a new life as a new person. She was finding her true identity. This transformation became evident in her dreams, which showed an increasing awareness of and connection to the Feminine within. One of her dreams reflected this very clearly. In it, she was in an office where she felt trapped and panic-stricken. She felt she was being persecuted by some type of "in-group" in the office and that she was "targeted for destruction." After she picked up a pair of glasses and put them on, she walked by a room where a meeting was being held and heard her name being called:

> I went in and three Chinese female employees were there. They told me that I am one of them. One said she remembered me back in childhood, that's why I am alright and I can be in the in-group. I felt relieved.

In this dream the negative, destructive Feminine represented by the original in-group is transformed into a positive, accepting one after Ruby put on the glasses. Since glasses help us "see more clearly" and change the way the world looks to us, they often stand for the moment when our perception or our view of reality changes. In this sense, they represent a new vision or a new way of seeing things. Another interesting aspect of this dream is that Ruby plus the three other women equal the number four. In several systems of thought, the number four represents totality. In the Jungian interpretation the number four, especially when it appears as one plus three, represents wholeness or completion. In fairy tales, this can be seen in the frequent motif of the King and three sons or, as in Cinderella, the wicked step mother and the three girls. In Cinderella, as in many such tales, the three negative female figures have to be transformed for the heroine to achieve wholeness.[3] This is exactly what happens in this dream when the three Chinese women and the dreamer together form the Feminine totality within which transformation can take place. This dream also reflects Ruby's psychic connection to her cultural heritage, as she never had

Chinese friends growing up in a racially homogeneous neighborhood with no other ethnic groups.

Ruby's newly gained vision was further reinforced by a dream that immediately followed:

> A young man in his twenties comes to see me and needs something to be done about his eyes. I am acting as his eye doctor, working with tools like a doctor's. He pays the cashier for my services.

Ruby as the dream ego restores vision, i.e. consciousness, to her inner Masculine and receives money, or energy, in doing so. A woman's positive animus is her guide to the unconscious. He represents her sword of discrimination which will give her a true sense of what she is. Through reflection, she gains meaning for her life's action and direction. In learning to accept and love herself, she finds and possesses herself. The growing feeling of wholeness gives her strength to trust in the moment and rejoice in the unfolding mystery of her life.

Soon after this Ruby related another dream that was indicative of these changes:

> I am in my childhood home. Mother was in the kitchen and was pleased to see me.

Kitchens are another type of image that often have deep significance in dreams. They are the place in the home where food is transformed by "cooking" from the raw and inedible to something that can be consumed and provide us with the sustenance and nourishment that we need. This dream then was a sign that the negative mother was well on her way to being transformed and that Ruby could establish a positive relationship with the inner Feminine which would, in turn, sustain and nourish her.

Up until this point in her analysis Ruby had been plagued by dreams that contained aggressive images of men; for instance, groups of tough high-school boys who challenged her knowledge of the reality of life and "a man running around shooting and causing trouble." In contrast to this, she now began to dream of "Chinese cooks cleaning the stove in the kitchen of Chinese restaurants." Her inner Masculine was going through the same process of transformation that the negative mother had gone through and was changing into a down-to-earth Chinese cook who was actively engaged in the process of transformation. Another dream soon followed, in which Ruby said:

> I am in a house which has a Japanese garden. There is a Japanese male gardener, who is planting as I watch.

In addition to its aesthetic beauty, a Japanese garden suggests refinement, contemplation, meditation – the attributes of a life lived with a deep awareness of the symbolic richness that exists both around and within us. Ruby's inner psychic structure, as represented by the house, now had a new spiritual dimension. The garden is a symbol of individuation; it depicts the evolution of human consciousness through spiritual development. The gardener, which in this case is the farmer who is raised to a higher spiritual level in cultivating his soul, is a symbol of wholeness. Ruby's sacrifice brings her the fruit of her suffering. In connecting with the Masculine spirit, she can now integrate her own creative energy and take responsibility for her own life. This energy must be grounded in the archetypal Feminine. That this had finally occurred for Ruby was suggested in the following dream:

> My maternal grandmother is in her bedroom upstairs. I go up to see her. She is sick. She speaks to me in English. I care about her. I am affectionate toward her. Someone has brought her green grapes. She wants me to have them.

In the dream, a strong bond existed between the older and the younger woman. In reality, Ruby had never spoken with her grandmother, who did not speak English and hardly knew her. She had only heard stories about this formidable lady. However, for Ruby, she embodied the chthonic power of the Chinese Earth from which Ruby was cut off due to her mother's rejection of her Chinese roots. This, then, is a powerful dream that connected Ruby to her ancestral heritage and her roots in Mother Earth.

As a symbol, grapes have long been associated with agricultural and fertility deities and represent wine, the blood of Life. Receiving grapes from her grandmother denoted in this sense a blessing from the Great Mother. Moreover, because of the deep association in Christian ritual between wine and the blood of Christ, grapes symbolize sacrifice and suffering.[4] These, in turn, are the prerequisites of the transformation conferred by Sophia, the giver of wisdom.[5]

In this dream the outworn Feminine principle, represented by the dying grandmother, needs to be redeemed by the younger woman. Through the grapes, the essence of the life experience of the grandmother is passed on to Ruby. Through the transformative power of this dream, Ruby now carried the psychic significance of her new self. In her earlier life as the musician she had never wanted to be, she had been complying with the rigid rules of fixed authority and had abandoned herself into non-being.

During the process of analysis Ruby managed to unravel the long cloth that bound her feet and find her own natural Feminine standpoint. From the depth of her soul, Ruby felt validated in her decision to leave her profession and her marriage, which was her unconscious attempt to save her life. Although she had sacrificed many years of her life, its real meaning was now finally being restored. She managed to cut away the Masculine that was dominating her life, discover her true self, and reconnect with the Feminine on a profound level.

Notes

1 For a brief history of the Chinese in Canada, see the following: Tom MacInnes, *Oriental Occupation in British Columbia*, Vancouver: Sun Publishing, 1927, p. 9; Anne M. Davidson, 'An analysis of the significant factors in the patterns of Toronto Chinese family life as a result of recent changes in immigration laws', M.S.W. thesis, University of Toronto, 1952; John Porter, *The Vertical Mosaic*, Toronto: University of Toronto Press, 1962, pp. 88–9; Donghai Li, *A History of the Chinese in Canada*, Taiwan: Zhonghua, 1967, p. 420 [text in Chinese]; Vivian Lai, 'The New Chinese Immigrants in Toronto', in Elliot, Jean L., ed., *Minority Canadians*, Toronto: Prentice-Hall, 1971, p. 123; Shirley Ma, 'Disunity in Toronto's Chinese Community', paper presented at the American Anthropological Association Annual Meeting, 1 December 1972; Peter S. Li, 'The Chinese Minority in Canada, 1858–1992: A Quest for Equality', in Evelyn Huang with Jeffrey Lawrence, *Chinese Canadians: Voices from a Community*, Vancouver: Douglas & MacIntyre, 1992, pp. 264–75.
2 Sibylle Birkhauser-Oeri, *The Mother, Archetypal Image in Fairy Tales*, Toronto: Inner City Books, 1988, pp. 34–6.
3 Marie-Louise von Franz, *Introduction to the Interpretation of Fairy Tales*, Houston, TX: Spring Publications, 1970, p. 140; *The Problems of the Feminine in Fairy Tales*, Houston, TX: Spring Publications, 1972, pp. 184–7.
4 Jean C. Cooper, *An Illustrated Encyclopaedia of Traditional Symbols*, London: Thames and Hudson, 1982, p. 76.
5 Eric Neumann, *The Great Mother: An Analysis of the Archetype*, New York: Bollingen, 1955, p. 252.

Chapter 10

Jade: unbinding and restoring her feet

Throughout this book we have been exploring the imagery associated with footbinding, how it can help us understand the ways we have allowed our true natures and heartfelt desires to be "bound" or restricted. We have also explored the ways a number of women have begun to unwind these bindings psychologically, in the process making it possible for them to reconnect with Mother Earth, the eternal Feminine, their deepest instinctual nature, and their true selves. An analysand whose story illustrates this process and summarizes many of the important points discussed throughout this work is a woman I'll call Jade. Born in Singapore and raised in Hong Kong, Jade went to university in America like thousands of other Chinese students during the seventies and eighties. An outstanding student, Jade received scholarships throughout her university years, then went on to graduate school and received an MBA. Once she entered the workforce she quickly began to excel in her field of specialization in banking and finance, and by the time she reached her thirties she was in the midst of a very successful career.

However, when Jade was 31, a long-term relationship she'd been in ended and things began to change for her. In the process of mourning the end of the reiationship, she began to suffer from depression. During this period she experienced frequent uncontrollable crying spells, bouts of nervousness and anxiety, and feelings of insecurity. She soon became overwhelmed by a sense of emptiness and of the futility of life. Her state of anxiety was accompanied by severe psychosomatic symptoms that eventually began to hinder her professional work. Suddenly, Jade – who had been so successful and so "in control" of her life – was thrown into a state of being that was entirely unfamiliar to her. Bewildered and lost, she entered analysis to find out what was "wrong" with her and to search for the deeper meaning of her life.

Jade's family history is a fascinating one. Her parents were originally peasants from southern China who met in a Japanese work camp in Southeast Asia during the war. After the war, poverty forced them to make their way to Hong Kong. As survivors, they were determined to "make it" in the world, and start a small business in their new home. They soon rejected their ancestors and adopted the Protestant faith. Deeply scarred by their experience of poverty, war, and camp life, they tended to look at their children as investment property and a means of advancement. The children were put to work in the family business as soon as they were able. Educating the children was also a means to an end for them in terms of their old-age security. Jade recalls returning home on her first day of school to be told by her mother, "Going to school will help you to achieve a good salary, half of which will belong to Mother."

Jade describes her youth as "burdensome" and full of responsibilities, both physical and emotional. As the eldest child, in addition to working in the business after school, Jade had the responsibility of looking after her four siblings. When she had the opportunity to continue her post-secondary education in the West, Jade was exposed to freedom and a sense of liberation from the bondage of family. She decided not to return "home" and subsequently took up residence in Canada.

By the time she had put herself through graduate school and established herself in her profession, Jade says she felt burnt out. In this context, her depression appeared as a clear signal to her that life could no longer continue if she didn't begin to reevaluate its meaning. Feeling that she may have deviated from her life path or *tao*, Jade took the courage to examine herself and search inward. Considering her action in psychological terms, it is clear that she consciously entered a period of introversion when she began analysis. This stage in analysis is also often referred to as "incubation," and it can be likened to a caterpillar entering a cocoon and staying there until ready to emerge as a butterfly. As soon as Jade felt "contained" and securely supported by the analytic relationship, she was able to begin deeply exploring her unconscious using dream analysis. She also sought out body work in order to help facilitate the process. This exploration was a long and challenging one for Jade but, as you will see, she persevered and managed to unravel the bindings that had restricted her for so long.

Jade began her analysis with the following dream. As happens frequently in the Jungian analytic process, the first dream was a very significant one:

> I am following my father and mother through a tunnel. They both appear young, in their twenties. I am my current age. Along the way, we pass by a caveman who has long, straight black hair covering his whole body. Then I am leading the way out of the tunnel, slightly ascending uphill to the opening on the ground. When I emerge from the tunnel into daylight, Dr. Yeung greets me as I shake hands with him.

This dream brings the dream ego back to childhood. Certain psychic issues from this period need to be made conscious and become assimilated. Her parents are leading her through the tunnel until they see the caveman. The tunnel can be understood as a symbol of the birth canal, suggesting the significance of what needs to be made conscious to allow for the birth of a new consciousness. The caveman in Jade's dream is first described in *Shan Hai Ching* (*The Classic of Mountains and Seas*), which delineated the original geomorphology of China since her mythic beginning. In it are described the strange creatures that were believed to have existed in China's primordial past.[1] Psychologically, the caveman represents the archetypal image of the Natural Man or the "Anthropos," which is a symbol of the Self.

At this point Jade felt that "what's wrong with her" was the sense of not being herself, not being really rooted on the ground, not being completely in the here-and-now and in Life. She commented: "I have never lived; I merely existed, performing my duties." The caveman reflects a need for psychological compensation to balance out her life: she had been driven to lead a one-sided life devoted to the intellect, cut off from her feelings as well as her peasant roots. This dream suggested the direction of her analysis, the need to go back to that primordial beginning, her original self, to find out what she was meant to be, rather than struggling to be what she was programmed to be.

To get to the caveman in her dream, she has to follow her parents, in other words, connect with her original peasant roots, in order to understand and differentiate her relationship with her parents. Then she can lead the dream parents out of the darkness of the tunnel into daylight, or consciousness. The dream ends with shaking hands, that is, establishing a bond, with Dr. Yeung. In the dream, Dr. Yeung is a practitioner of traditional Chinese medicine and represents a version of the primitive shaman-cum-alchemist from ancient China. This symbol had deep meaning for Jade for, when she was a child, her grandmother would take her to just such a practitioner for herbs and acupuncture.

For Jade, the shamanistic Dr. Yeung represented the traditional equivalent of an analyst.[2] This told her that she needed to bond with her analyst and direct her psychic energy on a journey that would take her deep within herself. Jung often referred to this as a *nekyia* or "night sea journey" and used the imagery of traveling alone on an ocean at night to describe it. However, it soon became apparent to Jade that the imagery associated with footbinding and the process of unwinding the bindings resonated more deeply for her. She saw herself, with every layer of the binding cloth that she unwound, going deeper and deeper within.

Although this dream was to occupy Jade throughout the course of her analysis, at this early stage the main challenge for Jade was to examine her relationship with her parents. Jade had virtually no relationship with her mother and her relationship with her father was complex and ambivalent. He emerged from the labor camp experience completely broken. His shame over what he had endured and the subsequent denial of how it affected him was a means for him of sealing the truth from the outside world. This resulted in him isolating himself in many ways. The consequent lack of social support and of therapeutic treatment made any type of rehabilitation impossible. During the course of her analysis it became clear to Jade that her father suffered from complex post traumatic stress disorder and that these symptoms over time degenerated into regressive impulses and psycho-pathological processes such as depression, rage, and paranoia.

This situation was exacerbated by the fact that mental illness in Chinese culture is perceived as a shameful reflection on the ancestors. Jade's father and the entire family tried to hide his condition and deny it – a conspiracy was created that demanded silence and banned communication. In Jade's family, relationships with outsiders were forbidden, and relationships within the family were characterized by physical and emotional abuse, mistrust, suspicion, and even surveillance. In addition to the lack of social rela-tionships within the extended family and with the community, there was no celebration of festivals or birthdays because of her father's volatile emo-tional state. His inability to express emotions often erupted in violent rage without any sense of the appropriateness of the situation. Laughter among the children often triggered resentment, leading to verbal and/or physical abuse. Every graduation or wedding was a traumatic event, as it was per-ceived as abandonment and betrayal. For example, when Jade's sister came home to give her parents the happy news that she was going to be married to a wonderful man, her father responded by going into a rage and beating her brutally. Since filial piety and kin responsibility are demanded in the Chinese family tradition, the whole family quietly bore the burden of her father's trauma. Because of this, Jade grew up feeling trapped in the prison of empty space that was shrouded in secrecy and circumscribed by fear, shame, guilt, loneliness, and isolation. In her words: "I have lived in the camp all my life!"

On the positive side, however, Jade saw that there was some part of her father that was still in touch with his peasant roots. This side of him was spontaneous and nature-oriented and Jade was drawn to it. At some point in the process of growing up, Jade identified with her father's suffering. Although she wasn't close to him in childhood, by the time she entered puberty, she had become in a certain sense his "spiritual companion." Often they spent long hours together talking over drinks. Like a therapist, Jade would listen to her father, feeling empathy with his emotional turmoil and his search for meaning in life. At some level, she devoted herself to healing him. Only later would she realize how this "devotion" inhibited her normal development as a woman and as a free individual.

Jade's father was a major influence in Jade's decision to study in the United States and in her dedication to the quest for knowledge. Both were an attempt to redeem "his unlived ambition." When the time came for her to leave to study abroad the decision was not free: her father made it clear that she was to "do it for him." Otherwise, he said, "he could just as well send her to work in a factory." As Jade pondered these aspects of her life in the early stages of analysis, she had the following dream:

> I am staying for the night in a luxury hotel where I am attending a big conference. I am wearing a three-piece suit in navy blue with white stripes. My father came in and, with my suit on, we went into the shower like lovers.

The dream ego is attending a conference in a ritzy hotel, suggesting a certain degree of professional achievement. The three-piece suit suggests a professional persona, since clothing generally denotes one's social position and attitude toward outer reality.[3] Blue sometimes symbolizes spirituality and white, purity and chastity. Jade associated the business suit with an armour for the battlefield of the business world. Instead of being naked, she wears this suit into the shower with her father. The erotic liaison suggests psychic incest, and its consummation is through the business suit. Water and washing, *ablutio*, represent the initial stage in the alchemical process of psychological transformation. Cleansing prepares the way for sorting, or differentiation and self-reflection, before integration can take place.[4] At this stage, Jade's analytical process had at its centre her persona, and the relationship of her persona to her chosen career – and her father's role in the direction her life had taken. These issues had to be explored before the naked truth could be addressed.

Jade was shocked by the incest motif in this dream. In essence, the business suit attested to her allegiance and total devotion to a cause she was fighting not for herself but for her father. Now she became aware that she had taken on the role of Hua Mu-lan who, as was discussed earlier, joined the army for her ailing father in the name of filial piety. Blinded by her devotion to both her father and the Father image, Jade was close to being stranded in the battlefield and risked losing her way back to her Feminine instinct. The business suit is the veil that represents an artificial bond between father and daughter; underneath it lies hidden the naked truth of betrayal.

On a deeper level, the business suit and the incest motif suggest animus problems in her psychic development. In a woman, the animus is the inherited collective image of the spirit, which is usually projected onto man, the father being the first carrier of this image.[5] Jade's associations with her father suggested that she had not been nurtured by her father's "Eros" during her development. In Jungian terms, Eros is used as an image that encapsulates all the inner "functions" that relate to the feeling side of our nature – emotion, sensitivity, tenderness, affection, love. Rather than bestowing these tender feelings on his daughter as a loving father normally would, Jade's father needed her to bestow affection on him – a need that was exacerbated by the absence of a loving relationship with his wife.

From her earliest years, Jade also lacked any type of meaningful relationship with her mother. This, along with other factors, resulted in her Feminine standpoint being significantly underdeveloped. In Jungian terms, this situation created a vacuum in her inner psyche and resulted in her being "possessed" in a certain sense by the animus. Psychologically, she fell victim to her father complex and passively submitted to her father's values and actions. Realizing the deeper meaning of this dream changed Jade's attitude towards her father. During the process of assimilating the dream, Jade discovered that her conscious love for her father covered a great deal of powerful negative emotion. This resulted in much emotional turmoil for Jade to deal with. Recent research on children of trauma survivors throws some light on Jade's experiences. It shows that children whose parents have suffered from complex post traumatic stress disorder suffer from the same symptoms.[6] Through dissociation, the horrors the parents once endured are visited upon their children and passed on both directly and indirectly.

Although Jade felt compassion for her father, then a broken old man who had never been given an opportunity for treatment and healing, she had come to the point where she realized that she was at times almost incapacitated by the rage she felt at him for dragging the whole family into the chaos of his camp experience, and for depriving her through this of her right to live a normal family life. Another dream soon followed:

> A famine has overtaken the land. But I am not afraid. Father has taught me how to make use of raw material in nature. He shows me how to cook by stir-frying the air-roots from the big old trees with ginger.

The tree symbolizes the union of the cosmic realm of the subterranean-chthonic, or terrestrial life, with heaven. In all cultures, the tree is ritually revered as the image of divine essence and as the residence of numinous powers. The big old tree is the symbol *par excellence* of individuation, the natural maturation of the personality. In the East, the air-roots that grow on very old trees have deep symbolic meaning. Called "*chi* root," they are believed to represent the life-giving power of *chi* because they exist in the realm of the sun and represent illumination and spiritual development. At the same time, because they hang downward, they represent our roots. Ginger, a medicinal herb, is one of the most important botanicals in the Chinese *materia medica*. This root is held to have great healing power and is often used for problems related to the female reproductive organs and to the digestive, cardiac, and circulatory systems.[7]

The dream ego is being shown a route to survival that involves a combination of air-roots from heaven above and ginger root from earth below. This is, in other words, a union of opposites that must be brought together through cooking – here, the analytical process – with fire, heat, and emotion.[8] This is a powerful clue for Jade that her one-sided intellectual development, devoted to the acquisition of Western scientific knowledge, may have given her success in the outer world, but it had caused inner suffering through spiritual starvation. It is the father's peasant wisdom, which represented a reconnection to the Mother Earth, that Jade needed to assimilate as a way of nourishing herself in her psychic famine.

These two dreams introduced considerable turmoil into Jade's emotional life. Her ambivalent feelings towards her father were pulling her in opposing directions. The intensity of this tension brought on the following dream, which had profound significance in Jade's healing journey.

I was in my childhood home. A man outside was calling for customers to buy his white-sugar-cake. I went out and saw that there was an old woman, about 70, also selling and in a quiet way, getting all the customers. The young man got angry and slapped her. She started to cry.

Two old women came along to console her and walked her home. As she walked away, one of her (black cotton) shoes fell off and she bent down to pick it up. The women helped her to put the shoe on. I noticed that her feet were bound in layers of white cloth.

I was then walking along an unpaved road in a village in China. I passed by a hut and saw an old woman inside, sitting by her bed. She had bound feet. I stopped at the door and asked her politely if she would let me see her feet.

She said: "That's a big secret, you know, a woman always keeps her bound feet to herself, never reveals them to anyone." But then she proceeded to unravel the cloth around her feet. I said in my grandmother's dialect: "I am amazed to still see women with bound feet." The cloth was removed and her feet revealed, two stumps. There were only traces of her [four] toes, her heels were small though intact. She said that her toes had grown inward.

Another old woman, her neighbor, came along and showed me her feet. The neighbor said she had bigger feet because she didn't start binding until she was 16. Her heels were closer to the natural shape but her toes were stretched in all directions due to the binding. I said: "Why bother?" The old woman said: "It depends on your father. If he said 'Yes', you'd have to do it. If he said 'No', then you don't have to."

It was too warm to wear the black cloth shoes in the summer and the neighbor had straw sandals made with lots of openings for her toes. I looked at her sandals and wondered how they would compare to my leather shoes which were hand-made and reinforced with much sole support.

Bewildered by the archaic motif of the women with bound feet, Jade pondered the deeper meaning of this dream. Increasingly shaken to the depths of her being, she continued to think about the feet, the stumps, and was led to question her own Feminine standpoint, her relationship to the earth and reality. This process brought her back to her Chinese roots and with this, the grief and rage of her life as a "filial daughter." She mourned for the unlived life of the silenced child whom she had left behind for the sake of her "ambition."

In the dream, although white-sugar-cake (a precious sweetmeat among peasants) was still being sold, the manner in which the selling was done, in other words the relationship pattern, was changing, with inevitable conflicts. The young man hustler and the old woman represent the collision between the old, simple way of life and the new, extroverted and aggressive Western approach toward living. The dream ego shows that the traditional way may still have its value, as represented by the silent receptivity of the old woman.

The repressed Feminine standpoint represented by the old women with bound feet suggests the various levels and intensity with which the "secret" may be assimilated. Jade associated age 16 with the period in which she had a close relationship with her father, whose influence gave her the motivation to study abroad. Her ambition and her acquired standpoint, though directly related to her father, came at a relatively late age; the deformed feet that are closer to natural shape therefore serve as images for this development. The deeper level of the Feminine, the original roots of the Earth Mother, find their symbol in the stumps with toes all grown inward. This is one of the first clues for Jade that her journey would involve the unbinding of her own feet, so that her toes – now deformed and grown inward – can change direction and grow outward so that they can touch Mother Earth the way they do when a child stands barefoot and "digs her toes" into the cool, damp earth. This image is the secret revealed to the dream ego, suggesting that she has the possibility of accessing and assimilating its symbolic meaning and, in the end, regaining her standpoint. The dream ends with the dreamer comparing the straw sandals of the women with her own leather shoes, a symbol *par excellence* of Western technology and materialism. For Jade, it remained to be seen if the Western standpoint was capable of containing her feet once she had unbound them or if there would be a good fit between her Chinese feet and the Western traditions and values she had been exposed to – in other words, whether Jade would be able to integrate Eastern and Western values in her life.

As Jade searched further inward, she confronted her own inner darkness, which had incapacitated her. She began to question the way her feet had been bound; she realized that having her "standpoint" bound was tantamount to having her whole being wrapped up in the binding cloth. Enshrouded in this darkness, she felt numb, suffocated. She struggled with every breath, which took her a step at a time into the void of her original existence. In encountering her darkness, she wrote in her journal:

> What is my standpoint? Do I have one? My parents used to boast to their friends of my usefulness. Only because I was an obedient child and faithfully catered to their needs. In the name of filial piety, the child in me was silenced before she ever uttered a word. Fear kept me quiet. Working and serving kept me busy. Doing a perfect job helped me to survive. How do I dare to know myself? All I wanted to say was No, No, NO! I want to play!

> My mother kept me as her investment so that I'd obediently hand her my salary with the expected gratitude. My father kept me as his "child bride," his glorified little achiever. They just want an obedient, dutiful slave. To allow me to grow up into an adult would be counterproductive and too threatening for them.

> Do I have any sense of direction in life when my feet don't even touch the ground, when my toes don't ever feel the earth? All these years of taking orders, I pleased the others but I have abandoned myself. I don't know who and what I am. I hate my parents but this feeling makes me feel guilty and "unfilial." It's futile to blame them and make them accountable. I must find myself.

Once convinced of the need to find her own direction in life, Jade embarked on her inner journey with total devotion. Her discipline and training became her most precious resources as she began to unravel the bindings and journey into the unknown. She started to live an introverted life, dedicating her energy to the psychic material that had emerged from her inner world. She withdrew into her own loneliness consciously, sinking into her innermost nature to connect with the unhurt virgin ground in her soul. Through body work and movement therapy, she concentrated on the somatic manifestations of her psyche. In this period of introversion or incubation, she tried to connect with her instinct, her feeling, her "toes that have grown inward," seeking her inner compass and the original oneness of her being. Supported by the structure of the analytical process, Jade's inner conviction gave her the faith and strength to embark further on this journey into the soul. In a recurring dream motif during this period, Jade saw herself walking on her own natural river bed. This lovely image encouraged her to continue her walks and to keep moving forward on her natural feet.

As she spent an increasing amount of time and money on her inner world – having bodywork done, taking workshops that deepened her awareness, and continuing with her analysis, she endured an increasing amount of criticism from the "outer" world. Some of her friends ridiculed her for "investing in herself instead of real estate." Her mother openly derided her and described her – an unmarried woman in her early thirties – as "an old maid gone crazy." In Jungian terms, this could be looked at as an onslaught from the collective shadow. Ironically, it is the natural wisdom that she inherited from her father that helped her connect with the deep meaning of sacrifice and come to terms with what she had to lose in order to regain her Feminine standpoint. In this search for her Feminine, Jade necessarily came into contact with the Mother image in her psyche and her relationship with her mother. She dreamt:

> I went to see my analyst, who took me into a submarine and we went down to the ocean floor. I saw the fish swimming by in the water. I have a long scarf with me that I have knitted in grade school. It is made up of two patterns, the plain stitch that my grandmother taught me and the cross stitch as taught by mother. I was to unravel the plain stitch and replace it with the cross stitch.

The ocean is the symbol of the unconscious, which contains the primordial beginnings of all life. To go down to the ocean floor suggests the depth of Jade's process at this stage of her analysis. The submarine represents the strength of the ego structure in her psychic journey at a time when unconscious contents are being activated. This is suggested by the fish – often a symbol for our unconscious thoughts – that are swimming around. The main task at this stage in Jade's identity search was symbolized by the scarf, representing the differentiation between her relationship with her paternal grandmother and her biological mother.

Jade was unable to say much about her feelings for her grandmother. When Jade was born her grandmother was only 46 years old and had been a widow since her early thirties. Soon after birth, Jade was given over to her grandmother as a substitute daughter. From birth until when Jade started school, she lived with her grandmother full time, and then for the next several years moved back and forth between her parents' home and her grandmother's. The grandmother was quite open that her intention in this was to cultivate Jade to provide companionship in her old age. Although allowing a child in a big family to be informally "adopted" by another family member has long been an accepted tradition in Chinese families, it still left Jade with feelings of confusion and abandonment. This was especially true because Jade felt no emotional connection with her whatsoever. One reason for this was that her grandmother, who had not converted to Christianity when the rest of the family had, became obsessed with Buddhism and spent countless hours making offerings, going to temples, and engaging in other Buddhist practice. Although Jade felt abandoned by this, she also absorbed some of her grandmother's spirituality on an unconscious level. She later discovered this to be a significant factor in her healing process.

Over time a power struggle over Jade developed between her grandmother and her mother. For this and a number of other reasons, Jade's relationship with her mother was precarious. As Jade began to explore this relationship, it became apparent that her mother emerged from the camp experience cold and ruthless. Jade described her as clever, efficient, controlling, and abusive. Married at the age of 17, she gave birth to two sons who both died in infancy. She treated their early deaths as a nuisance and didn't even bother to bury them. There was an intense power struggle between Jade's father and mother, who fought frequently over the control of their business. Inevitably, Jade became a "ping pong" caught in the power play between her parents. Her mother usually gained the upper hand, given her father's instability, and she was able to rule the family and the business with an iron hand. Eventually Jade's closeness to her father and her grandmother forged an alliance capable of counter-balancing the power of her mother in the family. Jade's relationship with her mother, whom she served obediently, was one of fear, dislike, and distant admiration.

The connection between Jade's feelings toward her mother as opposed to her grandmother, and the attendant conflicts, brought forth the following dream:

> I walk into a cathedral. At the vestibule, a big cross with Christ on it was laid flat on the floor. Christ then got up from the cross and walked along the aisle to the front toward the altar. In awe, I followed him, thinking: "what a beautiful body, I'd love to make love with him."

In this dream, the meaning of the crucifixion and the spirit of Christ becomes a living human reality, no longer an ideal to be worshipped. The crucifix symbolizes Christ's suffering, his death, and resurrection. Psychologically, crucifixion in Jung's words "is a symbolic expression for the state of extreme conflict, where one has to give up, where one no longer knows, where one almost loses one's mind. Out of that condition grows the thing which is really fought for . . . the birth of the self."[9]

The grounding of the crucifix reflects the reality of Jade's intense conflict, not merely intellectual understanding, but suffering to be endured. Christ coming off the cross and walking toward the altar suggests that the symbolic meaning of Christ as "divine essence within" offers the possibility of redemption. The progression toward the altar, the ritual ascent to the spiritual centre, reflects the direction of psychic energy toward the acceptance of death, suffering, and sacrifice. The desire of the dream ego for union with Christ is the longed-for sacred marriage, the *hieros gamos*, with Christ as the true bridegroom. The longing for the spiritual union is the search for the integration of the soul, for one's wholeness, and the possibility to live a full life.[10]

Confronting deeply buried insoluble conflicts, Jade had come face to face with Christ. The abandoned child in her knew the meaning of what he said on the cross: "My God, my God, why hast thou forsaken me?" An aspect of the symbol of the cross is the need for utter endurance of the conflict before the "solution" – what Jung calls "the third" – can emerge, through the passion of crucifixion and resurrection.[11] Paradoxically, this ritual ascent expressed in Jade's dream led her deeper into the abyss. The conflict was no longer in her head; it transcended verbal discussion. For hours, Jade's suffering could be expressed only in silence, as she mourned the abandoned child within herself. The terror of abandonment, its despair and pain, are reflected in a recurring dream motif of an abandoned baby on the roadside, naked and clad in diapers. The appearance of this dream often provoked a somatic reaction in Jade that resulted in bodily convulsions. In the midst of the ongoing pain, she dreamt:

> Everything has been taken away from me, I have nothing left. Even the jade gold ring that my aunt gave me is gone, gone, gone. I am naked, running along the road, crying at the top of my voice: *ah-ah-ah-ah!* Cars passed by, but they don't stop for me . . . I AM ALONE . . .

The ring made of jade and gold had deep significance, and not only because it was Jade's namesake. From time immemorial in China, jade has been considered the most precious of stones. It is a symbol of vital energy, cosmic forces, virtue, and beauty. It is also valued as the medicinal agent that grants immortality. It is even believed that it can protect the bodies of the deceased from decay. Gold is, of course, the most precious metal. As mentioned earlier in this book, it is associated with incorruptibility and immortality, and symbolizes consciousness in the alchemical transformation process. The ring is a symbol of union, that factor which creates relatedness and points towards the completion. Thus, for Jade, the jade gold ring expressed a positive connection with the world, the possibility of love, and creative activity.[12] It was clear she must find it.

In the depth and stillness of her despair, Jade remembered her connection to her aunt, who was also her wet nurse, from whom she received emotional parenting. In remembering, she was reconnecting to the love that was forcibly cut off by her mother once she became aware of Jade's affection for the aunt. As she began to remember the early bonding with her aunt and the nurturing she received from her, Jade became aware that this was virtually the only real emotional connection she had as a child. The only exception to this was the affection she received from the nannies she sometimes had – and these women were often fired as soon as Jade became attached to them.

Jade was aware that her mother did this not because she was afraid of losing Jade's love, but because she was worried that she might lose Jade's loyalty and with it the "future investment tool" that Jade represented to her. Thinking back on the way she felt when her mother began to use every means possible to keep her away from her aunt, Jade recalled: "I became like a lost puppy not knowing to whom I belonged." As Jade reconnected with the depth of this sense of abandonment, she also came face to face with her rage. She wrote in her journal:

> I feared and dreaded looking into my darkness, *the* darkness. This torment gave me no peace. All along it was the rage that kept me going. The layers of "binding cloth" kept me "in place." But every day I lived with the fear that this time-bomb would one day explode, releasing this rage that can kill, but would also annihilate myself.

At this point, struggling with her rage was an agonizing torture for Jade. Her torment and inertia started to erupt in severe body symptoms. The body functions related to the liver, the organ associated with anger in Chinese medicine, were thrown into upheaval. Her right leg, which is where the liver meridian is located, even became paralyzed. No apparent reason for this could be found by Western doctors. Psychologically, Jade felt the intensity of the devouring power of rage, as she wrote in her journal:

> This rage is Plutonian Rage. It is a powerful force that is much greater than myself, and I can't fight against it. I had to choose between death and the possibility of life. I have come to the end of the stairs, and the only way to go is to take the LEAP . . .

> All of a sudden, I see the rage in its entirety, the whole inherited rage of all Chinese women, my mother, my grandmother, my aunt, my nanny . . . who have all lived their dutiful lives with their concealed rage, merely struggling to survive from being annihilated and managing to stay afloat in the sea of their pain, in silent despair . . .

In surrendering to this power, Jade experienced the Self.

> For days, in this stillness, all I saw around me, smelt and felt in my guts was EARTH, EARTH, EARTH and nothing else. I asked myself if I was going crazy. In my deep solitude, my body symptoms disappeared and slowly I regained my bearings. I felt the Primal Feminine, the eternal essence of being a woman from the beginning. I feel the inner joy of being I AM.

As Jade sunk into the rage she felt, she experienced what in Jungian terms is known as *"enantiodromia,"* which literally means "running counter to." This refers to a phenomenon in which an extremely dominating emotion or tendency swings to the other end of the spectrum and is replaced by its opposite. It is almost as if the emotion, in this case the rage, holds within itself the seeds of its own transformation. An *enantiodromia* often fore-shadows a rebirth, and this was true in Jade's case.[13] She dreamt:

> I saw an attractive Chinese woman dressed in an official gown of a high-ranking mandarin. But she had small bound feet. I wondered what and who she was and hastened to get my camera to take a photograph of her.
>
> By the time I got my camera, she had changed into a bright red dress. It was in Chinese style with a high collar and slits on the sides. Her hair was tied up in a chignon. She looked very sexy. I noticed that she was in high-heel shoes that were about one and a half inches high, and her feet didn't seem as small or deformed as before. She was posing for me, dancing back and forth in a lively manner, enjoying the snap shots.
>
> I went into the front room and saw her with an old woman who was holding her in an embrace, walking with her back and forth as in a slow waltz. This was in the kitchen where they lived. They had a double sink and I saw clean dishes on the dish rack.
>
> I asked what the two were doing in the kitchen. The young woman told me that her mother was helping her to let out her feet by stretching, massaging her toes and walking her feet, which have made improve-ments. I was amazed that the bound feet could be let out. Compared with her appearance in her other outfit, her feet did seem bigger in the high-heeled shoes.

The woman in the scholar-official gown with bound feet embodies the ideal Confucian Masculine and Feminine, both of which have been robbed of their original standpoint by the rigid morals and institutions that governed Chinese society during the past two millennia. In a certain sense the ideal man was robbed of his standpoint by Confucian standards just as women were by footbinding. Personified in the scholar-official, this ideal man was completely defined by his mastery of the Confucian Classics and the achievement of bureaucratic office. Given this exceedingly narrow and constrictive definition of success and fulfillment, it is little wonder he wanted to exert control over family and in particular the women. The woman, in turn, was – as we have seen throughout the book – one who had no standpoint, who passively accepted the feminine ethics of obedience and loyalty as defined by the patriarchy. That the dream ego attempts to take a photograph of this disempowered figure who is no longer relevant in this age suggests her desire to make conscious its inherited impact in her psychic development.

Jade saw this embodiment in herself and struggled to redeem it. She felt that the liberation of woman from her traditional roles in the absence of an adequate alternative model merely channeled feminine energy into masculine roles. Jade realized that this was in fact a curse in disguise, for without her own natural Feminine standpoint, a woman risks being possessed by doing and achieving and becomes "a little man with bound feet." The transformation is personified in the young dancing woman.

This dream takes place in the kitchen, the place where food is chemically transformed. In China, cooking and the kitchen have been connected with alchemy since pre-Buddhist times. Psychologically, the kitchen is analogous to the stomach, which symbolizes the centre of emotion in its searing and consuming aspect. Also, the illuminating and warming functions found in the kitchen are often thought to symbolize how the light of wisdom comes only out of the fire of passion. In alchemy, the secret of psychological transformation is said to lie in rekindling the sacred fire within, the spiritual centre in oneself that gives meaning to one's life.

The double sink and the clean dishes in the dream also reflect the alchemical process of psychological transformation. It is a process of self-recollection through carefully discriminating, clarifying, integrating, and consciously assimilating inner psychic contents. It is a process necessary in the psychological development of the Feminine principle. In this sense, the "kitchen" in the dream is the place that helps promote the natural process of growth, transformation, and maturation in the psyche.

As Jade began to interpret the symbols in the dream for herself, she remembered learning that, since ancient times in China, the kitchen has been the centre of the house cults. On one level, she associated the young woman with the original hearth spirit, who according to some texts is dressed in bright red, resembling fire, and appears as a lovely, attractive maiden. For Jade, the old woman seemed to represent the soul of departed cooks, the most primitive kitchen deity, who was originally female.[14] At the mystical level, Jade saw the two women as personifying the primal image of the sacred fire in the centre. This was a powerful and positive image for Jade.

That the old woman represented the soul of departed cooks was another positive symbol for Jade, for she saw the "cook" as providing the psychological qualities of nurturance and transformation – elements that are necessary if a higher consciousness is to be attained. For Jade, the dancing young woman in red, traditionally a color worn by brides, represented spring and the emergence of a new libido that is in constant movement and in direct relationship to the earth. In the dream, the old woman was the mother who helped the younger woman, the daughter, to let out her bound feet, in other words to re-establish her repressed standpoint and her connection to the Feminine. As a symbol of the rejected and forgotten Earth Mother, the old woman also needed the daughter to come to light. In this way, the two figures constitute a binding relationship. From the mother, the daughter is reborn, while the daughter is the newly and consciously discovered self for the mother. The relationship between mother and daughter signifies the fullness of Life.[15]

With this dream, Jade became much more relaxed and centered. In her contemplations, she was able to muse over the paradox of her abandonment. Her experience of the Mother image had been split in three ways, between her biological mother, her grandmother who served as her spiritual mother, and her aunt (also her wet nurse) who was her nurturing and emotional mother. These three images plus that of her analyst – who provided the container for her journey – made the "four" and, thus, formed the Feminine totality within which transformation became possible.

As Jade considered the issues around her abandonment more deeply, she began to realize that it forced her to embark upon the process of individuation at an early age. She came to realize that abandonment was a deeply rooted problem in her family and perhaps in her culture. Her grandmother, who was born at the turn of the 20th century, was abandoned at the age of ten by her father who left for Thailand to search for better opportunities as countless young Chinese men did at the time. He never returned. She was soon betrothed in a match of convenience so that her mother could adopt a son to perform sacrificial rites after her death. By the time she was 31 her husband had died and custom forbade that she remarry. At that time, Jade's father was only a little boy of seven so he, too, experienced abandonment.

Jade's mother had fared no better. Born to a mother who was already 45, an age considered extremely old for motherhood in those days, she was thought of as an "accident." Enraged by the fact that the child was not a boy, she actually attempted to drown the infant. She then determined she would keep the girl child to serve as her maid in old age. To underscore this, she kept the child's head shaved throughout her youth. Like Jade's grandmother, her aunt was also abandoned by her father who also left China for Thailand in his youth and never returned. Trapped in an unhappy traditional marriage, Jade's aunt had no way out. As Jade became increasingly conscious of how these women had suffered, she began to feel great compassion for them and their life struggle.

Once Jade came to this state of compassion and understanding, she was able to utilize their strength to help her through the rest of her journey. The internalized spirituality of her grandmother was no longer idealized or abstract and could be brought into her consciousness. The intelligence and discipline that she learned from her mother, and the natural wisdom of her aunt's peasant roots, helped her to persist in finding her natural life path. In her search, Jade consciously entered introversion and surrendered to her inner process. In her solitude, she got in touch with her feelings and emotions, her own natural instinct as a woman, which had never been allowed in the Chinese culture. In the turmoil of her darkness, she finally saw the light. She dreamt:

> I realized that I have been living in Jung's house all this time and now the time has come to take my leave. I have to go through a ritual that takes place in the basement. I am to descend in an elevator down many floors to the basement where there is a pool. The first step of the ceremony is to immerse myself in water as in baptism. I have brought my bathing suit with me and also some casual clothing to wear afterwards, exactly the way it was when I was baptized in a Christian church in Hong Kong before leaving for the United States.

> The baptism was over, I felt the wet bathing suit on my body. Then I am swimming in a lake and for the first time in my life, I don't feel anxious in the water and was swimming back and forth in the vast expanse of water. My two younger brothers were also swimming close by me in the water. Then the lake was drained for some purpose and I was sitting on a rock on the floor of the lake, overwhelmed by the sight of the bottom of the lake, the mud, seaweed and bushes etc.

This dream suggested the completion of the journey which Jade had embarked on. Jade's encounter with the unconscious was contained and protected by the structure of the analytical process she went through which is symbolized in the dream by Jung's house. The distance from the basement of Jung's house to the floor of the lake reflects the depth of Jade's analytical work. She had taken the courage to plunge into the depth of her soul and emerged, transcendent, as a new person with her own inner authority. Jade had discovered her sense of inner autonomy and meaning.

This experience of the transcendent is what Jung calls "the third," which he said is arrived at through the passion of crucifixion and resurrection. Jung wrote:

> If one is sufficiently conscientious, the conflict is endured to the end, and a creative solution emerges which is produced by the constellated archetype and possesses that compelling authority not unjustly characterized as the voice of God. The nature of the solution is in accord with the deepest foundation of the personality as well as with its wholeness; it embraces conscious and unconscious and therefore transcends the ego.[16]

Jade had indeed endured and was ready to depart from Jung's house. Her departure was to be solemnized by baptism through immersion, which symbolizes the return to the primordial waters of life. It is an initiation for spiritual rebirth. As a rite, it purifies, revitalizes, and protects. For Jade, swimming in the lake meant getting back into the natural flow of life. Jade discovered that lakes are sometimes symbolically interpreted as the earth's "open eye." As both consisting of water and being a place where subterranean beings dwell, the lake is one of the most potent symbols of the Feminine, the unconscious, and the source of creative power. In this source of eternal Feminine power, Jade was re-united with her young brothers who here represent aspects of her newly found inner Masculine. Jade's feet were now well on the way to being unbound, she reconnected with the Feminine, and she replaced the old authoritarian Father image who controlled her life with a fresh, new, positive Masculine. She was clearly ready to stand on her own two feet and walk out of Jung's house, healed and whole, ready to meet the world on her own terms.

Through the process of unbinding her feet, Jade gained a living experience of the *tao* and with it, her reconnection to her ancient Chinese roots. Throughout this process the image of Dr. Yeung from her initial dream stayed with Jade. Increasingly this image reawakened the passion she had had in childhood for Chinese medicine. During the time she spent in analysis, Jade also explored Chinese alchemy and practiced T'ai Chi and Qigong. Soon after having the above dream Jade made the decision to enter the field of Chinese medicine. After a number of years of study, she graduated and started a clinic and did pro bono work every Friday. As a survivor, Jade found meaning in the healing professions. She continues to be amazed by the "miracle of the soul," and the resilience of the spirit, whose spark has sustained her throughout her life. On a personal level, with her heart wide open, Jade and her long-time partner finally tied the knot. In their conjugal bliss, they began to contemplate starting a family.

Notes

1 Lee Fung-lin, ed., *Shan Hai Ching*, Taiwan: San Min, 1987 [text in Chinese].
2 Marie-Louise von Franz, *Alchemy: An Introduction to the Symbolism and the Psychology*, Toronto: Inner City Books, 1980, p. 220.
3 Marie-Louise von Franz, *Introduction to the Interpretation of Fairy Tales*, Houston, TX: Spring Publications, 1970, pp. 140–1.
4 Ibid., pp. 171, 220–2.
5 Marie-Louise von Franz, *Individuation in Fairy Tales*, Houston, TX: Spring Publications, 1977, p. 41; *Shadow and Evil in Fairy Tales*, Houston, TX: Spring Publications, 1974, p. 264. See also Emma Jung, *Animus and Anima*, Houston, TX: Spring Publications, 1978.
6 Bessel A. van der Kolk, ed., *Traumatic Stress: The Effects of Overwhelming Experience on Mind, Body and Society*, New York: The Guilford Press, pp. 182–213.

7 Richard Lucas, *Secrets of the Chinese Herbalists*, New York: Parker Publishing, 1987, pp. 12–14, 144–6, 207.
8 Marie-Louise von Franz, *Introduction to the Interpretation of Fairy Tales*, op. cit., pp. 220–2.
9 Carl G. Jung, 'A Psychological View of Consciousness', in *Civilization in Transition*, CW 10, para. 856.
10 Marie-Louise von Franz, *Alchemy*, op. cit., p. 137; Marion Woodman, *The Ravaged Bridegroom*, Toronto: Inner City Books, 1990, pp. 101, 123.
11 Marion Woodman, ibid., pp. 65, 156.
12 Marie-Louise von Franz, *Introduction to the Interpretation of Fairy Tales*, op. cit., pp. 57–60, 87–8, 117; *The Psychological Meaning of Redemption Motifs in Fairy Tales*, Toronto: Inner City Books, 1980, p. 75.
13 Stephen Martin, 'Anger as Transformation', *Quadrant*, Spring (1986), pp. 31–45.
14 Carl G. Jung, *Symbols of Transformation*, CW 5, para. 663; Charles A. S. Williams, *Outlines of Chinese Symbolism and Art Motives*, third revised edition, New York: Dover Publications, 1976, pp. 210–11.
15 Marie-Louise von Franz, *The Problem of the Feminine in Fairy Tales*, op. cit., pp. 151–2; Carl G. Jung, 'The Psychological Aspects of the Kore', in Jung, Carl and Kerényi, Carl, eds., *Essays on a Science of Mythology*, Princeton, NJ: Bollingen Foundation, 1949, pp. 101–51; Carl Kerényi, 'Kore', ibid., pp. 156–65.
16 Carl G. Jung, 'A Psychological View of Consciousness', op. cit.

Chapter 11

Reflections on footbinding and the Golden Lotus

As I reflect on my life living in Zurich, I feel deeply moved by the encounter with the old Chinese lady whose bound feet helped revive my childhood memories of bound feet in various contexts. I became increasingly preoccupied with the Chinese custom of footbinding and pondered over the psychological meaning of the devaluation and repression of the Feminine as it relates to my own cultural roots. Eventually I was led to embark on an extensive exploration of the socio-cultural history of this phenomenon, in the hope of elucidating its impact on the psyche of modern Chinese women.

My exploration covers a long period and inevitably led me through the labyrinth of the cultural history of China, from the Shang dynasty (1520–1030 BC) to modern times. My principal aim was to decipher the psychological meaning of the practice of footbinding as symbolized in the image of the Golden Lotus. I circumambulate this image in order to obtain an overview and a more holistic understanding of the Feminine embodied within it. As if I were unravelling the "binding cloth," I attempt to reveal gradually the secret of this golden flower in its own natural rhythm, according to its own nature.

At the centre of this book is the paradox of an archaic, brutal practice persisting for over ten centuries in a culture known for its high level of sophistication. The term "Golden Lotus" carries a connotation of elevated spiritual value. Gold signifies immortality, the ultimate goal sought in Chinese alchemy. As an image of natural beauty, the lotus is a symbol for spiritual and mystical qualities. Unfolding from the centre, the flower portrays self-containment and divine bliss, a symbol of man's yearning for the spiritual aspect of the Feminine. Yet when we look at the reality of bound feet, the Golden Lotus is quite the opposite of this elevated spiritual image.

In psychology, the foot generally has a phallic or generative significance. Moreover, we stand upright on our feet to face the world, and our feet carry us in movement. Jung recognizes the feet as expressive of a person's standpoint *vis-à-vis* the external world, one's individual identity and relationship to reality. In addition, a woman's foot is a symbol of fecundity and fertility, in view of her connection to Mother Earth. The Golden Lotus is the deceptively lovely name given to the tiny, mutilated and deformed feet of women in traditional China. The practice of binding a young girl's feet to an ideal size of three inches in the prescribed shape of the New Moon is unique to China, without parallel anywhere else in the world. Such a mutilation cripples a girl for life, taking away the power and freedom of movement and physical strength, eliminating as well any possibility of independence and a self-sustained path in life. The miniature, deformed feet close off and seal a woman's existence within unnaturally restricted limits. Psychologically, footbinding means a suppression and distortion of the natural development of a girl's feminine identity. Yet an understanding of footbinding is compounded by its widespread historical practice, its social popularity, and cultural significance.

Over the millennia, the symbolic meaning of bound feet changed in accordance with the spirit of the times, and I believe its psychological impact is still alive today. As a symbol of filial piety – the basis of Confucian morality and ethics – the Golden Lotus represents the feared and repressed Goddess. It contains the inherited feeling and hidden identity of the violated Goddess that both Confucianism and Taoism shaped during the course of the millennia.

Major historical influences on the Chinese collective psyche contributed to the formation and development of the Golden Lotus. I explore influential images of women from China's past, including the creation goddess Nu Wa; the mythological motif of the last Shang Empress-fox; the ancient figure of Xi Wang Mu (Queen Mother of the West), the Great Mother and ruler of the cosmos; and the tragic, flamboyant 20th-century pioneer for the liberation of women in China, the poet and novelist Chiu Chin. In the course of my exploration, it becomes apparent that both Confucianism and Taoism exerted a considerable impact on the evolution of the collective attitude toward the Feminine and the position of women in society. But they shaped strikingly divergent images of women in the collective Chinese imagination.

During the Shang period, the Mother was the focal point in community life. Earth was revered as a numinous power, and life and death were viewed as a continuous process controlled by Mother Earth. The association of woman with Earth and with the cosmic vital essence of the universe, *chi*, gave woman a special power. The Shang Empress-fox expressed the archaic, elemental nature of the Yellow Earth, the primordial beginning – the nurturing, spiritual aspect as well as the chthonic – of the Earth Mother. This image of the Mother lingered in the Chinese psyche and was later canonized in Taoism.

The Shang world view, through its religious practices, reflected a close relationship between Man and Nature, and the supernatural and natural worlds. The myth of the last Shang Empress-fox binding her feet/paws in the 11th century BC symbolically suggests a changed attitude toward the

Feminine in the collective consciousness. Historically, it marks the fall of Shang to the nomadic Zhou conquerors, whose subsequent rule signaled the beginning of patriarchal consciousness. An indication of this shift is the re-arrangement in 1144 BC of the first two hexagrams in the *I Ching*, for the first time giving predominance to the *yang* principle over the *yin*. This change marks the beginning of a progressively negative attitude toward the Feminine and the inferiority of women in society.

It was during the Zhou dynasty (1030–221 BC) that the foundation of Chinese cultural heritage was consolidated. The Zhou masculine world view, characterized by an impersonal worship of *Tian*, or Heaven, and an emphasis on structure, hierarchy, law and order, governed all aspects of the socio-political organization of China for the next 30 centuries. The cross-fertilization of the masculine Zhou world view with the original Yellow Earth produced the "one hundred schools of philosophy." Among them, two major schools were eventually institutionalized in Confucianism and Taoism. Through political endorsement during the Han dynasty (202 BC–AD 220), Confucianism came to represent the dominant collective consciousness. But Taoism, with its roots in the primordial beginnings of the Earth and the soil, continued to nourish the collective psyche. Subsequently, Han Confucianism reinforced the patriarchal, patrilineal structure of Chinese society, in the service of a centralized unified empire. The Han initiative can be seen as a further step in masculine and cultural development in the collective consciousness. To enhance his power the Han emperor appropriated, as his new symbol of patriarchal authority, the emblem of the Dragon formerly associated with Xi Wang Mu, the ruler of the Cosmos. This re-arrangement of the myth reflects a definitive masculine bias.

Over the centuries, Confucianism and then Neo Confucianism have served the primary political function of ensuring the authority and continuity of the bureaucratic state. The patriarchal family was viewed as a miniature state, and ancestor worship was officially extended to all classes of society. The maintenance of the collective as a unified whole was given priority, and individualism was suppressed – at the cost of creativity and cultural development. This suppression culminated in cultural stagnation and the degeneration of Chinese society during the last two centuries, leading to the fall of the Qing dynasty in 1911, thus ending China's Imperial rule forever.

The May Fourth Movement of 1916, in attacking Confucianism and demanding major reforms in all institutions, signaled an expansion of consciousness. Partly the result of Western contacts and influences, this movement arose also out of the more basic recognition that new interpretations of the archetypes were urgently needed to bring them into accord with the changed spirit of the times. However, the young radicals who initiated this movement were imprisoned or killed. The right-wing New Life Movement of 1933 dealt with this crisis by eliminating the worship of many deities, including the ones of the Earth and soil, in favor of Christianity. The subsequent repeal of the Penal Code belatedly gave women their legal rights, but no mention was made of ancestor worship, which traditionally defined the status of women. The Chinese Revolution of 1949 eliminated ancestor worship altogether in favor of Marxism–Leninism. Thus, what began as the original religion of China, serving the people psychologically through rites of renewal, was eliminated in favor of a foreign god and a foreign ideology. China has been in a spiritual crisis ever since, and the original meaning of this ancient institution has yet to be recovered.

Taoism has filled the vacuum created in the collective psyche by the rationalistic ethical outlook of Confucianism. The revival of fertility cults devoted to Xi Wang Mu paved the way for the growth of the Taoist church. The Taoist alchemical opus represents a way of psychological liberation from the bondage of social and familial demands. The "inner elixir" aims for the experience of *tao*, the birth of a new consciousness, symbolized by the hexagram *fu*, returning–beginning. In this process, one returns to the Source, the root of one's original personality, to regain the beginning of one's life. This work seeks a reconnection to the pure *yin* as the source of the true *yang*. Returning to the Source is understood as reconnecting the Dragon to the woman as the embodiment of the Great Mother.

Unfortunately, over the years, sexual alchemy among certain sects lost its original meaning and degenerated into sexual exploitation of women. The treatment of women as sexual objects was justified by the "quest for the elixir." This magical belief fuelled the popularity of bound feet and the worship of the Golden Lotus as a love fetish. Taken concretely as the embodiment of Matter, the Golden Lotus reflects a regressive urge to the *yin* world. Even today, "the completion of *yang* through *yin*" is the slogan men use in their sexual exploits and their sojourns in brothels, and it is used in advertisements for the marketing of aphrodisiacs. The deeply rooted chauvinistic attitude helped to perpetuate the belief in the danger of the *yin* soul, and women had to carry the burden of its projection. The notoriety of fox-spirits and their association with women as incubi persists today as men's mistresses are often thus described.

Over the centuries, the dynamic interaction between Confucianism and Taoism produced divergent images of women in the collective imagination. Women came to be viewed as morally inferior, weak, subordinate, and sexually exploitable as well as sexually insatiable, powerful, and dangerous. Without a spiritual attitude, reconnection with *yin* is impossible and the true *yang* cannot be experienced. The Feminine thus remains in the shadow; the real woman remains imprisoned and untouched in the "inner chamber." The redemption of the Feminine has become a difficult, complicated, and arduous task.

Against this background, Chiu Chin (1875–1907), whose story is told in Chapter 7, was truly a pioneer in her career as reformer, political activist, educator, writer, and poet. She wholeheartedly fought for the emancipation of women against the oppressive family system and, in particular, the archaic practice of footbinding. Her life story echoed that of the heroine Nora in Ibsen's *A Doll's House*, which first appeared in China in 1911. The play was a big hit in those revolutionary times and Nora became a national symbol for the emancipation of Chinese women. The play was secretly passed through the hands of Shanghai's prostitutes and Nora became the epitome of the free woman for the prostitutes. The play spurred great debate among the population over the status of women in Shanghai. A few years earlier, Chiu Chin's revolutionary career had been cut short by her beheading. However, many believed that her martyrdom accelerated the revolution and paved the way for change and transformation for women. Under the new Republic, Chiu Chin was admired and praised as the incarnation of Nora even though, in reality, Chiu Chin was never exposed to Ibsen and knew little about Western individualism.[1] *A Doll's House* was first staged by the Spring Willow Troupe in 1914. It gained momentum and became one of the most frequently staged plays in the country. Today, Ibsen's Nora remains the foothold for the emergence of the feminist movement in China.

The May Fourth Movement that soon followed in 1916, the high point of the early women's movement in China, caused more Chinese women to not only unbind their own feet, but to walk out on their families in order to pursue a new world of independence and freedom. However, the future for the Chinese Nora did not appear to be as bright as they had imagined. The new generation of young, aspiring female writers in the 1920s and 1930s revealed in their writings how enormous the task of liberation had been for them. They had to fight to unbind their feet or against having their feet bound, against an arranged marriage, to get an education, to find ways of becoming financially self-sufficient, and so on. This generation of female writers wrote about their unlived adolescence and eventually their recognition of the impossibility of the task they had eagerly and courageously set for themselves. Not only did they have to fight an archaic and brutal custom that began ten centuries earlier, they had to fight their internalized Confucian values which carried the weight of over three millennia.[2]

Chinese women were brought up under the Confucian precepts of Three Obediences and Four Virtues. "When a girl, obey your father; when a wife, obey your husband; when a widow, obey your son." If a girl was reared to maturity before she was abandoned, sold, or given away, marriage was the only way to security and fulfillment by giving birth to a son. But to be marriageable, her feet had to be bound to the ideal size and shape of the three-inch Golden Lotus. In her socialization, she must live according to the feminine virtues of proper conduct, proper speech, proper presentation (of herself), and productivity. Physically, emotionally, and spiritually, a girl who survived her birth was entirely bound to the patriarchy in her body and soul. Can Nora take root in Chinese soil? Can Nora find her identity, freedom, and happiness against the institutional complexities of family and clan?

The struggle of Chinese women since 1900 reveals the psychology of the filial daughter trying to rebel against the Father and fight for her identity. Chiu Chin was a true pioneer in her efforts to give a voice to women's suffering. The enormity of her task in a lone voice made her martyrdom inevitable. In her despair, she prayed to Nu Wa and Xi Wang Mu for their support and blessing when she felt she was coming to the end of the road. She was a much-needed role model for women to have the courage to fight for their right to happiness and freedom.

The post-war years ushered in a period of growth and prosperity that witnessed the explosive growth of the Baby Boomers. The Chinese diaspora spread to Southeast Asia, North America and Europe. In Chapter 8, the story of Julia Ching (1934–2001) provides an example of how a Chinese woman metaphorically attempted to unbind her feet against the difficulties of her times, as a refugee finding a home in a foreign land. Julia's devotion to the patriarchy first through the Church and later the University led to fame and success but resulted in a one-sided development in which her Feminine and feeling side was neglected. In her memoir, Julia acknowledged that the neglect of her body probably resulted in the recurrent breast cancers that eventually took her life. She prayed to Nu Wa and Xi Wang Mu for their support and blessing. Her last dream, which showed her praying to the Madonna and Child, revealed her longing for connection with the Feminine. In her reflections, "butterfly healing" – the title of her memoir – was the last message that she shared with the world. It was an internal dialogue with the soul that encapsulates the self-realization of an accomplished woman who did not have sufficient time to enjoy her own hard-won Feminine wisdom.

The analytical process of several contemporary women told through the stories of Pearl, Ruby, and Jade (in chapters 4, 9, and 10) reveals in greater detail the complex psychic happenings and the inner dynamics of the psychology of footbinding, even though these women never had their feet bound like their grandmothers. The dreams and journals accompanying their inner journey reflected a psychology centered upon survival through adaptation to the environment at the expense of personal growth. Their experience suggests the psychology of the abandoned child whose "active doing" reflects an unconscious need for love and validation, and a struggle for self-worth.[3] In their upbringing, achievement and perfection formed the foundation of their self-esteem in adolescence and early adulthood, while fear, shame, and guilt became the central emotions associated with their authority-complex structure. Driven to perform and "to do a good job," these women developed a pattern of pleasing others, while they were filled with a sense of inadequacy and inferiority. Whatever they did, it had to be perfect – but it was never good enough. The striving to perform and please the Father had no limit; they were driven until the energy became autonomous, they panicked and plunged into the "black hole."

These young women suffered from a similar pattern of "possession," and they all entered analysis because of it. Their depression was the symptom of their struggle for life, as they feared being devoured by their own inner darkness, the void of their emptiness. Hidden in this darkness and emptiness is the abandoned child who needs to be redeemed. Research by Zurich Jungian analyst Kathrin Asper-Bruggisser on abandonment and narcissistic disorders suggests that the constant battle for a well-balanced feeling of self-worth would leave the abandoned child very limited freedom and energy to turn toward herself, to develop herself. Being uprooted early on in life, she would be cut off from the ground of her being and from the pattern of her own life. Uprootedness means self-alienation and an insecure footing. This situation may result in a rudimentary formation of the ego–self axis, and an apparently strong ego that is actually weak and needs to be solidified. The abandoned child survives through what Neumann calls an "emergency ego," which develops out of the need to combat the threat of annihilation both inwardly and outwardly.[4] The life experiences of these contemporary Chinese Noras suggest that they have concretely lived through the archetype of the abandoned child and have unconsciously searched for the divine child. This spiritual search has become the theme of their lives. They survived by adopting a perfectionist persona in which lies hidden their longing for recognition, acceptance, and love.

Their psychology of survival stems from a family constellation where the father is emotionally absent and narcissistically demanding, while the mother is without empathy, dominated by the Father world, its collective standards, opinions, and values. This family constellation creates in them their deep-rooted feelings of being "bad," unloved, and without the right to live. They learn to adapt, to compromise with external demands, and develop a strategy of survival. Driven to perform, they are psychologically turned into perfect geishas, with their perfectly sized little feet encased in those perfectly made and perfectly embroidered little shoes. But inwardly, they have been frozen, petrified in a static world of fixed laws and fixed authorities. In devoting their lives to justifying their existence, they have not lived but merely existed, without being in touch with their own Being. Behind their life-long striving lies hidden their intense insecurity and fear of life. Their repressed energy hidden in their terror and rage needs to be released and re-directed toward discovering and loving themselves.

Our heroines began their analysis with a professed "close" relationship with their father and explicit love for him. Analysis helped them to demystify their father, uncovering their experience of betrayal and their negative feelings, especially the feeling of being "used" and not loved for who they are. From an early stage, they learned to "tune in" to their father's emotional needs and "to give him of herself 100%." They became the "pearls in their father's palms." They belonged to father and they served father. Psychic incest is inevitable in a situation where the wife is not available to the husband, and the mother is not interested in the well-being of the daughter. Psychologically, the daughter is bound to her father as his child bride. Filial piety is thus a double-edged sword. From a deep psychological perspective, the total loyalty it demands in fact regulates the continual violation of the budding Feminine. She serves the patriarchy and is not allowed to grow to her natural potential. She becomes a bonsai. Blind filial piety is false consciousness. It retards growth and annihilates her soul.

The relationship between mother and daughter is precarious and conflicted. In the Chinese family, the mother's institutional interests lie in the welfare of her son and his agnatic kin. The daughter has no institutionalized role in the family. If a girl is reared to maturity before she is abandoned, sold, or given away, she literally exists at the sufferance of her parents. The hand of maternal love is constrained by the patriarchal family structure to be a hand in betrayal. The mother needs first to safeguard her own interests in the family before she can consider the interests of her daughter. Once married, the daughter is like water poured out of the door. As one who can never requite the expense of rearing her, the daughter does not provide any "return on investment."

Our heroines all reveal negative feelings toward their mothers, who are described as intelligent, efficient, overbearing, cold, and unfeminine. The loving, caring, nurturing qualities usually associated with the Positive Mother are absent. The Negative or Witch Mother rules the family. Jade's mother comes close to the fairy tale image of the witch in Hansel and Gretel who feeds the children in order to serve her unsatiated greed. Pearl's mother is more or less the evil queen in Snow White, dominated by her exhaustive demands to be adored and mirrored. Ruby's mother compares well with Cinderella's stepmother who, in a castrating way, demands obedience and service, but with no rewards.

These mothers all demand achievement through discipline and hard work toward a goal that has more to do with their own unlived ambition than with the reality of their daughters' life situation. Their unredeemed drives are the phallic energy that would symbolically apply the "binding cloth" ruthlessly to destroy their daughters' feet and their natural standpoint. Cut off from their own instinctive Feminine, they cannot allow, and in fact are incapable of allowing, their daughters to grow into their womanhood. The mother–daughter relationship is characterized by envy and competition. The personal mother is equally absent while the fate of the Positive Mother is precarious. The redemption of the Feminine becomes an arduous and almost impossible task.

In facing their dark night of the soul, our heroines endure pathological mourning experiences. Tears, forbidden and despised in their upbringing, pour out of them. They discover that "there is no need to be ashamed of tears, for tears bore witness that one had the greatest courage, the courage to suffer."[5] The basic experience and condition of this dark side is well described by Neumann in *The Child*.[6] In connecting with their own origin and growth, and in regaining their feelings, our heroines are then able to place themselves in the "here and now" and to keep that "standpoint firmly anchored to the earth." In the analytical process, they are confronted with the rage of the silenced child and with it, the release of repressed energy for further progression in life. Their process can be understood as finding home in oneself, as a discovery of inner affinity, and as a strengthening of self-love.

Through their analysis, our heroines come to see their ambivalent relationships with their personal fathers and with the Father principle, and they are enabled as a result to see their "careers" in context. Re-evaluating their relationships with their personal mothers and with the Feminine principle leads them to contemplate changes in their career that will accommodate their new attitude to life. They were abandoned by the father, but in their newly found Feminine self, they take the courage to abandon Father, in order to live a life that will be guided by their Feminine instincts, their natural yearnings and desires.

However, their close relationship with the Father principle is not entirely negative, for through it they come into contact with the Spirit and thus rediscover their own natural instinctive spirituality. In her dream image of the original kitchen god "as a young woman dressed in red and being cradled and rocked by an older woman who helped to unbind her feet in a slow dance," Jade was able to reconnect with her ancient peasant roots and experienced healing in her psyche. She returned to her childhood passions of Taoist alchemy, yoga, T'ai Chi, and herbal medicine. Pearl's renewed relationship with her mother provided a bridge to the Great Mother as her principal source of cultural identity and protection, especially in view of her family's uprootedness and the turbulent years of sojourn in various countries. She switched to part-time work, began to practice Zen meditation, and developed her own daily rituals of chanting, prayer, and playing the piano. Ruby, in receiving a blessing from her grandmother (with whom she never had contact in reality) in a dream, felt complete in her identity search. Through the dream image of new vision, she achieved a clearer picture of her life path. Ruby became more rooted in herself and confident in being who she is. Together with her partner, they moved to the west coast to begin a new life.

The challenge that our heroines experienced is to bridge the split between nature and spirit through a descent into the unconscious. It is also a descent into the instinctual world of Mother Nature from whom a new spirit can emerge.[7] According to Jung, "Nature itself has a spiritual aim."[8] A woman's life becomes barren if she cannot find spiritual meaning in it.

Through the Masculine spirit, our heroines reach the Feminine principle, which is their own true nature, a nature they had forgotten. Thousands of years of cultural evolution forced them to give up their relationship with this principle. Through the animus, they established a conscious relationship with this true base of their existence. Through dreams and messages from their body, our heroines submitted to their inner laws of nature and reconnected with their original wholeness.

All these young women suffered from psychological footbinding, and all, out of necessity, confronted their inner realms and took the courage to unravel the "binding cloth." In facing their inner darkness, they suffered symbolic death, the threat of inner fragmentation and dissolution. When consciously experienced as surrendering to the Self, symbolic death brings rebirth and psychic renewal. For them, it uncovered the angry, silenced child who can now begin to stand on earth and learn to walk in the "here and now" toward the future. The way will be directed by their own inner promptings as they become increasingly connected with their feelings as women. Jung conceived of depression as a power which presses a person down, but out of which one could emerge with new insights and attitudes. Depression led our heroines to encounter the dark night of their soul and to redeem their Feminine standpoint. In looking into their inner darkness, they also found the courage to be. Their "nigredo," or night sea journey, initiated them into their womanhood.[9]

My exploration of the psychological meaning of the Golden Lotus is an initial attempt to unravel the "binding cloth" that for centuries has been taboo. The traditional daughter endured the initiation of footbinding to become a (child) bride of the patriarchy. Her "career" was dictated by the need for survival and the fear of life. The modern woman needs to go through the initiation of "unbinding her feet" in order to find her Feminine standpoint and become the true bride. Her career is guided by her need for creative self-expression and the passion for life. I feel excited for Pearl, Ruby, and Jade as they embark on a new stage in their lives with their newly found autonomy.

As I ponder various possibilities in their futures, my fantasy keeps bringing me back to the face of the woman stranded in the street who I recalled in my childhood memories. That face is still the most beautiful face that I have ever seen. Its expression belongs to one who has never been exposed, who has lived all her life in the "inner chamber." My fantasy of her fate does not move on, as much as I try. But I am always brought back to her little feet in those beautifully embroidered shoes. My memory of her returns to my original queries about her fate and I come full circle.

However, the image of this woman changed when I moved to Asia after a sojourn of 40 years! Over the last couple of years, my dreams brought me to Asia where I began working with women from Hong Kong, mainland China, Macau, Taiwan, and Singapore. In Asia, I witness the suffering of

Chinese women who are under constant pressure to fight for a better life, who have to struggle for any available opportunities and improvements in their standard of living as well as their material well-being. Survival issues appear to override any considerations for sexism, feminism, and sexual equality. The challenges of life and of living are immediate and their uphill struggles appear endless. Witnessing the intensity of life brings me back to the face of the woman stranded in the street who I recalled in my childhood memories. I can still remember the terror in her eyes as she stared into empty space. But now I see her face everywhere, the same terror in the eyes, but that quiet dignity is gone. She is busy running around doing her errands, trying to get jobs done, getting deals closed and signed. She is multi-tasking, hiring, firing, planning, managing, organizing. She is everywhere yet nowhere, scattered, stressed out, there is no one home. But she is a common face in these Asian cities.

A few examples: A woman entered my consultation room, looking for counseling. A single, 42-year-old woman, she had a hysterectomy only six months earlier and a recent report indicated the presence of breast cancer. But she cannot reduce her work hours because she is a partner in her firm. She travels the rounds in Asia every month, monitoring the company's offices in the region. Another woman, aged 44, also single, had developed lymphatic cancer. A workaholic in banking, who has been successful throughout her life and has done all the right things in terms of working out in the gym, running marathons, healthy diet and various forms of self-care, she is skeptical about analyzing her dreams. She wants a quick fix and decided against therapy. She goes instead to see a fortune teller! Another woman, aged 32, suffers from depression but has no time to look into herself. Married with two young children, she has a full-time job administering a social welfare program while also studying for a doctoral degree and a certificate course. However, despite her accomplishments, she feels inadequate as a mother and as a program manager, and feels guilty for not doing more. She confides in me that she cannot out-perform her mother-in-law who is a high-achiever. Psychologically, these women have had their feet bound and their lives have been restricted to "performing" according to decreed roles and not according to their own inner needs.

However, a few of these women managed to find their way into my consultation room and took the courage to look into their soul. I feel humbled yet privileged by the encounters with them as their stories unfold in the course of their analysis. I learned that little girls are still being sold or given away by their mothers, or abused and ill-treated by their stepmothers and/or fathers; wives are still being bartered away, and treated as property and sexual objects. But the psyche is also vigilant in making its presence felt and its voice heard. For example, the motif of dismemberment is recurrent and powerful emotionally. A 25-year-old woman dreamt that she was cutting her mother into pieces with a saw. Another young woman dreamt that she had killed a young woman and cut her into pieces before holding a replica of herself in her own arms. The motif of dismemberment highlights the urgent need to understand oneself as a woman, and to differentiate the psyche's claims on one's body and soul.

Once these women take the courage to face their pain and suffering, they are supported by the Great Mother in a positive way. A young woman, after a few months in analysis, soon dreamt that a crane came to visit her in her new house. The bird walked around the house, made a full inspection and then left, leaving three feathers as souvenirs. She felt a strange and pleasant feeling of benevolence upon waking from the dream. As we know, the crane is an envoy of Xi Wang Mu, the Great Mother and originator of the Cosmos. The new house in the dream represents her new psychic structure, which expands with growing knowledge of herself. The gift of the feathers from the crane came to represent new ideas that she was able to integrate into her life. One of these ideas was to take advantage of the opportunity to study in a foreign country on a scholarship to further her professional development in a new direction.

Another woman, while suffering from post-partum depression, dreamt that she was flying in the sky among the clouds and suddenly found to her shock that she was in fact a dragon with sharp claws, strong shiny scales, and a thick muscled body. Although she was frightened by this dream upon waking, she was able to realize the immense importance of this dream with the recognition that motherhood has helped her to regain her innate power, the power of being a woman from the very beginning of existence, the power to give life and to be born. This is an initiation dream from the depth of her soul. It suggests the beginning of a new stage in her life and the emergence of a new identity.

The story of Crystal, told in Chapter 5, reflects the resilience of the human spirit in the face of extreme difficulties. Alone, depressed, and without a job, Crystal began to weave her story in symbolic forms with the threads she discovered in the market. The threads became a lifeline to her soul. She persevered in her aloneness, feeling soothed by the repetitive motion of winding the threads. In her solitude, she was able to connect with her rage and depression. Over three years, three balls of black threads were wound into shape, each weighing close to 30 kilos. They are symbolic of her real and essential suffering in concrete form, truly a testament to her deep journey into the Sol Niger, or black sun.[10] On the deep psychic level, working with the threads connected her to the myth of the Weaver Girl, the eternal aspect of Xi Wang Mu, the Great Mother. In this healing connection, Crystal's old self dissolved through her tears, while her new self was born. She eventually returned to the world with a new identity, that of an artist. The ball and labyrinth are prominent images in her art work.

From the analytic experience of these women in Asia, it can be seen that healing comes from the soul, from connecting to the Feminine, to the Great

Mother who is the Source and the Beginning. In Asian patriarchal cultures, connection to the Feminine is pertinent and necessary to prevent one-sidedness and to help promote feminine development. Healing comes from the Great Mother from whom we were born and to whom we will return in death. My analytic experience in Asia has given me new insight on feminine development as I witness the intensity of women's struggles to become conscious of themselves as women. Each will make the sacrifice and take the courage to find her own authentic path in life.

The stories of Pearl, Ruby, and Jade reflect their need and their per-severance in finding their identity and their position in the Western societies in which they live. They need to meet the challenges of ego development in a culture that puts much emphasis on the individual. These include charac-teristics such as goal-setting, discipline, achievement, competition, identity, assertiveness, self-esteem, personal fulfillment, and so on. However, these personal attributes are not valued in Asia, where the individual is not seen as a separate entity but as a member of the family, clan, group, or com-munity, with its relationship patterns inherent in its authority and power structure. Crystal's suffering and her inner transformation process remained a hidden secret: no one knew what happened to her, except that she left her family and disappeared for some time. The question of the meaning of individuation comes up again and again in my analytic sessions. A client, after a few months' analysis, began to experience inner conflicts and began to question not only her position in relation to authorities in her work place, but also her relationship to family members. Before analysis, she was more at peace with herself, her work, and her life in general. Naturally, she began to question her motivation in entering analysis, and if she should continue the analytic process! Her dilemma was probably compounded by the need to find a compatible definition of "individuation" which in her current state of consciousness, inevitably raises questions about group harmony and social integration. The term "self-realization" as presented in the Zen tradition's Ox Herding pictures may be more sympathetic to Asian sensibility.11 These pictures express in an art form the experience of satori or Zen enlightenment – a psychological reality *par excellence* – can be seen as portraying what C.G. Jung calls "the individuation process." My analytic experience in the last two decades suggests that Jung's psychology, which honors the Feminine as well as the soul, may be more appropriate for Asians. This is a challenging area of research and study that will require further reflection and contemplation. This task awaits the courage of more women and men to embark on their inner journey so that they will bear witness and bring light to the collective psyche.

In my exploration of the psychological meaning of footbinding, the thought strikes me that the Golden Lotus in feminine psychology means a struggle between life and death. As a symbol, it unites the backward and forward linkages to the Source. It contains the secret of immortality, which is of the highest value. For a woman, it means the challenge of the Aquarian Age, the development of androgyny. The Golden Lotus signifies what Jung considered "one of the most costly of all things – the development of personality. It is a question of yea-saying to oneself, of taking oneself as the most serious of tasks, of being conscious of everything one does, and keeping it constantly before one's eyes in all its dubious aspects – truly a task that taxes us to the utmost."[12] As Jung said: "Personality is Tao."[13]

Notes

1 Mary B. Rankin, 'The Emergence of Women at the End of the Ch'ing: The Case of Chiu Chin', in Wolf, Margery and Witke, Roxane, eds., *Women in Chinese Society*, Stanford, CA: Stanford University Press, 1975, pp. 49, 63.
2 Yi-Tsi Feuerwerker, 'Women as Writers in the 1920s and 1930s', in Wolf, Margery and Witke, Roxane, eds., op. cit., pp. 143–68.
3 Kathrin Asper-Bruggisser, 'Shadow Aspects of Narcissistic Disorders and their Therapeutic Treatment', *Journal of Analytical Psychology* 32 (1987), pp. 117–37; and *Depression – Dark Night of the Soul*, London: Guild of Pastoral Psychology, 1982; Toni Wolff, 'A Few Thoughts on the Process of Individuation in Women', *Spring* (1941), pp. 52–60.
4 Eric Neumann, 'Narcissism, Normal Self-Formation and Primary Relation to the Mother', *Spring* (1966), pp. 81–106.
5 Quoted in Marion Woodman, *Addiction to Perfection*, Toronto: Inner City Books, 1982, p. 68.
6 Eric Neumann, *The Child*, New York: Putnam, 1973.
7 Sybylle Birkhauser-Oeri, *The Mother, Archetypal Image in Fairytales*, Toronto: Inner City Books, 1988, pp. 155–9.
8 C. G. Jung, *Mysterium Coniunctionis*, CW 14, para. 21n.
9 Kathrin Asper-Bruggisser, op. cit.; Esther Harding, *The Value and Meaning of Depression*, New York: The Analytical Psychological Club of New York, 1970.
10 For a more thorough discussion of the black sun, see Stan Marlan, *The Black Sun: The Alchemy and Art of Darkness*, College Station, TX: Texas A & M University Press, 2005.
11 James N. Powell, *The Tao of Symbols*, New York: Quill, 1982, pp. 142–52. See also, 'Self-realization in the Ten Oxherding Pictures' by Mokusen Miyuki in J. Marvin Spiegelman and Mokusen Miyuki, *Buddhism and Jungian Psychology*, Arizona: New Falcon Publications, 1994, pp. 29–42.
12 C. G. Jung, 'Commentary on the Secret of the Golden Flower', in *Alchemical Studies*, CW 13, para. 95.
13 C. G. Jung, *The Development of Personality*, CW 17, paras. 288–9, 323.

Bibliography

Arroyo, Stephen, *Astrology, Psychology and the Four Elements*, Sebastapol, CA: CRCS Publications, 1975.

Asper-Bruggisser, Kathrin, *Depression – Dark Night of the Soul*, London: Guild of Pastoral Psychology, 1982.

Asper-Bruggisser, Kathrin, 'Shadow Aspects of Narcissistic Disorders and their Therapeutic Treatment', *Journal of Analytical Psychology* 32 (1987), pp. 117–37.

Ayscough, Florence, *Chinese Women, Yesterday and Today*, Boston, MA: Houghton Mifflin, 1937.

Birkhauser-Oeri, Sibylle, Sylvia, *The Mother, Archetypal Image in Fairy Tales*, Toronto: Inner City Books, 1988.

Bond, Michael H. and Hwang, Kwang-kuo, 'The Social Psychology of Chinese People', in Bond, Michael H., ed., *The Psychology of Chinese People*, Oxford: Oxford University Press, 1986.

Buck, Pearl, *The Good Earth*, New York: Bantam Books, 1975.

Cahill, Suzanne E., *Transcendence and Divine Passion: The Queen Mother of the West in Medieval China*, Stanford, CA: Stanford University Press, 1993.

Campbell, Joseph, *Oriental Mythology*, Toronto: Penguin, 1976.

Chan, Wing-tsit, *Source Book on Chinese Philosophy*, Princeton, NJ: Princeton University Press, 1963.

Chang, Chung-yuan, *Creativity and Taoism*, New York: The Julian Press, 1963.

Ching, Julia, *Chinese Religions*, London: Macmillan/New York: Orbis Books, 1993.

Ching, Julia, *Mysticism and Kingship in China: The Heart of Chinese Wisdom*, Cambridge: Cambridge University Press, 1997.

Ching, Julia, *The Butterfly Healing: A Life between East and West*, Maryknoll, NY: Orbis Books, 1998.

Christie, Anthony, *Chinese Mythology*, London: Hamlyn House, 1968.

Cirlot, Juan E., *Dictionary of Symbols*, London: Routledge & Kegan Paul, 1962.

Colgrave, Sukie, *The Spirit of the Valley*, Los Angeles: J.P. Tarcher, 1979.

Cooper, Jean C., *An Illustrated Encyclopaedia of Traditional Symbols*, London: Thames & Hudson, 1978.

Cusack, Dympha, *Chinese Women Speak*, London: Century Hutchinson, 1958.

Daly, Mary, *Gyn/Ecology: The Metaethics of Radical Feminism*, Boston: Beacon Press, 1978.

Davison, Anne M., 'An Analysis of the Significant Factors in the Patterns of

Toronto Chinese Family Life as a Result of Recent Changes in Immigration Laws', MSW thesis, University of Toronto, 1952.

Day, Clarence B., *Chinese Peasant Cults*, Shanghai: Kelly & Walsh, 1940.

De Vries, Ad, *Dictionary of Symbolism and Imagery*, Amsterdam: Elsevier Science, 1984.

Dworkin, Andrea, *Woman Hating*, New York: Dutton, 1974.

Eberhard, Wolfram, *Folktales of China*, London: Routledge & Kegan Paul, 1965.

Eberhard, Wolfram, *A Dictionary of Chinese Symbols*, New York: Routledge & Kegan Paul, 1986.

Edgerton, Clement, trans., *The Golden Lotus* (Chin Ping Mei), London: Routledge & Kegan Paul, 1939.

Eliade, Mircea, *Cosmos and History: The Myth of the Eternal Return*, New York: Pantheon, 1954.

Eliade, Mircea, *Shamanism: Archaic Techniques of Ecstasy*, New Jersey: Princeton University Press, 1964.

Feuerwerker, Yi-tsi, 'Women as writers in the 1920s and 1930s', in Wolf, Margery and Witke, Roxane, eds., *Women in Chinese Society*, Stanford, CA: Stanford University Press, 1975, pp. 143–68.

Fingarette, Herbert, *Confucius: The Secular as Sacred*, New York: Harper & Row, 1972.

Fung, Yu-lan, *A Short History of Chinese Philosophy*, New York: Macmillan, 1950.

Giles, Herbert A., trans., *Strange Stories from a Chinese Studio*, New York: Kelly & Walsh, 1925.

Granet, Marcel, *The Religion of the Chinese People*, Oxford: Blackwell, 1975.

Green, Liz, *Saturn: A New Look at an Old Devil*, New York, 1976.

Hamaker-Zondag, Karan, *Astro-Psychology*, London: The Aquarian Press, 1980.

Harding, Esther, *Woman's Mysteries, Ancient and Modern*, New York: Pantheon Books, 1955.

Harding, Esther, *The Way of All Women*, New York: C.G. Jung Foundation, 1970.

Harding, Esther, 'The Value and Meaning of Depression' (mimeograph), New York: The Analytical Psychological Club of New York, 1970.

Hsu, Francis L. K., *Under the Ancestors' Shadow*, New York: Columbia University Press, 1948.

Jackson, Beverley, *Splendid Slippers: A Thousand Years of An Erotic Tradition*, Berkeley, CA: Ten Speed Press, 1997.

James, Jean M., trans., *Rickshaw*, Honolulu: University Press of Hawaii, 1979.

Jung, Carl G., *The Collected Works of Carl G. Jung*, edited by Sir Herbert Read, Michael Fordham, Gerhard Adler and William McGuire. Translated by R. F. C. Hull (except Vol. 2), Princeton, NJ: Princeton University Press: Bollingen Series XX and London, 1953–76.

Jung, Carl G., *Freud and Psychoanalysis*, Volume 4.

Jung, Carl G., *Symbols of Transformation*, Volume 5.

Jung, Carl G., *Psychological Types*, Volume 6.

Jung, Carl G., *Two Essays on Analytical Psychology*, Volume 7.

Jung, Carl G., *The Archetypes and the Collective Unconscious*, Volume 9i.

Jung, Carl G., *Civilization in Transition*, Volume 10.

Jung, Carl G., *Psychology and Religion, East and West*, Volume 11.

Jung, Carl G., *Psychology and Alchemy*, Volume 12.

Jung, Carl G., *Alchemical Studies*, Volume 13.

Jung, Carl G., *Mysterium Coniunctionis*, Volume 14.

Jung, Carl G., *The Development of Personality*, Volume 17.

Jung, Carl G. and Kerenyi, Carl, *Essays on a Science of Mythology*, Princeton, NJ: Bollingen Foundation, 1949.

Jung, Emma, *Animus and Anima*, Houston, TX: Spring Publications, 1978.

Ko, Dorothy, *Teachers of the Inner Chambers: Women and Culture in Seventeenth-Century China*, Stanford, CA: Stanford University Press, 1994.

Ko, Dorothy, *Every Step A Lotus: Shoes for Bound Feet*, Berkeley, CA: University of California Press, 2001.

Ko, Dorothy, *Cinderella's Sisters: A Revisionist History of Footbinding*, Berkeley, CA: University of California Press, 2005.

Kohn, Livia, *The Taoist Experience*, New York: SUNY Press, 1993.

Kristeva, Julia, *About Chinese Women*, trans. Anita Barrows, London: Marion Boyars, 1977.

Kuhn, Franz, trans., *The Dream of the Red Chamber* (Hung Lou Meng), London: Routledge & Kegan Paul, 1959.

Lai, Vivian, 'The New Chinese Immigrants in Toronto', in Elliot, Jean L., ed., *Minority Canadians*, Toronto: Prentice-Hall, 1971.

Lang, Olga, *Chinese Family and Society*, Yale University Press, 1946; reprint, New York: Archon, 1968.

Lau, D. C. trans. [Chinese], *Mencius*, Harmondsworth: Penguin Classics, 1970.

Lau, D. C. trans. [Chinese], *Tao Te Ching*, New York: Alfred A. Knopf, 1972.

Layard, John, *The Lady and the Hare*, London: Faber and Faber, 1944.

Legge, James, trans., 'The Classic of Filial Piety' (Hsiao Ching); 'Analects' (Lun Yu) in *Sacred Books of the East*, London: Oxford University Press, 1879.

Legge, James, trans., 'The Doctrine of the Mean' (Chung Yung) in *Chinese Classics*, London: Oxford University Press, 1893–5.

Levy, Howard S., *The Lotus Lovers: The Complete History of the Curious Erotic Custom of Footbinding in China*, Buffalo, NY: Prometheus Books, 1992.

Levy, Marion Jr, *The Family Revolution in Modern China*, Boston, MA: Harvard University Press, 1949; reprint, New York: Athenaeum, 1968.

Li, Peter S., 'The Chinese Minority in Canada, 1858–1992: A Quest for Equality', in Huang, Evelyn with Lawrence, Jeffery, eds., *Chinese Canadians: Voices from a Community*, Vancouver: Douglas and MacIntyre, 1992, pp. 264–75.

Lin, Yu-tang, *My Country and My People*, New York: John Day, 1939.

Loewe, Michael, *Ways to Paradise: The Chinese Quest for Immortality*, London: George Unwin, 1979.

Lucas, Richard, *Secrets of the Chinese Herbalists*, New York: Parker Publishing, 1987.

Ma, Shirley, 'Disunity in Toronto's Chinese Community', Paper presented at the American Anthropological Association Annual Meeting, 1 December 1972.

Ma, Shirley, 'Golden Lotus: A Psychological Exploration of the Meaning of Chinese Footbinding', Diploma Thesis, C. G. Jung Institute, Zurich, 1989.

Ma, Shirley, 'Eastern Perspectives on the Relationship between Psyche and Body', in *Proceedings of the 13th Congress of the IAAP: Opening Questions in Analytical Psychology*, Einsiedeln, Switzerland: Daimon Verlag, 1996.

Ma, Shirley, 'Carl G. Jung and the Chinese Way', in Spiegelman, J. Marvin, ed.,

Psychology and Religion at the Millennium and Beyond, Phoenix, AZ: New Falcon Press, 1998.

Ma, Shirley, 'C. G. Jung and the Confucian Way', in *Proceedings of the European–North American Conference on the West and East Asian Values*, July, 1998, sponsored by the Sterling Currier Fund of Columbia University and Victoria College at University of Toronto, under the Patronage of the Royal Society of Canada.

Ma, Shirley, 'Carl. G. Jung and the East', in *Proceedings of the 14th Congress for IAAP: Destruction and Creation: Personal and Cultural Transformations*, Einsiedeln, Switzerland: Daimon Verlag, 1999.

Ma, Shirley, 'The I Ching and Psyche-body Connection', *Journal of Analytical Psychology*, 50 (2005), pp. 237–50.

MacInnes, Tom, *Oriental Occupation in British Columbia*, Vancouver: Sun Publishing, 1927.

Marlan, Stan, *The Black Sun: The Alchemy and Art of Darkness*, College Station, TX: Texas A & M University Press, 2005.

Martin, Stephen, 'Anger as Inner Transformation', *Quadrant*, Spring (1986), 31–45.

Miyuki, Mokusen, 'The Secret of the Golden Flower, Studies and Translation', Diploma Thesis, C. G. Jung Institute, Zurich, 1967.

Miyuki, Mokusen, 'Self-realization in the Ten Oxherding Pictures' in J. Marvin Spiegelman and Mokusen Miyuki, *Buddhism and Jungian Psychology*, Arizona: New Falcon Publications, 1994.

Needham, Joseph, *Science and Civilization in China*, Volumes 1 & 2, Cambridge: Cambridge University Press, 1954 and 1956.

Neil, Philip and Simborowski, Nicoletta *The Complete Fairy Tales of Charles Perrault,* Boston, MA: Houghton Mifflin Harcourt, 1993.

Neumann, Eric, 'On the Moon and Matriarchal Consciousness', *Spring* (1954), pp. 83–100.

Neumann, Eric, *The Great Mother: An Analysis of the Archetype*, New York: Bollingen, 1955.

Neumann, Eric, 'Narcissism, Normal Self-Formation and Primary Relation to the Mother', *Spring* (1966), pp. 81–106.

Neumann, Eric, *The Child*, New York: Putnam, 1973.

O'Hara, Albert R., *The Position of Women in Early China*, Taiwan: Mei Ya Publications, 1955.

Palmer, Martin and Zhao, Xiaomin, *Essential Chinese Mythology: Stories that Change the World*, London: Thorsons, 1997.

Paper, Jordan, *The Spirits Are Drunk: Comparative Approaches to Chinese Religion*, Albany, NY: SUNY Press, 1995.

Porter, John, *The Vertical Mosaic*, Toronto: Toronto University Press, 1962.

Powell, James N., *The Tao of Symbols*, New York: Quill, 1982.

Prager, Emily, *A Visit from the Footbinder*, New York: Vintage Books, 1982.

Pruitt, Ida, *A Daughter of Han*, New Haven, CT: Yale University Press, 1945.

Rankin, Mary B., 'The Emergence of Women at the end of the Ching: the Case of Chiu Chin', in Wolf, Margery and Witke, Roxane, eds., *Women in Chinese Society*, Stanford, CA: Stanford University Press, 1975.

Raphals, Lisa, *Sharing the Light: Representations of Women and Virtue in Early China*, Albany, NY: SUNY Press, 1998.

Rossi, William A., *The Sex Life of the Foot and Shoe*, London: Routledge & Kegan Paul, 1977.

Salaff, Janet, *Working Daughters of Hong Kong, Filial Piety or Power in the Family?* Cambridge: Cambridge University Press, 1981.

Salaff, Janet, 'Wage Earners in Hong Kong', in Sheridan, Mary and Salaff, Janet, eds., *Lives: Chinese Working Women*, Bloomington, IN: Indiana University Press, 1984, pp. 146–71.

Shimer, Dorothy B., *Rice Bowl Women: Writings by and about the Women of China and Japan*, Canada: Mentor Book, 1982.

Slote, Walter and DeVos, George, *Confucianism and the Family*, Albany, NY: SUNY Press, 1998.

Snow, Helen Foster, *Women in Modern China*, The Hague: Mouton & Co., 1967.

Tu, Wei-ming, *Confucian Thought, Selfhood and Creative Transformation*, Albany, NY: SUNY Press, 1985.

Tu, Wei-ming, *Centrality and Commonality: An Essay on Confucian Religiousness*, Albany, NY: SUNY Press, 1989.

Tu, Wei-ming, *The Living Tree: The Changing Meaning of Being Chinese Today*, Stanford, CA: Stanford University Press, 1994.

Tu, Wei-ming, *Confucian Traditions in East Asian Modernity*, Cambridge, MA: Harvard University Press, 1996.

Vance, Catharine, trans., *The Serenity of Whiteness* by Hong Zhu, New York: Ballantine, 1991.

van der Kolk, Bessel A., *Traumatic Stress: The Effects of Overwhelming Experience on Mind, Body and Society*, New York: The Guilford Press, 1996.

van Gulik, Robert, *Sexual Life in Ancient China*, Leiden: Brill, 1961.

von Franz, Marie-Louise, *Introduction to the Interpretation of Fairy Tales*, Houston, TX: Spring Publications, 1970.

von Franz, Marie-Louise, *The Problems of the Feminine in Fairy Tales*, Houston, TX: Spring Publications, 1972.

von Franz, Marie-Louise, *Shadow and Evil in Fairy Tales*, Houston, TX: Spring Publications, 1974.

von Franz, Marie-Louise, *Individuation in Fairy Tales*, Houston, TX: Spring Publications, 1977.

von Franz, Marie-Louise, *Alchemy: An Introduction to the Symbolism and the Psychology*, Toronto: Inner City Books, 1980.

von Franz, Marie-Louise, *The Psychological Meaning of Redemption Motifs in Fairy Tales*, Toronto: Inner City Books, 1980.

von Franz, Marie-Louise with Boa, Fraser, *The Way of the Dreams*, Toronto: Windrose Films, 1988.

Waley, Arthur, trans., *The Analects of Confucius*, London: Allen & Unwin, 1938.

Waley, Arthur, 'The Chinese Cinderella Story', *Folklore* 58 (1947), pp. 226–38.

Waley, Arthur, *The Way and Its Power*, New York: Grove Press, 1958.

Ware, James, trans., *Alchemy, Medicine, Religion in the China of A.D. 320: The Nei-pien of Ko Hung*, Cambridge, MA: MIT Press, 1966.

Watson, Burton, trans., *The Complete Works of Chuang Tzu*, New York: Columbia University Press, 1968.

Welch, Holmes, *Taoism: The Parting of the Way*, Boston, MA: Beacon Press, 1957.

Werner, Edward T. C., *Myths and Legends of China*, London: George Harrap, 1922.

Werner, Edward T. C., *A Dictionary of Chinese Mythology*, New York: The Julian Press, 1961.

Wilhelm, Helmut, *Eight Lectures on the I Ching*, Princeton, NJ: Princeton University Press, 1975.

Wilhelm, Richard, trans. [German], *The Secret of the Golden Flower*, trans. [English] Baynes, Cary F., New York: Harvest, 1962.

Wilhelm, Richard, trans. [German], *I Ching or The Book of Changes*, trans. [English] Baynes, Cary F., Princeton, NJ: Princeton University Press, 1975.

Williams, Charles A. S., *Outlines of Chinese Symbolism and Art Motives*, 3rd rev. edn, New York: Dover Publications, 1976.

Wolf, Margery, 'Women and Suicide in China', in Wolf, Margery and Witke, Roxane, eds., *Women in Chinese Society*, Stanford, CA: Stanford University Press, 1975, pp. 111–41.

Wolfe, Toni, 'A Few Thoughts on the Process of Individuation in Women', *Spring* (1941), pp. 52–60.

Woo, Terry Tak-ling, 'Emotions and Self Cultivation in Nü Lunyu: A Woman's Analects', *Journal of Chinese Philosophy* 36 (2009), pp. 334–47.

Woodman, Marion, *Addiction to Perfection*, Toronto: Inner City Books, 1982.

Woodman, Marion, *The Ravaged Bridegroom*, Toronto: Inner City Books, 1990.

Wu, Kuo-Chen, *The Chinese Heritage*, New York: Crown, 1982.

Ziegler, Alfred J., *Archetypal Medicine*, Houston, TX: Spring, 1983.

Texts in Chinese

Chen, Tung-yuen, *Chung-kuo fu-nu sheng-huo shih* (*A History of the Life of Chinese Women*), Shanghai: The Commercial Press, 1937.

Chin, Chiu, *Chiu Chin Chi* (*The Collected Works of Chiu Chin*), Shanghai: Zhonghua Publishing, 1960.

Chin Hua Tsung Chih (The Secret of the Golden Flower), in *Tao Tsang Chi Yao* (*Selected Works from the Taoist Canon*), 17th century.

Chiu, Tsan-chih, *Chiu Chin Ko Ming Chuan* (*A Revolutionary Biography of Chiu Chin*), Taiwan: San Ming, 1963.

Cho, Ju, ed., *Bing Xin*, Hong Kong: Joint Publishing, 1983.

Ding, Ling, *Ding Ling Hsuan Chi* (*Selected Essays*), Hong Kong: Wen xue chu ban she, 1955.

Fung, Yeh-tsai, *The Three-inch Golden Lotus*, Hong Kong: Asia Publishing, 1987.

Guo, Yanli, *Qiu Jin shi wen xuan* (*Selected works of Chiu Chin*), Beijing: People's Literary Publishing, 1982.

Guo, Yanli, *Qiu Jin wen xue lun gao* (*Literary Discussions on Chiu Chin*), Xian: People's Publishing, 1987.

Hsing Ming Kuai Chih (Secrets on the Cultivation of Life), transmitted by Master Yin, in *Tao Tsang Chi Yao* (*Selected Works from the Taoist Canon*), China, 1669.

Lee, Fung-lin, ed., *Shan Hai Ching*, Taiwan: Chin Feng Publishing, 1987.

Lee, Han-you, *Modern Introduction to the I Ching*, Hong Kong: Joint Publishing, 1983.

Li, Donghai, *A History of Chinese in Canada*, Taiwan: Zhonghua Publishing, 1967.

Siu, Tien-shih, *Introduction to the Studies on the Prolongation of Life in Taoism* (*Tao Chia Yang Sheng Hsueh Kai Yao*), Hong Kong: Tzu Yu Press, 1963.

Tu, Er-wei, *Researches on Confucianism, Buddhism and Taoism*, Taipei, Taiwan: Hau Ming Publishing, 1976.

Tu, Er-wei, *The Culture of Kun-lun and the Concept of Immortality*, Taipei, Taiwan: Xue Sheng Publishing, 1977.

Tu, Er-wei, *The Religious Systems of Ancient China*, Taipei, Taiwan: Xue Sheng Publishing, 1977.

Wei, Po-yang, Chou I Tsang Tung Chi (Meditation on Identity and Unity) in *Tao Tsang* (*Taoist Canon*), Volume Ying, China, AD 142.

Index

Page references in *italic* indicate illustrations.